Naturalism, Interpretation, and Mental Disorder

International Perspectives in Philosophy and Psychiatry

Series editors: Bill (K.W.M.) Fulford, Lisa Bortolotti, Matthew Broome, Katherine Morris, John Z. Sadler, and Giovanni Stanghellini

Volumes in the series:

Portrait of the Psychiatrist as a Young Man: The Early Writing and Work of R.D. Laing, 1927–1960
Beveridge

Mind, Meaning, and Mental Disorder 2e
Bolton and Hill

What is Mental Disorder?
Bolton

Delusions and Other Irrational Beliefs
Bortolotti

Postpsychiatry
Bracken and Thomas

Philosophy, Psychoanalysis, and the A-Rational Mind
Brakel

Unconscious Knowing and Other Essays in Psycho-Philosophical Analysis
Brakel

Psychiatry as Cognitive Neuroscience
Broome and Bortolotti (eds.)

Free Will and Responsibility: A Guide for Practitioners
Callender

Reconceiving Schizophrenia
Chung, Fulford, and Graham (eds.)

Darwin and Psychiatry
De Block and Adriaens (eds.)

Oxford Handbook of Philosophy and Psychiatry
Fulford, Davies, Gipps, Graham, Sadler, Stanghellini, and Thornton

Nature and Narrative: An Introduction to the New Philosophy of Psychiatry
Fulford, Morris, Sadler, and Stanghellini (eds.)

Oxford Textbook of Philosophy and Psychiatry
Fulford, Thornton, and Graham

The Mind and its Discontents
Gillett

The Abraham Dilemma
Graham

Is evidence-based psychiatry ethical?
Gupta

Thinking Through Dementia
Hughes

Dementia: Mind, Meaning, and the Person
Hughes, Louw, and Sabat (eds.)

Talking Cures and Placebo Effects
Jopling

Philosophical Issues in Psychiatry II: Nosology
Kenneth S. Kendler, Josef Parnas (eds.)

Philosophical Issues in Psychiatry III: The Nature and Sources of Historical Change
Kenneth S. Kendler, Josef Parnas (eds.)

Discursive Perspectives in Therapeutic Practice
Lock and Strong (ed.)

Schizophrenia and the Fate of the Self
Lysaker and Lysaker

Responsibility and Psychopathy
Malatesti and McMillan

Body-Subjects and Disordered Minds
Matthews

Rationality and Compulsion: Applying action theory to psychiatry
Nordenfelt

Diagnostic Dilemmas in Child and Adolescent Psychiatry
Perring and Wells (eds.)

Philosophical Perspectives on Technology and Psychiatry
Phillips (ed.)

The Metaphor of Mental Illness
Pickering

Mapping the Edges and the In-between
Potter

Trauma, Truth, and Reconciliation: Healing Damaged Relationships
Potter (ed.)

The Philosophy of Psychiatry: A Companion
Radden

The Virtuous Psychiatrist
Radden and Sadler

Addiction and Weakness of Will
Radoilska

Autonomy and Mental Disorder
Radoilska (ed.)

Feelings of Being
Ratcliffe

Experiences of Depression: A study in phenomenology
Ratcliffe

Recovery of People with Mental Illness: Philosophical and Related Perspectives
Rudnick (ed.)

Values and Psychiatric Diagnosis
Sadler

Disembodied Spirits and Deanimated Bodies: The Psychopathology of Common Sense
Stanghellini

One Century of Karl Jaspers Psychopathology
Stanghellini and Fuchs

Emotions and Personhood
Stanghellini and Rosfort

Essential Philosophy of Psychiatry
Thornton

Naturalism, Hermeneutics, and Mental Disorder
Varga

Empirical Ethics in Psychiatry
Widdershoven, McMillan, Hope and Van der Scheer (eds.)

The Sublime Object of Psychiatry: Schizophrenia in Clinical and Cultural Theory
Woods

Alternate Perspectives on Psyciatric Validation: DSM, ICD, RDoC, and Beyond
Zachar, St. Stoyanov, Aragona, and Jablensky (eds.)

Naturalism, Interpretation, and Mental Disorder

Somogy Varga

OXFORD
UNIVERSITY PRESS

OXFORD
UNIVERSITY PRESS

Great Clarendon Street, Oxford, OX2 6DP,
United Kingdom

Oxford University Press is a department of the University of Oxford.
It furthers the University's objective of excellence in research, scholarship,
and education by publishing worldwide. Oxford is a registered trade mark of
Oxford University Press in the UK and in certain other countries

Published in the United States of America by Oxford University Press
198 Madison Avenue, New York, NY 10016, United States of America

British Library Cataloguing in Publication Data
Data available

Library of Congress Control Number: To come

ISBN 978–0–19–874725–3

Acknowledgments

Throughout the course of the research and writing required to complete this book, I had the support and benevolence of numerous people. I can probably never fully discharge the debt of gratitude that I owe to my family, friends, and colleagues for their generous help. As early as the proposal stage of this book, and later when writing the first draft of many of the chapters, I benefited from detailed comments from Peter Zachar, Jennifer Radden, George Graham, Matthew Ratcliffe, Achim Stephan, Shaun Gallagher, and Albert Newen. It is my sincere hope that I have produced a book that does justice to all their advice and at least approximates a result that repays their help. Naturally, I am under no illusion that further improvement is impossible.

I presented some of the material in this book as a visiting speaker at Macquarie University, the University of Copenhagen, Ruhr Universität Bochum, Universidad National de Colombia, and Freie Universität Berlin. I would like to thank all of these institutions for inviting me, and I am grateful to all who participated in the events and provided insightful comments that enhanced the quality of this book. I have greatly benefited from informal conversations with friends around the world and with colleagues at the University of Memphis, in particular Stephan Blatti, Heidi Samuelson and Deborah Tollefsen. I have also taught a graduate course on this subject at the University of Memphis, which enabled me to rethink many important aspects of this book. I thank my students for their enthusiasm, lively participation, and useful commentaries.

Finally, I owe a profound debt of gratitude to my wife, Bettina, and to my children, Vincent, Isabel, and Edgar, for their continuous encouragement and loving support, without which this book and indeed my life would be infinitely poorer. This book is dedicated to them.

Contents

Part 1

Philosophy of psychiatry

Chapter 1

Introduction: interpretation, naturalism, and the aims of this book

Most people understand philosophy as an academic discipline that relies on the use of reason and logic to comprehend reality and existence, and to answer essential questions about knowledge, morality, and human nature. Whereas for the ancient Greeks, who originally coined the term, the study of philosophy amounted to seeking answers to "big questions" about the meaning of life, the sources of morality, and secure knowledge, the spectrum of questions is significantly broadened in current philosophy. Today it is widely acknowledged that philosophical work can take a great number of different forms. One particular, and increasingly popular, form of philosophical inquiry leans toward empirically informed theorizing, which productively integrates scientific material. Although the umbrella of "empirically informed philosophy" designates a cluster of quite different domains of inquiry, one common aspect is the pursuit of questions that have a straightforward bearing on practical matters and do not typically focus on problems that only occur in highly theoretical reflection. Drawing a parallel with the development of the sciences, one might maintain that, just like the sciences, philosophy has evolved, and many of the subdisciplines are now dedicated to investigating special areas. Almost every significant scientific field of inquiry is accompanied by a branch of philosophy, usually referred to as "the philosophy of" that field. The main purpose of the philosophy of *X* is to investigate the nature of the subject matter of *X* and to account for its aims and methodology (Shapiro 1983). At its best, such work is not a one-way application of philosophical knowledge and methods, but rather a two-way encounter where both philosophy and empirical fields can benefit from one another.

This book is about such a special area, the *philosophy of psychiatry*, which is concerned with those philosophical issues that arise from within the academic and clinical discipline of psychiatry. Guided by such "practical" problems, in the field of *philosophy of psychiatry* philosophical theories are brought to bear on the particular questions that relate to the concept of mental disorder and the explanation of impaired thinking and behavior. Consequently, the considerations in this book are largely guided by problems of a philosophical nature that arise in various settings of mental healthcare.

Although it is helpful to place the philosophy of psychiatry in the group of "philosophies of," the view will be defended that the philosophy of psychiatry is in a number of respects a unique area of research. Partly due to its connection to socio-political and ethical issues, the depths of the conceptual problems in the philosophy of psychiatry are genuinely unique. In addition, and complicating the picture further, it seems that epistemological and normative issues are deeply connected when it comes to the nature of health and disease. As well as the normative implication of questions that arise in this field, these implications are also closely connected to a number of social and policy issues. Consider, for instance, the question "Do disorder categories objectively pick out something real, or do they function as convenient labels used for grouping certain people together for certain ends?" Questions like this, and the lack of really good answers, have contributed to the fact that no other medical subspecialty has faced so much criticism not only for being unscientific (for lacking a unified account of mental disorder, reliable biological criteria, and diagnostic classification system), but also for unfairly functioning as a normalizing socio-political force (Szasz 1965, 2000; Horwitz and Wakefield 2007).

Some of the reasons why the philosophy of psychiatry can be seen as a unique area of research stem from the very nature of psychiatry and mental health phenomena. It is quite simply the nature of the subject matter that leads to rather unique methodological challenges. While there are many such unique challenges, this book focuses on those that concern processes of interpretation and understanding. In many ways these questions are more challenging than in "somatic" medicine, as the symptoms of mental disorder are far more diverse, and as no "gold-standard" laboratory tests or biomarkers are available. However, given the nature of these challenges that partly stem from the unique position of psychiatry as a scientific discipline, it is likely that the new perspectives generated will not only benefit the two disciplines involved, but also philosophical work in this area might be expected to have potential ramifications for areas of study way beyond the field. Thus, while the depths of the philosophical problems are genuinely unique, so is the range of possible answers and new perspectives that might be generated in attempting to answer them.

This book is intended to speak to the academic readership that is interested in issues relating to human behavior and questions about mental health—a fact that is also reflected in the choice of methodology. The inquiry draws on different traditions, such as philosophical hermeneutics and analytic philosophy, with the methodological aim of moving beyond the analytic versus non-analytic divide. Although some of the main arguments are based on work in *philosophical hermeneutics*, ideas from this particular tradition are merely used as points of departure for developing hypotheses that speak to readers who are versed in both traditions. The book is intended for a wide audience, but it is likely to be most stimulating to mental health professionals, philosophers, and intellectuals in general who share at least to some extent the motives by which this book is driven, namely sensitivity and skepticism. Specifically, this group would include those who are concerned with questions about the mind and mental health, but who are nevertheless somewhat skeptical about the notion of naturalism, and cannot accept the idea of retreating to the supposedly objective biological and statistical findings of scientific psychiatry.

1. The aims of the book

This book has several aims, and it is worthwhile to distinguish between a set of general and specific aims. One of the most important general aims of the book is to generate a constructive impact on psychiatric thinking, and thus on the lives of people who are involved in the numerous settings in which mental healthcare is practiced. It is hoped that the critical philosophical engagement with psychiatry as a medico-scientific discipline that is presented in this book will advance philosophical debates and inspire further work at the intersection of philosophy and psychiatry.

A more specific aim is to contribute to existing debates in the philosophy of psychiatry and to explore new areas and opportunities that have not yet been exploited. In particular, the intention is to make a detailed attempt to integrate a hermeneutically informed perspective into current debates in the philosophy of psychiatry. Whereas phenomenology has been successfully incorporated into many works in the field of philosophy and psychiatry, hermeneutics has not received the attention that it merits. Although there has traditionally been a link between hermeneutics and psychiatry—at least since Karl Jaspers took over Dilthey's concept of understanding (*Verstehen*) as a mode of comprehension (Jaspers 1963)—it has never been fully developed. A few authors have published articles that touch on this subject (Gadamer 1996; Phillips 1996; Sass 1998; Arnason 2000; Miller 2008), while others have briefly addressed it in books that are broader in scope than what is proposed here. This book aims to make a more comprehensive attempt to enlighten currents debates from a hermeneutically informed perspective.

Such an aim is in agreement with the work of philosophers who argue that, due to the unique standing of medicine along deductive forms of scientific explanations, there is a need for a specific *hermeneutics of medicine* (Leder 1990; Svenaeus 2000). The point they aim to convey is that processes of understanding characteristic of clinical settings do not clearly fit into the realm of the natural sciences. These authors argue in favor of a "hermeneutics of medicine," but my point is that, due to the particular challenges of interpretation in psychiatry, there is a need for a specific "hermeneutics of psychiatry." This need arises because, in the field of psychiatry, the processes of interpretation and information organization are arguably even more problematic than in medicine, as the symptoms of mental disorder are far more diverse than in the case of "somatic" disorders. That is, whereas the symptoms of "somatic" disorders are largely limited to sensations, perceptions, and movements, the symptoms of mental disorder comprise a wide range of thoughts, behaviors, emotions, desires, beliefs, perceptions, volitions, personal identity, and so on. In addition, given that many areas of medicine rely on technology, the scope for the interpretation of clinically relevant facts is relatively narrow. Noticeably in mental healthcare, which lacks "gold-standard" laboratory tests or biomarkers, the possible interpretations of symptoms are multiplied.

2. **Hermeneutics and naturalism**

Although numerous philosophical issues arise in the study of psychiatric phenomena, only some of them concern processes of interpretation and understanding.[1] According to a standard definition, hermeneutics is the theory of interpretation—the theory of achieving a proper understanding of texts and utterances. Although the term "hermeneutics" was first employed in a theological context in the seventeenth century, it has since acquired a cross-disciplinary importance, and it is now understood as encompassing a wide variety of interpretations. For instance, we do not only speak about interpretation when we attempt to uncover the meaning of a particular passage in the Bible or in a literary work. We also interpret juridical codes to determine the application of law and sets of scientific data to find explanatory regularities (Leder 1990). In such general terms, and specifically in such forms as commentary and exegesis, hermeneutics looks back on a long tradition. Increased attention was brought to bear on hermeneutics in the wake of the Reformation, as canonical interpretations of the Bible were questioned, and as the responsibility for interpreting the biblical texts became individualized.

[1] With a view to establishing the goals of this book, I shall not attempt to provide a comprehensive survey of the field of modern hermeneutics, but instead to focus on some of the main ideas.

The question of how to understand the Bible gave rise to interpretative investigations and debates, and, in response, hermeneutics evolved as a distinct field of inquiry that aimed to identify the rules by which interpretation should be directed. In other words, hermeneutics was to a large degree motivated by diverging interpretations of the Bible. The context in which the principles of a hermeneutic investigation were developed was the encounter of biblical texts with obscure or unacceptable meanings. Friedrich D. E. Schleiermacher, one of the main figures of Romantic hermeneutics, famously emphasized that misinterpretations, and hence misunderstandings, naturally arise due to the time span that separates the author from the interpreter. In this "gap," concepts and words might change their meanings due to historical events or changing traditions that have to be taken into account by any adequate interpretation. Therefore only a reflective and methodologically underpinned interpretation can reveal the meaning of a text.

Under its development over the course of the nineteenth and twentieth centuries, the scope of hermeneutics significantly broadened beyond the narrowly prescriptive questions of textual interpretation, and beyond situations in which we encounter meanings that resist instantaneous comprehension and require interpretative effort.[2] With regard to the aims of this book, it is especially important to emphasize two aspects that are related to this expansion. First, the approaches developed by thinkers such as Martin Heidegger and Hans-Georg Gadamer no longer focus on identifying rules of interpretation, but direct attention to the nature, structure, and conditions of possibility for human understanding (Linge 1976; Gallagher 2004). Hermeneutic thinkers resist the idea that the individual is a "wordless and timeless source of insight" (Wachterhauser 1986, p. 5), and argue that we should think of all human understanding as deeply embedded in historically and linguistically constituted horizons of intelligibility. It is in this sense that hermeneutic thinkers argue that language and history both enable and limit human understanding. As Gadamer (1989, p. 43) argues, understanding is not so much the activity of a subject as "the entering into an event of transmission in which past and present are constantly mediated." In contrast to Kant's work that sought to identify the necessary conditions of three demarcated types of understanding, thinkers from the hermeneutic tradition tend to argue that the "historicity" (*Geschichtlichkeit*) of understanding is at odds with the idea of strictly differentiated realms of comprehension.

---

[2] This is why Linge (1976, p. xii) maintains that hermeneutics has its origins in the "breaches of intersubjectivity."

Second, in Heidegger and post-Heideggerian hermeneutics, perhaps most tangibly in the work of Charles Taylor, hermeneutics is no longer confined to understanding texts and utterances in interpersonal communication, but also includes the idea that humans are essentially "self-interpreting animals" (Taylor 1985a, 1985b). The relationship between being a human being and being "thrown" (as Heidegger would say) into a particular historical situation and social community is essential rather than accidental. What we are is itself historical in the sense that it cannot be reduced to some noumenal core. Thus philosophical hermeneutics here emphasizes that the sources of normativity should be sought in the existential structure of our being embedded in the world. Importantly, such embeddedness is itself shaped by the range of our concerns, which themselves are interpretations that are indivisibly linked to the question of what it is to be a human being. In the wake of this development of hermeneutical thought, the human capacity of interpretation, and particularly self-interpretation, is attributed *ontological significance*. Rather than being given to us, our existence as human beings is such that who we are is (at least to a major degree) constituted by the manner in which we interpret ourselves. Consequently, who we are is intertwined with our "care" and concern for the meanings that things have for us. Just as the process of interpretation is for Gadamer (1989), self-interpretation is an ongoing process that cannot be finalized, or somehow concluded. Throughout his work, Taylor carefully develops this idea, emphasizing that the condition of our ability to constitute ourselves is our being embedded within horizons of significance—a collectively shaped background of a particular historical–cultural context. The self-understanding that this everyday practice of collective self-interpretation provides us with is not a set of axioms that we are free to choose; rather, it is a milieu made up of culturally shared notions, narratives, and historically shaped values that we further unfold (Gadamer 1989).[3] Our identities are constituted by the way that we situate ourselves in such a cultural context, which we achieve by using the language of evaluative contrasts, assessing what is desirable by a qualitative characterization of options as higher and lower, noble and base, virtuous or vicious, more or less refined, profound or superficial, and so on (Taylor 1985a, 1989, 1991a).[4]

[3] This view is shared by Habermas (2003), who adds that in self-interpretation we reflect on what it means to be a human being, not merely as members of a certain cultural, religious, or national community.

[4] A subject who only evaluates weakly—that is, who makes decisions such as whether to eat now or later, or to take a holiday in the north or in the south—might be described as a simple weigher of alternatives. In weak evaluation, "for something to be judged good it is sufficient that it be desired" (Taylor 1985a, p. 18; 1991).

Thus, far from merely being a methodological doctrine for the humanities and social sciences, hermeneutics has evolved to include fundamental reflections about what it means for human beings to lead a practical life. At least prima facie, it is not difficult to see that such considerations are relevant to the philosophical questions that arise in psychiatry.

However, it should be noted that, in this book, hermeneutical thought will also be used in a selective manner, often in critical opposition to what could be called a general attitude of "naturalism" in psychiatry. The first point to mention is that, possibly to an even greater extent than is the case with hermeneutics, "naturalism" is applied in such a variety of contexts within philosophical thought that it is very difficult to pin down its principal tenets. As Papineau (1993, p. 1) fittingly remarks, "nearly everybody nowadays wants to be a 'naturalist', but the aspirants to the term nevertheless disagree widely on substantial questions of philosophical doctrine." In the context of this book, it is acknowledged that a precise demarcation would itself require philosophical reflection and argument, and it is not claimed that naturalism is something like a consistent philosophical position with epistemological, metaphysical, and ethical dimensions. Papineau (1993) notes that, for some philosophers, naturalism is simply characterized by the rejection of dualism, for others by the denunciation of supernatural orders, and for yet others by the commitment to an externalist epistemology. It is not these varieties of naturalism that this book will critically engage. Rather, naturalism is seen as a general philosophical "attitude" with some discernible commonalities. The most important of these commonalities are the granting of unique cognitive authority to the empirical sciences, and striving to firmly base philosophical views about society, politics, and psychology in scientific fields such as evolutionary biology. Occasionally, such a position is combined with the claim that the entire range of physical and social aspects of reality are accounted for by the causal order of nature. Although critical of this kind of naturalism, the overall position that is defended in this book is not anti-naturalist in the sense that it wants to counter the position that properties related to our minds are ontologically dependent on entities in the natural world. No such claim is made here. Rather, the position defended in this book is skeptical about attempts to render philosophical approaches as entirely continuous with scientific methods and principles and that accept science as the highest tribunal for knowledge. The kind of naturalism that is opposed here is one that holds that science alone should tell us what mental disorder is, and that distinguishing between mental health and mental disorder is an objective matter that does not require taking into account value judgments. While critical toward a certain branch of naturalism, the position proposed in this book is "realist" in the sense that it acknowledges that mental disorders exist and that they cannot be reduced to mere conventions that aim to classify individuals as subjects of such disorders.

Since naturalism is regarded as a general philosophical "attitude," it does not seem entirely unfair to label some philosophical views as "naturalistic," even though they do not explicitly discuss the role of science. A view that denies the importance of historicity, socio-cultural situatedness, and the primacy and irreducibility of interpretation, or that posits a direct, non-interpretative access to the contents of our minds, counts as naturalist.

3. **Outline of the book**

This book falls into two parts that each draw on different strands of hermeneutic philosophy. Part I, consisting of Chapters 1 to 4, draws on work on interpretation related to texts and utterances, and focuses on problems of understanding in research and therapeutic settings. Part 2, consisting of Chapters 5 to 10, draws on the broadened notion of interpretation (particularly on the idea that humans are essentially "self-interpreting animals"), and presents a new take on the concept of mental disorder.

Chapter 2 demonstrates that psychiatry has a unique position "torn between" (medical) science and the humanities, and therefore faces unique methodological challenges with regard to both clinical practice and research. After a brief account of the relationship between science, psychiatry, and philosophy, the field of the *philosophy of psychiatry* is introduced by discussing some of its historical developments and current challenges. The chapter conveys a sense of the variety of philosophical issues that arise in the study of psychiatric phenomena, while emphasizing philosophical issues linked to interpretation and rejecting a specific version of "scientism." Having introduced psychiatry as a discipline with a unique standing in science, the chapters that make up Part 1 highlight the philosophical challenges that arise pertaining to interpretation, focusing on problems related to texts and utterances. The overall conclusion of Part 1 is that focusing on the role and character of interpretation is crucial in order to avoid inaccuracies and misunderstandings both in research and in clinical settings.

Chapter 3 starts out with the observation that knowledge about historical aspects of diseases is often useful for achieving a full understanding of the conditions in question. In the case of mental disorders, because there is a lack of "hard" evidence stemming from the discovery of fossil records, textual evidence is usually the only clue to which researchers have access in order to reconstruct disease activities in the past. Drawing on earlier work (Varga

2013b, 2013c; Radden and Varga 2013), it is argued that this leads to unique methodological challenges with regard to how to engage with historical sources. For instance, some conditions that we today refer to as mental disorders have covered a far wider spectrum than that covered by description of pathological states (Radden 2000). Thus it is first argued that one of the most pressing issues in this regard—the hermeneutical question about *continuity or discontinuity* (or comparability) between texts—is neglected in current debates. In order to provide the most robust comprehension of the relevant text, researchers must *properly interpret* them—a process that involves not only a careful assessment of the quality of the source and its representativity, but also a thorough understanding of the linguistic aspects and cultural horizon of the community from which the text originates. It is then indicated that the problem presents itself in two disguises—as a question about the continuity or discontinuity not only between historical and contemporary texts, but also between different genres of contemporary texts (autobiographical testimony, patient reports written down by clinicians, etc.). Chapter 3 conveys the decisive extent to which the knowledge of *cultural–historical embeddedness of the text* and the *genre of the text* influences its meaning and, lastly, how that knowledge plays a decisive role when trying to settle the question of continuity. To disregard these aspects might reasonably be assumed to incur the risk of drawing unreliable conclusions.

Chapter 4 continues the focus on interpretation, showing that challenges analogous to those discussed in Chapter 3 also present themselves in everyday clinical–therapeutic encounters. The chapter commences with a general reflection on some of the processes that are involved in clinical–therapeutic encounters. Subsequently, the focus is on cognitive behavioral therapy (CBT), as advocated by Beck et al. (1979), Beck and Alford (2009), and J.S. Beck (1995), which is among the most commonly used approaches for understanding disordered psychological processes and is promoted as the therapy of choice for many affective disorders. It is shown that CBT builds upon flawed assumptions about the nature of mental states and, most importantly, about the *meaning* of mental state reports. These assumptions, it is then argued, constitute numerous sources of misunderstanding that require attention. One of the main aims of this chapter is to clarify two processes that are crucial for an extensive understanding in a therapeutic setting, regarding *self-interpretation* and *conversation*. In the final section of the chapter it is demonstrated that taking more seriously these processes between client and therapist can ameliorate understanding in a therapeutic setting.

Whereas Part 1 of the book focuses on interpretation related to texts and utterances, analyzing problems that occur in different guises in research and therapeutic settings, Part 2 of the book deals with *the concept of mental disorder*, arguing that a hermeneutically informed perspective is also fruitful when applied to the concept of mental disorder itself. The critical dialog in Part 2 is with a naturalist position—often referring to classificatory systems in chemistry and biology—which maintains that mental disorder can be defined by relying exclusively on "pure" facts. Naturalists, according to this view, are those who aim to provide a scientific and value-free concept of mental disorder and a connected classificatory system that picks out objective differences between types of mental disorder that are theoretically significant. Part 2 thus critically engages with "naturalism" and its philosophical assumptions, interlinking the clarification of interpretative processes with the critical exploration of claims put forward by naturalistic approaches. This discussion is of crucial importance, as the concept of mental disorder is in many ways important for psychiatric research and practice, with far-reaching consequences for diagnosis and interventions. However, although the question of where to draw the boundaries between health and disease is difficult to answer in medicine, it is even more challenging when it comes to mental health. For the psychiatrist, in Gadamer's words, "the category of illness … is not simply given in the same way as it is for other forms of medical diagnosis" (Gadamer 1996, p. 168). In addition to having to deal with diagnostic uncertainty, psychiatry is further away than other medical subdisciplines from the type of knowledge that characterizes the domain of the natural sciences. As the Introduction to Part 2 demonstrates, a satisfactory answer to these challenges is especially pressing, given the wide range of severe criticism launched against psychiatry as a medico-scientific discipline. Psychiatry has been attacked by a wide variety of philosophers, sociologists, psychiatrists, feminists, psychologists, social workers, and political scientists, who often present a fundamental critique targeting the very concept of "mental disorder." One of the main criticisms is that instead of picking out real entities in the world, psychiatry exerts social control by converting normal forms of suffering and deviant behavior into psychiatric conditions.

Chapter 6 starts out by overviewing the theoretical landscape and observing that while many agree that a strongly naturalist (essentialist) understanding of mental disorders as *natural kinds* is inadequate, two interesting alternatives have emerged in the work of Rachel Cooper and Richard Boyd. According to both authors, the motivation is to recognize the inadequacies of the essentialist understanding of natural kinds, while salvaging some form of naturalism, along with the idea that the special sciences investigate natural kinds in their respective domains. First, it is argued that Cooper's account of mental disorders as natural kinds (Cooper 2005) must ultimately introduce too many conventionalist elements. Second, the chapter deals with Boyd's account of the "homeostatic property cluster" (HPC) model and with the idea that a scientific taxonomy reflects the mechanistic structure of the world (Boyd 1991, 1999). It is argued that there is a problem connected to two common strategies in the sciences, namely "splitting" and "lumping" (Craver 2009). These strategies are relevant whenever a cluster of properties connected to a putatively distinct kind is explained by several mechanisms, or whenever several putatively distinct kinds are explained by the same mechanism. Two interpretation-related dilemmas arise, and it is argued that the elimination of the dilemmas occurs at the price of embracing *conventionalism*. At the end of the chapter, arguments are put forward in favor of a hermeneutically informed *pluralistic view*—what a legitimate scientific kind is might turn out to be contingent on the parameters and interests of the particular scientific enterprise.

Chapter 7, which has the title "Naturalizing biological function," explores an influential attempt to objectively identify a particular condition as disease. Advocates of *natural function naturalism* have recourse to the notion of "natural function." Central to this approach is that value-laden evaluations are not necessary in order to decide whether there is a dysfunction. The chapter first explores Christopher Boorse's "biostatistical" account of natural function (Boorse 1976, 1997, 2014) and a recent modification of Boorse's theory proposed by Manesh Ananth (2008). This debate is especially important, as Boorse (2014) has recently replied to critics and provided more details of and context to some of his earlier thoughts. In the last part of the chapter, a particularly stimulating version of natural function naturalism is discussed. Jerome Wakefield's prominent "hybrid" account of mental disorder (Wakefield 1992, 1999a, 1999b, 2007) is examined, which both accepts a value component (harm) and embraces an objective, evolutionarily informed account of natural functions. The point is that natural functions are objectively discoverable, because our physiological and psychological systems were naturally selected to execute certain functions. Overall, the goal of Chapter 7 is to critically assess the arguments that support this version of natural function naturalism.

Chapter 8, which has the title "Having it both ways," deals with less strict accounts of mental disorder. Fulford (1989, 1991, 2005), Thornton (2007), and Graham (2010, 2013) reject the widely held dichotomy between value-laden and value-neutral (scientific) accounts and the connected Szaszian claim that bodily disease is value-free, whereas mental illness is normative.[5] Thornton

[5] For instance, Hempel (1961) has influentially argued that in order to secure scientific status of a psychiatric classification, "valuational aspects" have to be avoided.

(2007) and Graham (2010, 2013) opt for what is referred to as a "having it both ways" account, accepting that (just like the concept of somatic illness) the concept of mental disorder is value-laden, while rejecting the idea that this has to be interpreted as a sign of scientific deficiency. In other words, the authors accept that the concept of mental disorder is value-laden, while simultaneously maintaining that there are objective truths about mental disorder attributions. Starting from such shared ground, Graham (2010, 2013) and Thornton (2007) develop their positions in different ways.

Graham (2010) presents a prototypical account of mental disorders, according to which a mental disorder implicates a partial impairment in the operation of at least one of the basic psychological capacities of a person. A set of symptoms or a condition is clinically significant and thus qualifies as a mental disorder if there is an impairment of a *fundamental psychological competence*, which is basic, because leading any kind of a "decent or personally satisfying life" requires it (Graham 2010, pp. 131–132). Graham (2010, pp. 147–149) utilizes Rawls' thought experiment to argue that basic mental capacities are like "primary psychological goods."

Thornton (2007) attempts a different approach to "having it both ways," largely inspired by McDowell's secondary property realism and "relaxed naturalism" on which values can be objective. According to this view, some values are not merely projections into a value-free world, but constitute genuine parts of the world and are open to evaluative experience. The fact that they conceptually depend on experience and human sensibility does not preclude the possibility that they are genuine parts of the world. Thus Thornton argues that accepting allows us to "have it both ways"—securing the scientific validity of psychiatric judgment while at the same time acknowledging the value-ladenness of the concept of mental disorder.

The overall conclusion of Chapters 6, 7, and 8 is that although these accounts provide unique perspectives that help us to understand a wide range of aspects of the concept of mental disorder, they ultimately fail to provide an adequate concept of mental disorder. This leads to the proposal and defense of the idea that the key to understanding the failure of both naturalist and (quasi-)value theorist accounts lies in the nature of a group of concepts to which "mental disorder" belongs. Chapter 9 then sets out and defends the idea that the concept of mental disorder is *identity-tied.* Taking seriously the claim that who we are is (at least in large part) constituted by the manner in which we interpret ourselves, and that certain concepts such as rationality are crucial to our self-understanding, it is argued that "mental disorder" stands in an *asymmetrical supervenience* relation to our identities. Demonstrating that the concept of mental disorder is identity-tied and making explicit the manner in which it supervenes on our self-interpretation help to explain its elusive and dynamic nature. However, perhaps the most important implication of this thesis is concerned with the limits of empirical discovery connected to mental disorder. If this thesis is correct, then it would follow that there cannot be anything like a purely empirical discovery of the boundaries of mental disorder. But, this does not mean that nothing can prevent the slide into a detrimental relativism about mental disorder. The suggested position is situated *between* naturalism and relativism, making possible a reflection on mental disorder that steers clear of the pitfalls to which naturalism and relativism fall victim.

Chapter 2

The philosophy of psychiatry: historical developments and current challenges

> It is … particularly in periods of acknowledged crisis that scientists have turned to philosophical analysis as a device for unlocking the riddles of their field.
>
> (Kuhn 1970, p. 88)

This chapter aims to introduce the philosophy of psychiatry, to highlight central aspects of its historical development, and to draw attention to some current challenges. "Philosophy of psychiatry" suggests a field of inquiry that encompasses two different intellectual engagements with the world—science and philosophy. These two disciplines are distinctive enterprises that have made unique and significant contributions to the development of Western thought since the time of the ancient Greeks. In the first part of the chapter, an attempt is made to outline some of the main characteristics of the relationship between science and philosophy, and to argue against a specific version of "scientism" that aims to render philosophy superfluous. Proponents of "scientism" maintain that science will ultimately answer all genuine questions about the nature of the world. The associated claim is that any questions that might remain unanswered by science are not genuine questions but simply products of fallacious thinking. However, as will be shown, "scientism" relies on assumptions that are inherently philosophical in nature.

In the second part of this chapter, the peculiar status of medicine within the natural sciences is discussed. It is argued that medicine is a uniquely relevant domain for philosophical inquiry, due to the intertwinement of science and praxis-related issues with normative implications. It is then demonstrated that while medicine occupies a unique position among the sciences, psychiatry is also unique as a medical subdiscipline. In other words, as a subdiscipline of medicine, psychiatry has a *doubly unique standing*, which explains some of the reasons why philosophical–conceptual issues are inextricably linked to its study and practice. Overall, as well as providing a brief overview of the development of psychiatry and its relationship to medicine and philosophy, one major goal of this chapter is to show that the philosophy of psychiatry is a very promising, albeit emerging, field of investigation. As such, the field will no doubt face challenges. However, the results are likely to be of significant interest in relation to areas of study beyond this field.

1. Science and philosophy

In his widely read introductory text, *Philosophy of Natural Science*, Carl G. Hempel (1966, p. 2) rightly pointed out that the enormous prestige that empirical science enjoys in contemporary Western societies can be largely attributed to its remarkable successes and the wide reach of its applications. Different scientific branches have provided the basis for associated technologies and have thus successfully put the findings of scientific investigations to practical use. However, although science clearly helps humans to gain control over their environment by providing reliable predictions and applicable knowledge, Hempel also notes that science answers a more "disinterested" urge, namely the desire to attain an increasingly profound understanding of the world. It is not difficult to see that, as far as this objective is concerned, there is a clear parallel between science and philosophical inquiry. Accordingly, some contemporary philosophers consider that there is no clear-cut division between philosophy and science. According to such a view, scientific inquiry is a continuum that extends from speculative methods in philosophy to practical–empirical methods in science—both aim at truth and are universal in subject matter. The divide is really of a methodological and stylistic nature (Searle 1999).

Others regard philosophy and science as radically different enterprises with goals that are far from congruent. Some might even go so far as to claim that speaking about the *philosophy of science* amounts to something like a contradiction in terms. The point is that whereas philosophy seems to focus primarily on profound problems such as the meaning of our most basic concepts, fundamental beliefs that are rationally justified, and "eternal questions" that are essentially unresolvable, science is preoccupied with concrete matters of fact and with questions that are resolvable. According to this view, there are features that are unique to philosophical questions. For instance, it is commonly accepted that philosophical questions tend to focus on conceptual matters and, more specifically, on the relationship between our concepts and the world. Another point is that philosophical inquiry is often concerned with questions that are characteristically *uncertain*—we lack not only a clear answer but also an understanding of what would constitute a suitable answer in the first place (Blackburn 1999). When philosophy reaches the point of having certain knowledge about what would constitute an adequate answer to a question, and how to answer the same question in a systematic manner, the question changes from a philosophical to a scientific one. This view might be supported by a certain historical narrative about the relationship between science and philosophy, which typically frames that relationship as a "narrative of partition." According to this view, science and philosophy were once in the same discipline, but science gradually became independent from philosophy and developed into a separate discipline. This gradual development had already started by the time of the ancient Greeks, when Euclidean geometry evolved into a "science of space" that was studied independently from philosophy in Plato's Academy. Other notable examples of this partition include the separation of physics from philosophical metaphysics in the seventeenth century, the development of biology separately from philosophy in the nineteenth century, and the emergence of psychology as a separate discipline in the early twentieth century (Rosenberg 2005, chapter 1). Moreover, as science began to specialize and focus on specific problems, certain philosophical questions started to be viewed as relevant but no longer essential to the discipline. For example, when biology developed into the science of living organisms, the "fundamental" question of what constitutes life (i.e., the question of whether life requires something in addition to those physical and chemical processes that are absolutely necessary for it) was consigned to the periphery of the discipline and became perceived as a question that belonged to philosophy rather than to biology. One important point made by those who view philosophy and science as radically different enterprises is that such fundamental questions remain unanswered by science. This is because the nature of the questions themselves is different from the nature of scientific inquiry.

However, there are several reasons for resisting the temptation to interpret the partition between philosophy and science as a total separation. Although empirical science presents empirically testable hypotheses to account for natural phenomena, certain areas of science remain dependent on genuinely philosophical reflection. Not only does philosophy provide continuous inspiration for new scientific hypotheses, but also philosophical presuppositions are inherent in the scientific method. As Norris (2011) argues, philosophy has long been offering important guidelines with regard to empirical evidence, validity, inductive warrant, corroboration, falsification, hypothesis testing, causality, probability weighting, and many other issues. Questions such as "How does one distinguish deductively valid and/or sound arguments from invalid and/or unsound ones?" or "How does one ascertain the reliability, strength, and cogency of inductive arguments?" are crucial to scientific inquiry, but at the same time cannot be answered empirically by means of experiment and observation. Philosophical logic has historically addressed such questions, and the fact that many scientists today are familiar with these issues should not overshadow the fact that such familiarity is the result of philosophical thought. Other examples of the importance of philosophical presuppositions can be found in the debates about the general scientific method and its application to the special sciences (such as medicine and biology). Many of these questions of application cannot be settled empirically, because they require philosophical reflection. For example, can phenomena in medicine and biology be reductively explained by chemistry? And should phenomena in chemistry be ultimately reductively explained by physics? Just as the question of warrant is relevant with regard to scientific methods, questions concerning reduction are similarly crucial to science (Barker and Kitcher 2013). In addition, it is worth noting that the basic question about the nature and boundaries of science is itself of a philosophical nature. Karl Popper (1962) has famously called attention to this issue and described it as the "demarcation problem."

An important upshot of all this is that some of the problems that arise in empirical science are not just of a genuinely philosophical nature, but can be included among the fundamental problems of philosophy. Hence there are many issues of a non-empirical nature that are pertinent to the *philosophy of science*—a branch of philosophy that deals with questions that arise from science, but which are not themselves scientific.

1.1. **Science and scientism**

Although the emerging sciences left certain "fundamental" questions to philosophy, the extraordinary success of science during the last three centuries generated many new questions, which influenced philosophers' views and guided their choice of topics of interest. For instance, the success of Newton's work propelled forward the philosophical discussion about determinism. If it is the case that simple laws govern the motion of all matter with potentially calculable positions at certain times, and if the human body is a complex constellation of matter, then it seems by no means clear that free will can exist. This is how the philosophical question of free will and determinism arises anew in the wake of a particular scientific advance. To take a more contemporary example, functionalism in philosophy was inspired by the rapid advances in computer science and technology (Appiah 2003, p. 128).

While scientific advances have continuously inspired philosophical work, there have been other times when a genuine interweaving of science and philosophy has been apparent. That is, some scientific revolutions were at the same time revolutions in philosophical thinking, and one could probably not have occurred without the other. As Dennett notes:

> Darwin's new perspective turns several traditional assumptions upside down, undermining our standard ideas about what ought to count as satisfying answers to this ancient and inescapable question. Here science and philosophy get completely intertwined.
>
> (Dennett 1996, p. 21)

However, Dennett is also well aware of the fact that not everybody agrees with the idea that, at least in some cases, philosophical reflection is indispensable to successful scientific practice:

> Scientists sometimes deceive themselves into thinking that philosophical ideas are only, at best, decorations or parasitic commentaries on the hard, objective triumphs of science, and that they themselves are immune to the confusions that philosophers devote their lives to dissolving. But there is no such thing as philosophy-free science; there is only science whose philosophical baggage is taken on board without examination.
>
> (Dennett 1996, p. 21)

The fact that Dennett finds it necessary to issue this warning reveals something about the historically discordant nature of the relationship between science and philosophy. This disharmony eventually led to a debate about the fragmentation between humanities and science, as a divide between what the British chemist and novelist C. P. Snow referred to as "two cultures." On the centennial anniversary of Darwin's *Origin of Species,* Snow delivered the famous "Two Cultures" lecture at the University of Cambridge. In it he addressed the relationship between the sciences and the humanities, and the lecture had an exceptional and lasting impact. Snow lamented what he identified as the continuously growing schism between these two areas of human intellectual activity:

> I believe the intellectual life of the whole of western society is increasingly being split into two polar groups. ... Between the two a gulf of mutual incomprehension—sometimes (particularly among the young) hostility and dislike, but most of all lack of understanding.
>
> (Snow 1990, p. 169)

To avoid the loss to our societies that this "gulf of mutual incomprehension" would eventually cause, Snow invited practitioners on both sides to build intellectual bridges for the sake of advancing knowledge. Alas, Snow's appeals for bridge building fell on deaf ears. Half a decade after his lecture, the historically unique relationship between the (special) sciences and philosophy seems to be even more compromised. Rather ironically, some of the harshest contemporary criticism of philosophy comes from another Cambridge scientist,

Stephen Hawking. In *The Grand Design*—a widely read book, co-authored with Leonard Mlodinow—Hawking argues that philosophy has been rendered useless by the advancing sciences:

> Living in this vast world that is by turns kind and cruel, and gazing at the immense heavens above, people have always asked a multitude of questions: How can we understand the world in which we find ourselves? How does the universe behave? What is the nature of reality? Where did all this come from? Did the universe need a creator? ... Traditionally, these are questions for philosophy, but philosophy is dead. Philosophy has not kept up with modern developments in science, particularly physics. Scientists have become the bearers of the torch of discovery in our quest for knowledge.
>
> (Hawking and Mlodinow, 2010, p. 5)

It certainly rings true that a large number of philosophers would agree that scientists are indeed "the bearers of the torch" with regard to new discoveries. However, Hawking unjustifiably turns the success of science into a flawed, dogmatic "scientism." We might say that the extraordinary success of science has perhaps overshadowed the founding assumptions and intellectual achievements upon which this success was built. Hawking and Mlodinow not only ignore the philosophical foundations of the sciences, but also fail to realize that their wholesale rejection of philosophical work is itself philosophical in nature. This amounts to a self-contradiction in Hawking and Mlodinow's claims that cannot be sidestepped by invoking scientific advances. Ironically, after their dramatic declaration of the demise of philosophy, the authors engage in a good deal of philosophical reflection. When they evaluate conflicting models of reality and develop what they refer to as a "new picture of reality," they do not proceed on rigorously scientific grounds. Rather, they build this "new picture of reality" with a series of characteristic inferences (specifically inferring non-empirical conclusions based on empirical issues) and extrapolations. This sort of reasoning is the hallmark of philosophical thought. Further problems arise if we look at the nature of the questions that they pose. Although a question such as whether the existence of the universe and human beings requires a sentient creator may appear to be empirical, because the proposition that "a creator does/does not exist" admits of truth or falsity, the question itself is actually deeply philosophical. In fact a philosopher could address this question in two steps. First, she could grant that the question of the existence of a being capable of such an act of creation is an empirical matter. The next step would be to identify the contradiction involved in the premise that a sentient creator is needed to explain existence. To make this case, the philosopher could argue that creation *ex nihilo* is precluded by the principles of causation and non-contradiction.

Hawking and Mlodinow might think that philosophy is superfluous because science will eventually answer all genuine questions and expose those that remain as simply meaningless, generated by incorrect thinking. However, it bears repeating that Hawking and Mlodinow need to assume that there cannot *in principle* be genuine questions that are not answerable by science. This assumption is not only false, but it is also unquestionably philosophical in nature. In any case, uncritical deference to the authority of scientific knowledge may, as Snow predicted, result in further polarization and stagnation.

2. Science, medicine, and philosophy

Although the main aim of this chapter is to introduce the philosophy of psychiatry and highlight important historical development and current challenges, some introductory comments about the relationship between science and philosophy were necessary to provide the context. However, before going any further, more needs to be said about psychiatry as a branch of medicine—a scientific discipline that has a unique standing among the sciences and its own particular relationship with philosophy. Some argue that the close relationship with (natural) philosophy in Greek medicine from the beginning of the fifth century resulted in a cross-fertilization that has essentially altered the course of medicine (Miller 1949). One such view, "natural philosophy," with its focus on finding rational explanations and universally applicable laws, has provided the framework for the evolution of medicine into a true science. In the development of medical theory that is associated with natural philosophy, it appears that it was Greek medicine that could first be characterized as "scientific" in the contemporary sense. At the same time, both Hippocrates and later Galen understood medicine as a uniquely composite discipline that encompassed practice, medical theory, and philosophy. Galen believed that a good physician was also a philosopher, who was able to master logic, physics, and ethics (Magner 2005, chapter 4).

Medicine has maintained a long-standing dialectical relationship with philosophy, and some of the most characteristic aspects of medicine arise from the intertwinement of scientific, philosophical, and praxis-related issues. With the establishment of medicine as a unified science of disease that relies on the methodology of the natural sciences to obtain and apply knowledge, philosophy no longer competed with medicine. Rather, philosophical reflection came to operate on a meta-level, taking the medical approach to illness and disorder as its proper object of analysis (ten Have 2000).[1] It is against this

[1] Some of the treatises contained in the Hippocratic Corpus, especially *On Ancient Medicine*, argue that medicine should be strictly empirical and observation based, and they highlight what is seen as the disruptive influence of natural philosophy that might endanger medical science. In fact, *On Ancient Medicine* makes the case for the

background that the philosophy of medicine has come to deal with metaphysical, ontological, ethical, and epistemological examinations of particular forms of medical knowledge and practice (Marcum 2008, p. 8).[2] Edmund D. Pellegrino has aptly described the near relationship between the humanities and medicine in the following way: "Medicine is the most humane of sciences, the most empiric of arts, and the most scientific of humanities" (Pellegrino 1979, p. 17).

However, at least partly due to such an intertwinement, medicine has traditionally occupied a special—and in many ways unique—position in the landscape of the emerging sciences. Aristotle noted that medicine does not completely correspond to what the Greeks called *techne*—that is, a specific form of technical knowing pertaining to a skill used to produce things. The development of the Greek understanding of medicine clearly shows that medicine involved the accumulation of both practical skill (*techne*) *and* a body of "scientific" knowledge. The latter, as Hans-Georg Gadamer (1996, p. 31) argues, involves grasping the universal (usually in terms of causes and effects or general laws) and the eventual application of the universal to the specific. In other words, there are two types of knowledge involved in medicine. On the one hand, medicine has a clear explanatory goal that aims to gain a theoretical understanding of biological processes in the human body. Clearly here the ambition is to provide (causal) explanations of illness in exclusively physiological terms. On the other hand, medicine is also described as an "art." It is literally a "practice" that involves personal encounters and aims to improve the health of individuals and groups. Here physicians do not merely understand their patients according to general scientific laws. Rather, the encounter often involves active, "prudential" engagement from the physician.

> ... medicine represents a peculiar unity of theoretical knowledge and practical know-how within the domain of the modern sciences, a unity moreover which as such cannot be understood as the application of science to the field of praxis. Medicine itself represents a peculiar kind of practical science for which modern thought no longer possesses an adequate concept.
>
> (Gadamer 1996, p. 39)

It is not difficult to see that the difference between the two types of knowledge, and between theory and practice, gives rise to unique methodological

independence of medical science, maintaining that medicine and philosophy are separate undertakings, with different methods and aims.

[2] Philosophy of medicine as a subfield emerged in the nineteenth century, as huge advances in medicine were being made. Elisha Bartlett's *Essay on the Philosophy of Medical Science*, published in 1844, was one of the first academic books on this subject.

issues within the health sciences. These issues came to the fore in the early eighteenth century—the period during which medicine emerged as a genuine scientific field. Gadamer has persuasively argued that, due to this rupture, and to its difference from other fields, modern medicine is in a both *exceptional and problematic* position. In addition to particularly challenging conceptual, epistemological, and methodological questions about the extent to which standard meta-scientific concepts apply to this discipline, significant questions of normative nature arise. In other words, the position of medicine in the sciences is also exceptional and problematic due to the fact that "nowhere else do the advances of modern research enter so directly into the socio-political arena of our time" (Gadamer 1996, p. vii).

Having started this chapter by pointing out some genuine philosophical issues within the realm of science, the goal of this short discussion was to show that medicine has a peculiar status among the sciences. The unique intertwinement of science and praxis-related issues, coupled with substantial normative implications, make medicine an especially appropriate site for philosophical inquiry.

2.1. Medicine, psychiatry, and philosophy

While medicine thus occupies a distinctive and somewhat uncertain position among the sciences, it may be argued that psychiatry's position is even more unique (Gadamer 1996, p. 163). Since the advent of psychiatry in the nineteenth century (significantly later than that of many other medical subdisciplines), it has occupied a peculiar—and in many ways contested—position within medicine. This position has generated an even broader range of philosophical questions. The German philosopher and psychiatrist Karl Jaspers, author of one of the landmark texts in psychiatry, *Allgemeine Psychopathologie* (*General Psychopathology*), has pointed out that one prominent philosophical issue relates to the question of understanding and explanation. To simplify this somewhat, we can say that because it deals with mental phenomena, psychiatry relies on scientific approaches as well as more interpretive methods. Specifically, it relies on the two principles of "knowing" that Wilhelm Dilthey (1989) has called "explanation" (*erklären*) and "understanding" (*verstehen*). On the one hand, along with the more scientific understanding of mental disorders (sometimes referred to as the "medical" or "biological" approach), psychiatry attempts to comprehend these disorders by *explaining* them in terms of *causes*. According to this approach, it is typically hypothesized that the causes of mental disorders are related to impaired brain functioning. Accordingly, the goal is to understand mental disorders by seeking correlations between brain processes and "mental symptoms," which are considered to signal a neurobiological impairment. On the other hand, the more interpretative approach emphasizes psychological mechanisms of the mind, seeking *reasons* for mental disorders. Hence the scientific, biological approach seeks a causal *explanation* that connects mental events to brain events, whereas the interpretative approach seeks psychological *understanding* by establishing meaningful connections between mental events (Phillips 2004).

Elaborating on Dilthey's distinction, Jaspers argued that both the "realm of causes" and the "realm of meanings" had to be taken into account in psychiatry. Such meaning-based approaches can be found not only in historical–hermeneutical disciplines, but also in psychoanalysis (interpretation) and the method of phenomenological psychopathology (emphatic understanding).[3] The acknowledgment of the fact that psychiatric enterprises are inextricably bound to forms of reflection that are not wholly scientific (or biological) led Jaspers to highlight philosophical questions that are connected to psychiatric research and practice. Although he witnessed achievements in neuropathology and biological psychiatry in a period marked by breakthroughs in understanding neurosyphilis and Alzheimer's disease, he argued that without genuine philosophical reflection an adequate comprehension of psychopathological phenomena could not be achieved:

> Many a psychiatrist has said that he did not want to burden himself with a philosophy and that this science had nothing to do with philosophy. But the exclusion of philosophy would nevertheless be disastrous for psychiatry: firstly, if we are not clearly conscious of our philosophy we shall mix it up with our scientific thinking quite unawares and bring about a scientific and philosophic confusion. Secondly, since in psychopathology in particular the scientific knowledge is not all of one kind, we have to distinguish the different modes of knowing and clarify our methods, the meaning and validity of our statements and the criteria of tests—and all this calls for philosophic logic. ... To sum up: If anyone thinks he can exclude philosophy and leave it aside as useless, he will be eventually defeated by it in some obscure form or another.
>
> (Jaspers 1963, pp. 769–770)

Jaspers emphasized that the nature of the study of psychopathology dictates an interdisciplinary approach, and he placed a distinct emphasis on the significance of training in philosophy (Jaspers 1963, p. 36). He compelled clinicians to create in themselves a "universe of different approaches." To use

[3] Jasper's analysis of the philosophical underpinnings of psychiatry and the distinction between explanation and understanding, and between causal meaningful and connections, cannot be avoided today by anybody wanting to engage with the philosophy of psychiatry. Jaspers has undoubtedly made an enormous contribution to the view that psychiatric clinical practice, research, and theorizing involve certain accepted philosophical assumptions.

Snow's words, Jaspers called for a unification of "two cultures" and aimed to provide a foundation for psychopathology that would close the gap between the "vocabulary of the brain" and the "vocabulary of the mind": "Whenever the object studied is Man ... we find that psychopathology comes to be not only a kind of biology but also one of the Humanities" (Jaspers 1963, p. 36).

It is interesting to note that the distinct emphasis on the significance of philosophy for psychiatry was by no means restricted to Germany. In 1948, Aubrey Lewis, the leading British psychiatrist and professor at the Institute of Psychiatry, warned that the diminished role of philosophy in psychiatry has negative consequences:

> Psychiatry has not been able to refrain since then from many a backward glance at the older philosophy she once swore by, and she has been much influenced by the philosophies of later times: she has—doubtless in punishment for her defection—become entangled now and then in bad, unrecognized philosophy of her own making.
>
> (Lewis 1949, p. 99)

Despite the fact that Lewis was concerned with the status of psychiatry as a reputable branch of medicine that emphasized biological explanations and quantitative evaluative methods, he was nevertheless convinced that philosophy ought to have a role in the discipline. He wondered "how it has come about that psychiatrists, who of all doctors might be expected most to value philosophic training and thought, do not as a rule think much of philosophy" (Lewis 1949, p. 100).[4]

Overall, both Jaspers and Lewis were not only convinced by the general contribution of philosophical inquiry, but also believed that philosophical training should form part of education in psychiatry. The point is that rather than trying to turn psychiatry into a scientific discipline that resembles neurology, one should acknowledge that psychiatry, as a medical specialty, is an amalgamation of disciplines and approaches. The unified perspective that Jaspers has specifically called for involves the substantial task of bridging the gap between the "vocabulary of the brain" (used by those researching brain processes and possible drug treatments) and the "vocabulary of the mind" (used by psychiatrists and psychologists involved in counseling and psychotherapy). These two approaches reflect a split

---

[4] Moreover, Lewis does not believe that the relationship between philosophy and psychiatry is unidirectional. He also acknowledges the importance of psychiatry for philosophy and maintains that "it is scarcely to be denied that the phenomena which the psychiatrist studies throw light on many questions of great interest to philosophy, especially those touching on theory of knowledge" (Lewis 1949, p. 103).

within psychiatry insofar as they represent very different ways of reflecting on mental disorder.

3. Psychiatry and philosophy: a short history

Although many issues, such as the unique position of psychiatry and its accompanying challenges, place psychiatry in close proximity to philosophy, the relationship has been one of varying intensity. This is partly due to lack of interest among philosophers, but also due to the aim of psychiatrists to gain recognition as a medical subspecialty on equal footing with any other medical subspecialty, such as cardiology. In the following brief historical survey the aim is to sketch the "dialectic" between the forces that draw psychiatry either toward medical science, or toward the humanities, and to philosophy in particular. It is shown that in the course of the history of psychiatry there were several periods during which one of these two approaches was more dominant than the other. Moreover, the case is made that there were periods during which psychiatry was more or less open to the idea that psychiatric enterprise is bound to forms of philosophical reflection. It is perhaps not too surprising that the interpretative approaches were more positive about the role of philosophy in psychiatry. Once it is acknowledged that the psychiatric enterprise is inextricably bound to forms of reflection that are not strictly biological–scientific, a certain degree of openness toward specifically philosophical questions in psychiatry seems like a natural consequence. For this reason, a brief historical overview is useful here, as it helps to explain some of the challenges that the philosophy of psychiatry faces today.

3.1. The first "biological phase" of psychiatry

Psychiatry developed into a "scientific" endeavor when the view became accepted that insanity was—much like psychical diseases—best understood as a "disease state" (Berrios 1996; Markova and Berrios 2012). Before then, specialists dealing with mental disorder within the walls of the asylums were referred to as "alienists." The alienist's work was administrative and therapeutic in nature, with a focus on the creation of a therapeutic environment within the institutional setting. This was accomplished by implementing rules to govern space, time, movement, diet, and so on (Engstrom 2003, p. 88). By contrast, the new generation of academic psychiatrists at the end of the nineteenth century had a very different ideal regarding their professional role. Many young psychiatrists had some experience of the research that was being conducted in the new laboratories, and they envisaged psychiatry as a scientific discipline closely related to neuropathology. In Germany, Wilhelm Griesinger played an important role in psychiatry's break from its alienist roots. He critiqued the alienist tradition for being both scientifically untenable and unwilling to embrace new medicine firmly rooted in scientific principles. As Griesinger became the Chair of both the neurological and psychiatric wards at the renowned Charité hospital in Berlin, he successfully advocated for linking psychiatry with the field of neurology and extending natural–scientific methods to the study of mental disorder (Engstrom 2003, p. 90). Griesinger's work has certainly played an important role in popularizing a view of psychiatry as a scientific discipline linked to neuropathology and in the promotion of a scientific, biological understanding of mental illness. However, such a view has been around since the establishment of psychiatry. Although early psychiatrists such as Philippe Pinel and Jean-Étienne-Dominique Esquirol accepted that socio-cultural factors play an important role, they ultimately interpreted mental disorders as failures of biological function. During the first half of the nineteenth century, French psychiatrists in particular made significant advances using different methods to study mental disorder. Antoine Laurent Bayle and Louis-Florentin Calmeil described pathologically altered brain structures in patients with dementia, which resulted in the acknowledgment of general paralysis as a nosological category (Gach 2010). Importantly, as another result of the success of the new methodology, this clinical syndrome became widely recognized as an exemplary model of mental disease. In other words, nineteenth-century psychiatrists began to understand mental disorder as an organic malfunctioning, or a "brain disease."

In Germany, a similar development occurred, although it took a slightly different form. This was partly because psychiatric reflection became influenced by the Romantic movement's ideas of nature and mind. These ideas were hostile to the biological reductionism that characterized the work of psychiatrists such as Bayle and Calmeil. Nonetheless, by the middle of the nineteenth century the idea that mental disorders are, in essence, brain diseases appeared in the work of J. B. Friedreich and Wilhelm Griesinger, founding figures of German scientific psychiatry. On the one hand, Griesinger can be interpreted as an archetypal proponent of the clinical movement that emphasized empirical approaches in biological neuropsychiatry and, in doing so, reduced the value of psychological concepts in the understanding of mental diseases. On the other hand, it is not easy to place Griesinger in a theoretical landscape. He was also keenly aware of a certain type of philosophical line of thought that demonstrates the limits of such a reductionist scientific approach. He noted what philosophers today refer to as the "hard problem of consciousness" (Gach 2010, p. 382) when he maintained that "how a material physical act in the nerve fibres or cells can be converted into an idea, an act of consciousness, is absolutely incomprehensible" (Griesinger 1871, p. 6).[5] According to one interpretation, he might be seen as navigating between the domains of highly speculative (Romantic) and anti-theoretical (materialist) medicine (Mishara 1996). Nevertheless, in the same passages, Griesinger also posits that the relationship between the faculties of the mind and the body is ultimately similar to the relationship between function and organ. Thus, for Griesinger, cognitive and conative skills are functions of the brain, "just as transmission and reflex action are considered the special functions of the nerves and spinal cord," and it is valid to "consider the soul primarily and pre-eminently as the sum of all cerebral states" (Griesinger 1871, p. 6).[6]

This view of psychiatry as a scientific discipline linked to neuropathology and the scientific, biological understanding of mental disorder gradually became widely accepted, partly due to Griesinger's considerable influence in German psychiatry. His influence was also reflected in the fact that psychiatry and neurology were clustered together in medical schools. However, the way that Griesinger viewed mental disorders in terms of underlying biological "diseases" was also instrumental in the development of British psychiatry. The *Manual of Psychological Medicine* (Bucknill and Tuke 1858), which quickly became a standard text in the English-speaking world, reflected Griesinger's view of mental disorders as diseases of the brain that affect mental faculties.

Overall, the establishment of psychiatry as an academic medical discipline went hand in hand with the view that mental disorders are "diseases of the brain," and thus essentially similar to neurological diseases. However, the attempts made by biologically oriented psychiatrists to demonstrate the underlying brain disease in psychoses have not led to the kind of success that was achieved by Bayle and Calmeil. Except in a few cases, such as

5 I am using Gach's translation (Gach 2010, p. 382). The original passage is as follows: "Wie ein materieller, physicalischer Vorgang in den Nervenfasern oder Ganglienzellen zu einer Vorstellung, zu einem Acte des Bewusstseins werden kann, ist vollkommen unbegreiflich, ja wir haben keine Ahnung, wie auch nur eine Frage nach dem Vorhandensein und der Art von vermittelnden Vorgängen zwischen beiden zu stellen wäre" (Griesinger 1871, p. 6).

6 Again, however, Griesinger's position is more complex than a simple reductionist one. In fact he notices that when it comes to the relationship between body and mind, we enter the domain of philosophy: "Vom empirischen Standpunkte aus ist zwar vor Allem die Thatsache der Einheit von Leib und Seele festzuhalten und muss es dem Apriorismus überlassen bleiben, die Seele ohne Beziehung auf den Leib, eine leiblose Seele, zu untersuchen und sich mit abstracten Betrachtungen über ihre Immaterialität und Einheit im Gegensatz zur Vielheit der Materie etc. zu begnügen" (Griesinger 1871, p. 6).

senile psychoses and general paresis, the structures of the brain failed to reveal traces of pathological alteration. It is this mismatch that led Jaspers (1963) to critically remark that some psychiatrists embraced a "brain mythology," because they assumed the reducibility of mental disorder to brain disease without a solid empirical foothold. The failure of pathology to robustly link mental disorder to brain disease stood in stark contrast to the simultaneous strides in scientific knowledge about physiological processes and their relationship to medical diseases. On top of this, despite the fact that neurology was on the rise and included eminent figures such as Pavlov and Alzheimer, research in biological psychiatry yielded only modest results that could advance etiological, diagnostic, or therapeutic practice.

Given these failures, it is understandable that by the first decade of the twentieth century the focus on the underlying biological components of mental disorders had diminished somewhat (Angel 2003). On the one hand, this can be explained by the emergence of functional concepts of mental disease. These concepts were able to address behavioral disorders without palpable brain pathology. In many cases this involved a change of focus away from brain pathology, and attention was increasingly directed to interpreting the dysfunctional behavior and the experience of patients. The emergence of functional concepts even prompted consideration of the possibility that life events and psychological factors might be causally responsible for mental disorder. On the other hand, the reduced emphasis on the biological elements of mental disorder can partly be explained by the rise of psychodynamic approaches, which came to dominate American psychiatry in the post-war decades. With these new approaches, the explanatory vocabulary of psychiatry expanded to encompass psychological terms alongside reductionist explanations.

3.2. The triumph of psychopharmacology and neuroscience

However, the period after the Second World War is usually considered to have seen significantly less interaction between philosophy and psychiatry.[7] This

[7] This is to a large extent a valid observation, but it is not to say that philosophy has completely neglected issues pertaining to psychiatry. For example, in Germany, and especially in Heidelberg, phenomenologically informed philosophy and psychiatry flourish to this day. In the mid-1950s, the Joint Commission on Mental Illness and Health assembled a group of experts on mental illness and health. Various disciplines were represented, and the renowned philosopher Charles Morris was asked to represent philosophy. The task assigned to him was to present current philosophical work relating to mental health and the factors that cause or contribute to the development of mental illness. Morris completed the task and prepared a report during a stay at the Center for Advanced Study in the Behavioral Sciences, at Stanford University, California. The work was published in

can be partially explained by a number of events. The first is surely the success of psychopharmacology, which began in the 1950s with the discovery of the antipsychotic effects of chlorpromazine. This drug was able to efficiently regulate and reduce the flamboyant and psychotic symptoms in schizophrenia without massively anesthetizing the patient. Chlorpromazine had a sufficiently stabilizing effect to enable the patient to benefit from psychotherapy. Then, only a decade later, a group of extremely popular benzodiazepine-based psychopharmaceuticals came on the scene. This class of drugs proved to be very effective against anxiety. The success of benzodiazepines was only outmatched by the tricyclic antidepressants (TCAs) and monoamine oxidase inhibitors (MAOIs) that arrived on the scene during the last two decades of the twentieth century. Due to their supposedly having fewer side effects, selective serotonin reuptake inhibitors (SSRIs) eventually supplanted MAOIs and TCAs. The ostensible triumph of psychopharmacology was accompanied by a new preference for understanding neurogenic disorders as manifestations of biological causes, rather than as a response to psychological conflicts. In other words, as during the period in which psychiatry was established as a medical discipline, the view of mental disorders as "diseases of the brain" was again gaining popularity.

Second, the pharmaceutical victories further contributed to the interest in the emerging neurosciences. Following the rapid development of the neurosciences in the second half of the twentieth century, philosophers and psychiatrists came to believe that the ultimate trajectory of psychiatry was to develop into a form of applied biological science. Today, some believe that psychiatry will in the future become a form of clinical neuroscience (Reynolds et al. 2009). In any case, the arrival of neuroscience and its initial successes led

Philosophy and Phenomenological Research (Morris 1959). Although Morris conceded that a great deal of philosophical work specifically addresses mental illness, he seemed to be in agreement with Lewis's assessment of philosophy when he stated that "I doubt whether philosophers, on their side, have paid much attention to psychiatry." Nevertheless, Morris noted that "the interest of philosophers in the field of mental health and illness is rapidly growing, and the interaction of philosophers and psychiatrists is notably on the increase." He envisaged a common ground for philosophers and psychiatrists and reflected on the various ways in which philosophy can be relevant to psychiatry and mental health: "an extension of the philosophic concern with signification and significance into the domain of psychiatry would not make less important the logical, methodological, and normative activities of the philosopher in this area" (Morris 1959, p. 52). While Morris thus acknowledges the relevance of psychiatry to philosophical inquiry, many might press this claim and agree with Bolton (2008) that no philosophical understanding of the mind can be comprehensive without first taking into consideration those aspects of the mind that reveal themselves in the context of mental disorder.

many philosophers and psychiatrists to conclude that the mechanisms that were active in mental disorders could be explained in the "vocabulary of the brain." Linked to this was the hope that if such an understanding of mental disorder was possible, psychiatry could at last share the same scientific (and thus privileged) status as other areas of medicine.

Third, there was a growing dissatisfaction with the methodology and practice of psychoanalysis and its dominance after the Second World War. This aspect is far more complex than the first two. In the 1950s and 1960s, medicine and psychiatry had developed in different directions, partly due to significant scientific advances. Medicine changed from being a practicing "art" to a scientific field that was grounded in biology. Within approximately the same time period, psychiatry underwent its own transformation and began to assimilate the insights of psychoanalysis. What began as a medical subdiscipline turned into a psychoanalytically based therapeutic "art." Psychoanalysis was initially applied to "neurotic" conditions, but psychoanalytically informed therapy eventually came to influence virtually every treatment of mental disorder, including disorders with psychotic features. During the decades that followed the Second World War, psychoanalytically informed psychiatry had become dominant (Kandel 1998).[8] Given the psychodynamic explanations of symptoms in the first two editions of the American Psychiatric Association's *Diagnostic and Statistical Manual of Mental Disorders* (DSM), there was no need to work out elaborate and precise classification systems. Symptoms were not viewed as signs of underlying disease entities that could be understood in scientific, causal terms. Rather, they were understood as expressions of underlying dynamic tensions triggered by life events and therefore as only meaningful in the light of the individual's situation and history. This emphasis, together with the exceptionally minor role that diagnosis played in dynamically informed psychiatry, had provoked criticism for being medically unscientific and thus overly subjective. Philosophers such as Karl Popper famously objected that psychoanalysis was non-falsifiable and therefore unscientific. Doubts arose about both the effectiveness of psychoanalysis and its discordance with scientific approaches, and psychoanalysis eventually moved toward the periphery, despite its once dominant position.

Partly in reaction to widespread concerns about the reliability of psychiatric diagnosis, considerable efforts were made to develop a psychiatric taxonomy.

[8] Kandel quotes a Harvard Medical School Department of Psychiatry faculty member's summary of the state of psychoanalytically oriented psychiatry in 1964: "In the past 40 years, largely under the impact of psychoanalysis, dynamic psychotherapy has become the principal and essential curative skill of the American psychiatrist and, increasingly, a focus of his training" (Kandel 1998, p. 458).

From the 1980s onward, a symptom-based, descriptive approach to psychopathology began to gain ground. The descriptive approach changes the focus from underlying psychodynamic events to the study of discernible symptoms and behavioral phenomena. One theoretically and practically significant change that this approach brought about can be found in the third edition of DSM (DSM-III). Inspired by a diagnostic model from medicine, mental disorders were no longer categorized as broad, etiologically defined entities that were continuous with normality. As Mayes and Horwitz (2005) note, this radical change from psychoanalysis to symptom-based (descriptive) diagnoses was not so much the result of growing scientific knowledge as a reflection of professional politics, increased government involvement, marketing efforts of pharmaceutical companies, and pressure from health insurers to demonstrate therapeutic effectiveness. By contrast, some prominent figures in psychiatry interpreted the changes that DSM-*III* brought about as a victory for the scientific approach to psychiatry (Klerman et al. 1984; Sabshin 1990). The hope was that such a victory would allow the development of a standardized system.

Overall, a couple of factors might help to explain the relatively small amount of interaction between philosophy and psychiatry in the period after the Second World War. Pharmaceutical successes, interest in the emerging neurosciences, and the symptom-based descriptive approach to psychopathology (and the "disease" model of mental disorder) have helped to create an intellectual climate to which philosophical thought might have seemed unlikely to be able to contribute. In a general academic climate that has been deeply influenced—consciously or not—by these developments, it has become common to imply causal relationships between biological and psychological phenomena, despite the fact that the concrete functioning of the relevant mechanisms may remain unknown. For instance, it is nowadays widely customary to apply a naive reductionism (i.e., that neural events have a direct causal relationship to psychological phenomena) to depression by speaking about depression as "a chemical imbalance," or about a psychotic disorder such as schizophrenia as a "brain disease" (France et al. 2007; Miller 2010). Although some psychiatric textbooks acknowledge that such hypotheses are unproven, the former Director of the US National Institute of Mental Health (NIMH) has maintained that mental disorders are diagnosable and treatable "brain disorders" (Hyman 1998; Miller 2010).

3.3. Disappointment with psychopharmacology and neuroscience and the new critique of psychiatry

By the end of the twentieth century, the initial enthusiasm about psychopharmacology and the neurosciences was starting to wane. Despite the early optimism, the neurosciences that shaped the "Decade of the Brain"[9] have not provided biomarkers or diagnostic laboratory tests that can confirm the diagnosis of even the most common psychiatric disorders. Those disorders with an undeniable biological disease or genetic defect catalogued in DSM-IV-TR (e.g. Alzheimer's disease, certain forms of dementia, Rett's disorder) now fall under the authority of neurology (Murray 2006). It is not surprising that some prominent psychiatrists have become more vocal in their criticism of the widespread hope that neuroscience will be able to provide solutions to psychiatric questions:

> The past 30 years have produced no discoveries leading to major changes in psychiatric practice. The rules regulating research and a dominant neurobiological paradigm may both have stifled creativity. Embracing a social paradigm could generate real progress and, simultaneously, make the profession more attractive.
>
> (Priebe et al. 2013, p. 319)

One of the problems with a strictly neurological explanation of mental illness is, as Gregory Miller puts it, that "a mental disorder need not be triggered by, due to, or explained by brain pathology any more than a software bug must be a consequence of hardware failure" (Miller 2010, p. 736). In other words, even in seemingly clear-cut cases where it could be demonstrated that the etiology of a disorder involves a causally active brain mechanism, it remains a possibility that the mechanism involved is itself causally affected by psychological events. Expressing his pessimism about a simple biological etiology of mental disorders, Frances (2010) argues that there are probably a wide variety of pathways that lead to disorders such as schizophrenia.[10] We need to bear in mind that such disappointment with neuroscientific progress is not a dominant view. Indeed, it seems that the general tenor of current research is still grounded in the claim that mental disorders are best understood and treated as brain disorders (Insel and Quirion 2005).

Nevertheless, optimism about psychopharmacology and trust in the pharmaceutical industry's claims are dwindling. In recent years, evidence has surfaced that has disconfirmed the most commonly used antidepressants. Moncrieff and Kirsch (2005) have criticized the pharmaceutical industry's exaggerated claims about the effectiveness of some of the available psychopharmacological products. Drawing on meta-analyses,

[9] The 1990s were designated the "Decade of the Brain" by the US Congress.

[10] Frances is rather pessimistic about diagnostic classification, which "is the result of historical accretion and accident without any real underlying system or scientific necessity. ... Our mental disorders are not more than fallible social constructs (but nonetheless useful if understood and applied properly)" (Frances 2010, p. 6).

they argue that, when compared with placebo, SSRIs fail to exhibit clinically significant benefits. Moreover, even the slight superiority shown over placebo can be explained by the choice of methodology. After successful petitioning, a significant amount of the negative data for antidepressants became available to the public. Naturally, this increased doubts about the benefits of popular antidepressants. Furthermore, similar doubts have been raised with regard to antipsychotic medication. The National Institute of Mental Health (NIMH) came to the conclusion that it could not be demonstrated that more recent, atypical antipsychotic medications outperform conservative antipsychotic medications (Murray 2006). An interesting study by Leff et al. (1992) compared schizophrenic patients in developing and developed countries. It was demonstrated that patients in developing countries experienced a higher rate of recovery, even though only 16% of them received antipsychotic medicine, compared with 61% in the developed countries (Whitaker 2004). In fact, an empathetic psychosocial milieu and little or no medication were found to be among the best predictors of recovery (Bola et al. 2005). Although these findings certainly cannot be interpreted as knock-down arguments against certain medications, they have definitely contributed to the skepticism about the efficacy of psychopharmacological products.

It seems understandable why a growing number of researchers such as Kendler (2005) are advocating explanatory pluralism in the light of the discouraging results of neuroscience and psychopharmacology. Kendler argues in favor of abandoning the idea that simple, linear explanatory models can be developed, and claims that psychiatry ought instead to accept that etiological pathways will always be complex. In fact, the new DSM-5 seems to want to take into account the increasing evidence for the role of psychosocial factors,[11] thus attempting to acknowledge the intertwinement of psychological and biological factors in mental disorder. However, it remains neutral about the causal relationship between such factors. The current approach understands mental disorder as a psychological or behavioral syndrome that expresses or *reflects* an underlying dysfunction of a psychobiological nature (Stein et al. 2010).[12]

[11] Not everyone would agree with this. Some would maintain that the fact that *DSM-5* eliminated Axis IV and psychosocial factors (now covered through an expanded set of V codes) points in the opposite direction.

[12] The NIMH has withdrawn support for *DSM-5*, criticizing its symptom-based diagnosis, in favor of a broad-spectrum approach that shows an explicit preference for biologically based methods.

The question of whether psychiatry is a "genuinely scientific" discipline has been raised in view of myriad factors that seem to influence diagnostic practices. As evidenced by the debates relating to DSM-5, psychiatry is once again accused of being unscientific. According to this view, psychiatry lacks objective biological criteria even in the case of the primary disorders. It operates with an inferior and often changing diagnostic and classification system, and lacks a unified account of mental disorder. Moreover, critics contend that psychiatry inappropriately medicalizes otherwise normal reactions to life events. Given the growing criticism from prominent psychiatrists, including Frances (2010) and Spitzer (2011), it is fair to say that psychiatry is currently undergoing a major "identity crisis." As one critique argues, there is a

> national trend toward gradually increasing openness to the idea that psychiatric diagnosis (A) is largely unscientific, (B) is highly subjective and political, and (C) can cause untold harm, ranging from the patients' lowered self-confidence to loss of custody of children to loss of health insurance (because any psychiatric label can be considered evidence of a pre-existing condition) to loss of the right to make decisions about their medical and legal affairs.
>
> (Caplan 2012)

Indeed, one could claim that psychiatry's descriptive (symptom-based) diagnostic categories appear too crude when they are directly compared with the etiological models used in medicine. Whereas scientific advances in physiology, bacteriology, etc. have led to progress from descriptive to etiological categories in medicine, psychiatry has not yet witnessed the same degree of progress. Undoubtedly, if one were to use the same standards of measurement in psychiatry as one would employ in the case of other medical subdisciplines, then by all accounts psychiatry would appear to suffer from scientific immaturity. However, the crucial question is whether it is adequate and fair to use the same standards in psychiatry as in medicine, given the differences between psychiatry and medicine.

One way to reduce the impact of this criticism is to "pass the buck." One might say that, akin to psychiatry, although to not nearly the same extent, neurology in part relies on descriptive categories due to the relatively slow rate of progress in the brain sciences. Another, and better, line of defense was hinted at over the course of this discussion. We may recall Gadamer's remarks about the unique status of psychiatry among the medical subspecialties. Apart from the complex empirical challenges that it shares with neurology, psychiatry must face additional conceptual challenges because it addresses a wider range of symptoms. Neurological and "somatic" disorders are typically confined to sensations, movements, and perceptions. By contrast, psychiatric disorders include emotion, volition, actions, desire, motivation, belief, thought, personal identity, intersubjectivity, and behavior. There is thus a vast difference in complexity between symptoms that occur in "somatic" disorders and those that occur in "mental" disorders. As Fulford (1989) and Fulford et al. (2006) have noted, the further removed a psychiatric disorder is from a bodily disorder, the greater the number of potential conceptual difficulties that arise. For instance, certain types of controversial disorders, such as hypochondria or hysteria, are further removed from bodily illness than organic disorders such as dementia. The controversies arise not only because of the lack of solid biological evidence, but also because their status as genuine disorders is dubious. They are suspiciously close to characteristics that can be evaluated as immoral. It is not entirely clear whether a person's habits are signs of disease or just signs that the person has an extremely hedonistic view of life. It can be similarly difficult to draw meaningful distinctions between a person who is often anxious and a person who suffers from an anxiety disorder. Likewise, a person who has the lifestyle of a "career criminal" may not necessarily suffer from psychopathic personality disorder. The more heavily the diagnostic criteria for a mental disorder rely on judgments that are potentially value-laden, the more contested will be its status as a legitimate mental disorder.

For example, consider the case of conduct disorder. This condition is diagnosed against a background of a sustained pattern of antisocial behavior that results in a clinically significant deficiency in social or occupational functioning. However, the criteria for antisocial behavior are evaluative (moral, social, etc.) in nature, rather than factual. Examples of social–evaluative criteria include serious violation of laws and of social and moral norms (e.g. destructive and aggressive behavior, deceit, thievery). Given the natural variations of laws and social norms that occur between groups, the overly broad formulation of diagnostic criteria, and the lack of biomarkers (for a review, see Moffitt et al. 2008), the necessary and sufficient diagnostic criteria for conduct disorder are highly contestable and ambiguous. Other diagnostic categories that are partly defined in terms of violation of social norms include paraphilias. For instance, masochism is defined in DSM-IV as the repeated urge to be beaten, humiliated, bound, etc. The ambiguities inherent in the diagnostic criteria for conditions such as conduct disorder and masochism have serious implications in relation to the possibility of involuntary treatment. If there is a lack of objective diagnostic measures outside of subjective social–evaluative criteria, it becomes extremely difficult to determine whether individuals diagnosed with conditions such as conduct disorder should be subjected to involuntary treatment.

In addition to these aspects, new socio-political issues have come to the fore in recent discussions of the changes made in DSM-5. One example of such a change is the proposed removal of the "bereavement exclusion" in major depressive disorder. Removing this exclusion runs the risk of pathologizing a normal grief response. Another socio-political issue concerning DSM-5 is the controversy over whether or not racism should be listed as a disorder. One possible effect of introducing racism as a disorder is that it would become an "individual problem." Thinking of racism along the lines of individual pathology might further contribute to the socio-political forces that create and sustain racism. Issues such as these demonstrate the degree to which metaphysical and epistemological difficulties occur at the boundaries between distress and disorder. These complications exacerbate the ethical, jurisprudential, and political problems that arise in psychiatric practice.

Overall, with the waning enthusiasm about psychopharmacology and neurosciences and the lack of biomarkers and diagnostic laboratory tests to confirm the diagnosis of psychiatric disorders, the question of whether psychiatry is a "genuinely scientific" discipline has again been raised. In the debates relating to DSM-5, we see that psychiatry is accused of being unscientific, with a frequently changing diagnostic and classification system that pathologizes normal conditions based on unscientific grounds. However, given the differences between psychiatry and medicine, and the unique position of psychiatry that has been emphasized in this chapter, it seems justified to question whether it is adequate and fair to use the same standards in psychiatry as in medicine.

4. **A new situation and the interest in the philosophy of psychiatry**

In the face of growing disappointment with neuroscientific and psychopharmacological advances, the complications associated with diagnostic practice discussed earlier once again point to two alternative ways of understanding the nature of psychiatry. One approach is to maintain the "vocabulary of the brain," attempt to strengthen the scientific nature of psychiatry, and insist on placing psychiatry on an equal footing with other medical subspecialties. Some consider that this could be achieved by bringing psychiatry closer to the life sciences. For instance, it has been suggested that psychiatry should be considered a "clinical neuroscience." Another approach is to recognize that psychiatry also needs the "vocabulary of the mind." This view acknowledges the limitations to the scientific nature and validity of the current categorical system. According to this view, these limitations stem in part from the ways in which neuroscience progresses, but they are also the result of conceptual problems inherent in psychiatry. Put simply, the opinion is that no neuroscientific evidence or psychopharmacological invention will be able to resolve these conceptual roadblocks. Many psychiatrists in this camp argue in favor of explanatory pluralism, seeking a constructive encounter with the humanities and with philosophy in particular. Just as Jaspers and others have argued, the view is that psychiatry is exceptionally likely to benefit from philosophical contributions. The realm of the "mental" necessitates the kind of systematic reflection that is unique to philosophy. Moreover, there is growing acknowledgment of the fact that many of the issues linked to the everyday practice of psychiatry have been addressed within the rich history of philosophy.

Largely due to the work of psychiatrists, psychologists, and philosophers in this latter group, the new interdisciplinary field of philosophy of psychiatry has begun to develop and flourish within the last three decades (Fulford 2000; Fulford et al. 2003). Inspired by both Anglo-American analytic and continental philosophical traditions, philosophers, psychologists, and psychiatrists working in this area are striving to gain a deeper understanding of both psychiatric issues and mental healthcare. Within the field of philosophy of psychiatry, we may distinguish between three overlapping areas of special interest (Graham and Stephens 1994; Murphy 2008). The first area consists of a body of work on the special issues that arise in psychiatry as a "special science." Here researchers draw on the methods and concepts of philosophy of science to reflect on the nature of psychiatric explanation and classification. To a certain extent this is a continuation of a philosophical concern with the evidential status of psychoanalysis. The second area deals with ethical issues in psychiatry. One of the main ethical issues considered in philosophy of psychiatry concerns the rationality and self-determination of patients, and the conditions under which the deprivation of their liberty and coercive treatment might be justified. Surprisingly, this area of philosophy of psychiatry has received relatively little attention from the field of medical ethics. It may very well be the case, as Fulford et al. (2006) have argued, that the analytical instruments which have been developed in bioethics do not match the complexity of the issues presented in psychiatry. Finally, the third area covers work related to psychopathology and the philosophy of mind. For instance, the philosophical issue of personal identity has benefited from empirical material on disorders such as multiple personality disorder (Mackie 1985; Wilkes 1988; Humphrey and Dennett 1989). The majority of psychiatric disorders, and particularly those involving altered bodily self-consciousness, prompt philosophical questions about the relationship between the mind and the body.

The World Psychiatric Association has recognized the value of this emerging discipline and established a new section for the field of philosophy of psychiatry. Meanwhile, Oxford University Press established the International Perspectives in Philosophy and Psychiatry (an international book series), and has since published the *Companion to the Philosophy of Psychiatry* (Radden 2004) and the *Oxford Textbook of Philosophy and Psychiatry* (Fulford et al. 2006; see also Banner and Thornton 2007). In addition, with assistance from the Association for the Advancement of Philosophy and Psychiatry, the journal *Philosophy, Psychiatry and Psychology* (*PPP*) was launched almost two decades ago. The MIT Press has also acknowledged the surge of interest in this subject and established a new book series under the label Philosophical Psychopathology. Researchers are able to meet and cooperate at the annual series of International Conferences on Philosophy, Psychiatry, and Psychology. Finally, together with all of the publication activity within the discipline, the establishment of Masters programs in philosophy of psychiatry in the UK shows that this discipline is more than just a temporary trend. Lest this assessment be considered too optimistic or speculative, it should be pointed out that leading figures in the field have managed to establish international research forums and teaching programs, both of which are crucial to preserving interest in the emerging field.

As we have seen over the course of this chapter, the new interdisciplinary field of philosophy of psychiatry began to develop and flourish within the last three decades, and the expansion of interest in this field is not surprising when one considers the challenges that are faced by present-day psychiatry. However, there might be a slightly different way of explaining this development that provides additional support for some of the points discussed in this chapter. Kuhn (1970, p. 88) has famously noted that it is "particularly in periods of acknowledged crisis that scientists have turned to philosophical analysis as a device for unlocking the riddles of their field." Following his analysis, a crisis emerges due to the occurrence of a series of anomalies that amount to a cluster of challenges that cannot be addressed with the current paradigm. Philosophical inquiry, and particularly the philosophical analysis of the most fundamental rules and suppositions of the field, makes a unique contribution to the transformational process that co-occurs with the emerging paradigm. To support this compelling observation, Kuhn points to two major shifts in physics, namely the emergence of Newtonian physics in the seventeenth century and quantum mechanics in the twentieth century, both of which were "preceded and accompanied by fundamental philosophical analyses of the contemporary research tradition" (Kuhn 1970, p. 88). Against such a background, we might indeed ask ourselves whether the increasing attentiveness to the philosophy of psychiatry can be interpreted as a response to a developing crisis in the guiding paradigm of psychiatry. It seems indisputable that, after the advances in the neurosciences and pharmacology in the last two decades, there are significant issues that have proved resistant to straightforward resolution within the existing paradigm.

4.1. The applied "philosophies of ..."

Up until now the focus of this discussion has been on the changes within psychiatry that have contributed to interest in the emerging interdisciplinary field of philosophy and psychiatry. However, genuine cooperation between the disciplines is only sustainable if there is solid commitment from both disciplines. To complete the picture of the factors that have contributed to the development of the philosophy of psychiatry as a field of inquiry, we also need to consider some of the relevant changes that philosophy has undergone in recent decades.

The fact that there is now a growing body of philosophical research that has a direct bearing on areas of practical concern is partly the result of a trend that has been discernible over the last couple of decades. For instance, in the philosophy of mind, the interest in the "pure" investigation of psychological concepts with the help of thought experiments has diminished. Much philosophical inquiry began to lean toward forms of empirically informed theorizing, productively integrating empirical material. After some initial resistance from philosophers, this general tendency has led to the emergence of a variety of philosophical enterprises that are described as "applied." "Applied philosophy" involves the application of philosophical knowledge and methods to certain problems.

While this may at first glance seem like a reasonable label, it carries some unfortunate connotations that might lead to misunderstanding. The term "applied" tends to imply a one-way application of philosophical knowledge and methods, thus suggesting that these "applied" fields are in significant ways derivative. However, this is not entirely correct, as the methods and theoretical approaches that philosophers may apply to empirical fields are altered by their application. Therefore it is better to think of applied philosophy as a two-way encounter in which philosophy and empirical fields can benefit from each other. This two-way interaction is well documented, in particular if one recalls the conundrums that both philosophy and the special sciences face when reflecting on the nature of causation. One puzzling question that is often generated in biology, psychology, economics, etc. concerns the relationship between correlation and causation. In order to address such a conundrum within a special science, the biologist, psychologist, or economist first needs to take a stand on philosophical accounts of causation. Similarly, philosophers working on general issues relating to causation consult the special sciences for real-life examples that might challenge, test, and correct some of their hypotheses. Much progress, whether it is scientific or philosophical, is propelled by the open dialog between the two realms.

The subfields that today make up a long list of “philosophies of …” aim to offer a profound understanding of the theoretical and conceptual underpinnings of the respective (sub)fields by means of the critical–analytical approach that is characteristic of philosophy. In these fields, philosophers frequently establish links between the particular, local concerns of specific disciplines and those of philosophy in general. At their best, these domains of philosophy attempt to build a mutually beneficial bridge across what Snow described as a “gulf of mutual incomprehension” between the two sides. Critics such as Hawking and Mlodinow (2010) ignore the increasing number of areas in which fruitful cooperation between philosophy and the sciences can occur.

Although the list of “philosophies of …” is growing, there are specific reasons why philosophical interest in psychiatry is on the rise. Certainly the anti-psychiatry movement played a prominent role in generating philosophically skeptical interest in psychiatry. The radically skeptical claim that mental illness does not exist was advocated by some of the most prominent anti-psychiatric figures, such as Thomas Szasz. This claim was supported by what were, in essence, philosophical arguments. Such skeptical arguments prompted philosophically informed discussions about the evaluative nature of psychiatric diagnoses, in addition to a great deal of philosophical work on the very concept of mental disorder. However, as was stated previously, there is a two-way relationship between philosophy and psychiatry. For these reasons, we may also speculate that the nature of the phenomena that are dealt with by psychiatry enables a cooperation that is beneficial to philosophy. It is easier to see this benefit if we locate psychiatry within the landscape of the “philosophies of …”

4.2. Philosophy of psychiatry in the landscape of "the philosophies of …"

The philosophy of psychiatry thus occupies a unique position on the long list of “philosophies of …” We have already seen how medicine has a special status among the sciences and how psychiatry stands out within medical subdisciplines. To see why the philosophy of psychiatry has a special position among the “philosophies of …,” it is helpful to divide “philosophy of …” fields into two groups—those with a “direct” bearing and those with an “indirect” bearing on a particular scientific field. Put simply, “indirect” philosophical contributions to scientific investigation are those that address the fundamental elements of scientific methodology, types of inferences, and research practices. These philosophical contributions analyze central notions, such as knowledge and evidence, that are dealt with in the special sciences. By contrast, "direct" philosophical contributions to scientific investigation are those that discover new features of the particular object of study.

Philosophy of psychiatry is distinctive in the sense that it makes both "indirect" and "direct" philosophical contributions to the science of psychiatry. "Indirect" philosophical research can provide a more profound understanding of the ideas, practices, types of knowledge, inferences, concepts, and values that are inherent in mental healthcare. For instance, ideas from the philosophy of science can illuminate the nature of psychiatric explanations for a given set of symptoms. In addition, since the object of study in psychiatry is the human mind, it is very likely that philosophy can also offer a "direct" contribution by revealing features about the human mind. These features can include human consciousness, behavior, emotions, cognition, mental causation, etc. Here philosophy of mind can help to clarify those aspects of consciousness, emotions, and cognition that seem to be impaired by various mental disorders. This makes a constructive encounter between philosophy and psychiatry more probable. If the philosophy of psychiatry is successful, its contributions can have a significant effect on the lives of both patients and professionals involved in the various mental healthcare settings.

Overall, the philosophy of psychiatry is a recently developed field that has unique potential for the constructive two-way enrichment of both disciplines. Since the object of study in psychiatry is the human mind, both "direct" and "indirect" contributions are possible. Moreover, due to the fact that, unlike biology, physics, or chemistry, a normative notion of health is unavoidably implicated in psychiatry, philosophy is likely to be able to make a broader contribution. Philosophy also stands to benefit from advances made by psychiatry as the study of the human mind. Specifically, philosophy of mind can receive essential input from disordered cases, while the philosophy of science can be enriched by psychiatry's attempts to address problems of explanation and causation in clinical practice. Thus, although the philosophy of psychiatry clearly shares ground with several other "philosophy of ..." fields, there are also a number of aspects that make this field distinctive. The nature of these distinctive characteristics will probably push the field toward dynamic development. Such development is also likely to be fueled by the fact that the specific conditions for a systematic inquiry into the philosophical questions connected to psychiatry have radically changed since the time when Jaspers had "only" phenomenology at his disposal. Today the philosophy of psychiatry has access to a wide variety of conceptual tools. These range across the discipline of philosophy and include both the European tradition of the philosophy of subjectivity and the Anglo-American tradition of the philosophy of mind and science (Spitzer et al. 1988, introduction). However, the perplexing philosophical questions that confront psychiatrists remain fundamentally unchanged.

4.3. Resistance and objections

The philosophy of psychiatry definitely has the potential to become a broadly accepted subdiscipline. However, there may be resistance from both sides. Philosophical reflection about the mind and behavior can seem like an intellectual luxury in the context of the urgent distress of patients that psychiatrists encounter on a daily basis. In addition, psychiatry is currently facing a crisis of reputation, unable to attract excellent students, or to convince psychiatric trainees to choose research-oriented careers (Reynolds et al. 2009). Given this background, one could object that psychiatry has enough trouble as it is, so it does not need to burden itself with puzzling over problems related to abstract notions such as causation.

The resistance from philosophy could take a different form. Although philosophers welcome and appreciate the concern to make philosophy relevant to the "real" world, some might worry that branches of applied philosophy (such as the philosophy of psychiatry) may not represent a properly philosophical form of engagement. Indeed, this seems like a reasonable concern, given the restructured educational "market" that has put increased pressure on departments to prove themselves "useful" in terms of attracting students. Many philosophy departments have reacted by offering an increasing number of courses in applied philosophy. Some of them focus only on practical aspects of a given field and neglect traditional philosophical reflection and the history of philosophy (Noonan 2003).

Although this might be the case, this concern does not mean that there is something *necessarily* unphilosophical about the idea of applied philosophy. Thus under certain circumstances it would indeed be possible for branches of applied philosophy to "dilute" the discipline. This would be the case if the inquiry would somehow negate or undermine some of the features that are unique to philosophical questions. For instance, one could envisage that a process of "dilution" might be generated if applied philosophical inquiries became strictly outcome-oriented and blind to the characteristically uncertain nature of some philosophical knowledge. However, so long as such aspects of genuine philosophical engagement with the world are respected, there is no reason to suppose that branches of applied philosophy "dilute" the discipline. Furthermore, such concerns about "dilution" of the discipline are, at bottom, committed to the notion of a "pure" discipline. However, given the historical developments, the notion of a "pure" practice of philosophy may turn out to be something of a fantasy.[13]

5. Conclusion

Rather than attempting to provide a comprehensive account of the relationship between science and philosophy, or between psychiatry and philosophy, the aim of this chapter was to present the field of the philosophy of psychiatry by discussing some aspects of its historical development and current challenges. The opening sections of the chapter illustrated some of the main characteristics of the relationship between science and philosophy. As a subdiscipline of medicine, psychiatry can be described as historically "torn" between (medical) science and the humanities. As a branch of medicine, psychiatry has a *doubly unique standing*, as it is fundamentally concerned with philosophical questions. Given psychiatry's unique standing, the philosophy of psychiatry holds a special position among the "philosophies of ... ." Its peculiarity is the source of both major challenges and considerable promise. The extent of the philosophical–conceptual problems is matched by the range of possible answers and new perspectives that might be generated in attempting to resolve them. Due to both the much debated position of psychiatry as a scientific discipline, and the productive reciprocal relationship between philosophy and psychiatry, it is likely that the new perspectives generated will not only benefit the two disciplines involved, but also have potential ramifications for areas of study way beyond the field. As we have seen in the final sections of this chapter, it is likely that the philosophy of psychiatry will evolve into a fertile field characterized by mutual interest. Although it clearly shares ground with all the other "philosophy of ..." fields, the aspects that make this field unique are those that make it likely that the field will grow and develop. The questions that psychiatry raises are not only important to philosophers,

[13] Similarly, the search for a "pure" science seems to be proving elusive. This is partly evidenced by a change in scientific paradigm away from hard-nosed naturalism (Horst 2007). Although it would seem that science aims to describe the world from an "objective" standpoint, the idea of a value-free observation of reality has come under scrutiny. There is now an acceptance of the view that all observations are theory-laden. What this means is that observation will not "carve nature at its joints." Rather, our pre-existing framework of ideas shapes the content of a given perception into the context of a meaningful whole. The recognition of the concept and theory-ladenness shows that science may not be able to achieve the level of "absolute" objectivity that it strives for. Thus those who protest against "applied" philosophy on the grounds that it dilutes the discipline would be hard pressed to find a similar level of "purity" in the sciences.

but also immediately relevant to distinctly human concerns that go beyond philosophy and psychiatry.

There are many types of philosophical questions that arise in the philosophy of psychiatry. However, in this book the focus is on those questions that concern interpretation and understanding. Importantly, it has also become clear that it is the doubly unique standing of psychiatry that gives rise to some of these philosophical questions. The remaining chapters of this book will attempt to make a contribution to the field of philosophy of psychiatry by exploring some of these issues, asking new questions, and providing new answers. Now that psychiatry has been introduced as a discipline with a unique standing in science, Chapters 3 and 4 will highlight the philosophical challenges that arise with regard to interpretation. As will be demonstrated, challenges arise with regard to three different contexts in research and therapeutic settings. Focusing on the role and character of interpretation is crucial in order to avoid inaccuracies and misunderstandings both in research and in clinical settings.

Chapter 3

Interpreting psychiatric texts

Historical inquiry may in many cases help us to acquire a fuller understanding of a condition. Investigating the available historical sources may reveal how the frequency and distribution of the condition correlate with environmental changes, types of human activity, or population density. Gathering such data not only enables a richer understanding of the condition in question, but may also help to predict future occurrences and thus allow preventive measures to be taken. For instance, it is well known that in several areas of central Asia the bacterium responsible for human cases of bubonic plague (*Yersinia pestis*) can still be found in its hosts, in wild populations of small mammals. Studies of the history of plague outbreaks have aided our understanding of the impact of climate changes on wildlife reservoirs and how this is linked to the outbreak of human epidemics. Furthermore, the knowledge that plague activity in a particular region has historically correlated with climate fluctuations enables researchers to predict the extent to which the changes linked to climate change are likely to affect future plague epidemiology. There are no convincing reasons why this should not apply to both somatic and mental disorders. In addition to the personal costs for sufferers, mental disorders such as depression incur significant economic and social costs for societies (Greenberg et al. 2003). Consequently, especially at a time when the incidence of mental disorder is increasing, it would be valuable to gather information about some of its historical aspects, such as its frequency, distribution, and correlation with changes in the natural or social world.

In the case of somatic diseases, researchers utilize a number of methods of gathering data in their investigation of past diseases. They often rely on the skills of paleopathologists, who locate and prepare the skeletal or mummified remains of infected individuals or hosts and identify the cause of death. Of course, interpretation of the relevant data is not immune from problems of reliability, as the information provided by fossil records can be misleading in a number of ways, and as different types of remains (such as skeletons) have different conditions of preservation. Furthermore, the evidence relating to the cause of death can often be interpreted in various ways. Therefore, in order to reduce the likelihood of drawing erroneous conclusions, fossil records are best interpreted in combination with other types of evidence. In many cases, an additional historical–contextual knowledge of the geographical location of the skeletal or mummified remains is desirable, as are descriptions which demonstrate that the symptoms of the disease in question were in fact present in that community. Such knowledge might be available in the form of historical artifacts, such as written texts, or works of art, such as paintings, mosaics, or sculptures. Combining these two sources of evidence helps to increase the reliability of the results of the investigation.

To add to the challenges of understanding the history of a particular condition, researchers who are exploring the history of somatic disorders often do not have access to "hard" evidence from fossil records. Written evidence might in these cases very well be the only clue available to researchers for reconstructing disorder activities in the past. In such cases, in order to produce the most robust and reliable understanding of the relevant text, researchers must carefully interpret it—a process that involves not only a careful assessment of the quality of the source and its representativeness, but also a thorough understanding of the linguistic aspects of the text and the cultural horizon of the community from which the text originates. In other words, the proper interpretation of these textual sources of knowledge requires skills that can unveil the codes and cultural meanings that are attached to and shape texts.

While these requirements seem to involve rather substantial hurdles, they are even more challenging in the case of mental disorders. This is not because there is less written material available about mental disorders, or because the quality or representativity of these sources is more questionable than in the case of other disorders. Rather, as we shall see in this chapter, it is because the meaning of mental disorder as depicted in historical texts and different genres of contemporary texts is more ambiguous. As mental disorders are deeply ingrained in the cultural life of communities, they tend to take on special roles and gain different meanings that increase the level of ambiguity.

Overall, it seems that there are good reasons for highlighting the importance of developing our knowledge of the historical aspects of mental disorders. In this chapter, the aim is to shed light on two problems that are faced by current research on historical and contemporary textual descriptions of mental disorders. The challenge is to determine how to engage in this endeavor while at the same time ensuring that the ambiguities related to the interpretation of the relevant texts are minimized.

The first problem concerns the interpretation of texts about mental disorders in current and past populations. We may refer to this as the problem of the *historical continuity* of certain mental disorders. To demonstrate the extent of this challenge, the example of depression and melancholia will be considered. Although the term "depression" first appeared in the seventeenth century (Shorter 2005, p. 79), many prominent researchers, such as Stanley W. Jackson, Nancy C. Andreasen, Allan V. Horwitz, and Jerome C. Wakefield, argue that what is now termed *depressive disorder* is in fact more or less the same condition as that which has generally been referred to as *melancholia*.[1] The view is that major depression is well known within medicine, having been portrayed in medical texts since ancient times. However, the question that arises is whether such a view, maintaining a historical continuity between melancholia and depression, is warranted. Whereas I have elsewhere argued in favor of a *modest continuity view* (Varga 2013c), here the focus is on demonstrating the extent to which knowledge of extra-textual elements changes the meaning of the text and, ultimately, whether or not we can speak about continuity.

The second problem concerns the understanding of contemporary and recent texts about mental disorder. Researchers have recently discovered the rich variety of autobiographical writing (memoirs) about mental disorder that has become available in recent decades. These memoirs inform psychiatric understanding in several ways. Researchers value the experiential descriptions as being richer and more revealing than the information that is available in patient reports in clinical settings and in third-person descriptions. Although we should certainly appreciate this attention to autobiographical testimony, it also presents a special methodological challenge that has not been dealt with in the literature (see Radden and Varga 2013). Unlike the first problem, the challenge in this case is linked to the text belonging to a specific *literary genre* (rather than to a specific cultural constellation). In other words, the question of continuity and discontinuity now arises between patient reports in clinical settings and rich descriptions in autobiographical writing. Two questions arise. First, what do memoirs really reveal about mental illness? And second, even more importantly, is the information that is revealed by memoirs continuous and compatible with patient reports?

The two parts of this chapter thus aim to make two interconnecting points about understanding descriptions of mental disorder. The first part demonstrates to what decisive extent the knowledge of *cultural–historical embeddedness of the text* changes the meaning of the text and, ultimately, whether or not we can speak about continuity. The second part demonstrates to what decisive extent knowledge of the *genre of the text* changes the meaning of the

[1] It should be noted that melancholia has maintained a place in psychiatric classification and currently refers to a specific *melancholic* subtype of major depression (American Psychiatric Association 2000, p. 419).

text and, ultimately, whether or not we can speak about continuity. Over the course of this chapter, arguments are presented in favor of a particular position on how to interpret the relevant material and how to address two types of problems relating to continuity and discontinuity in order to minimize ambiguity. However, it should also become clear that any inquiry that aims to develop our knowledge of mental disorders must take these factors into account.

These aspects make the case of mental disorders particularly challenging, and highlight some of the ambiguities linked to understanding historical texts. Hence, in order to obtain reliable historical information about mental disorders, a thorough engagement with both the texts and the cultural horizons and social practices in which they were created is necessary. The appropriate interpretation of these textual sources of knowledge requires the unveiling of the cultural meanings that are linked to mental disorder.

1. A "plurality of melancholies"

If one is skeptical about the continuity between melancholia and depression, one might start by seeking to establish whether there is any single feature that actually unites all of the various phenomena that are historically linked to melancholia. One might point out that the range of states encompassed by the term "melancholia" includes a wide spectrum of normal mental states and dispositions, as well as pathological states that express mental disturbances (Radden 2000, 2009). In addition, melancholia not only included the well-known group of affective states (anxiety, sadness, and despair), but also states of despondency, dejection, and even profound boredom. Surely, however, one of the most confusing points is that it also covered a range of states and dispositions that Western cultures traditionally value as contemplative and as important means of reflection on and articulation of the human condition:

> the potency of the notion of melancholy has been partly explained as the result of a blending of two traditions: the Hippocratic view, according to which melancholy is an unpleasant disease caused by the overabundance or deterioration of a humor, and the (pseudo-)Aristotelian tradition of Problems, according to which melancholy is a necessary condition of genius. Particularly in Ficino and Agrippa of Nettesheim, whose interpretations became the most influential statements of this blend, ideas of melancholic genius are in turn supported by the Platonic notion of the poet working in divine rapture.
>
> (Schleiner 1991, p. 335)

Due to this blend of the Hippocratic and Aristotelian views, melancholia has come to include the realms of the normal, the pathological, and the exceptional. As Schleiner (1991) notes, the basis of the famous association of genius (or admiration for a socially significant deed) with melancholy stems from a statement in Aristotle's work that later dominated Western cultural history up until the Romantic period:

> Why is it that all those who have become eminent in philosophy or politics or poetry or the arts are clearly of an atrabilious temperament, and some of them to such an extent as to be affected by diseases caused by black bile, as is said to have happened to Heracles among the heroes? For he appears to have been of this nature, and that is why epileptic afflictions were called by the ancients 'the sacred disease' after him. That his temperament was atrabilious is shown by the fury which he displayed towards his children and the eruption of sores which took place before his disappearance on Mount Oeta; for this often occurs as the result of black bile.
>
> (Aristotle 1984 edition, p. 226)

Interestingly, and further complicating the picture of melancholia, Aristotle understood more severe forms of the condition as involving frenzy and epilepsy, which may be interpreted as referring to the ancient belief that godly inspiration flows through individuals suffering from epileptic episodes. It is from such a view that, during the Renaissance, sometimes described as the "golden age of melancholy," melancholy came to constitute the dominant "mood" of literature and cultural production (Starobinski 1962). In addition, the Aristotelian view had a decisive impact on Elizabethan and early Stuart England, where melancholy became something akin to a "fashionable disease," lauded as accruing cultural capital, heavily featured in literary representations, and much in vogue among intellectuals (Babb 1951). Clark Lawlor (2011, p. 27) argues that "melancholy has been a fashionable condition across a number of centuries, if not millennia," while John F. Sena (1971) maintains that during the eighteenth century more of the leading poets were melancholic than during other periods in the history of English literature. However, this leads to an inevitable question. How can we even begin to talk about the historical continuity between melancholia and depression, if melancholia encompasses both pathological and non-pathological features? Further fueling the skeptic position, this matter can become even more complicated if we look at a terminological issue and the way in which melancholia functions as a concept.

First, as Stanley W. Jackson (1986) maintains, well into the eighteenth century divergent meanings were attached to the terms "melancholy" and "melancholia." They were applied to designate both the disease and the black bile itself. It was only with the emergence of clinical psychiatry in the eighteenth and nineteenth centuries, and the growing requirement for more precise terminology, that the term "melancholia" became progressively restricted to the disorder. At the same time, the term "melancholy" continued to denote both the disorder and dissimilar, non-pathological states of mind.

Second, we should note that melancholia is what we could term a "complex functional concept"—that is, a concept whose meaning can only be fully comprehended if we understand the complexity of its function. This may sound confusing at first, but the underlying idea is relatively simple. To illustrate this, it is useful to think of Shakespeare's descriptions of a wide variety of melancholic states in *As You Like It*. When he speaks of the "scholar's melancholy, which is emulation," "the musician's, which is fantastical," "the courtier's, which is proud," "the soldier's, which is ambitious," and "the lawyer's, which is politic" (Shakespeare 1890, p. 211), it becomes clear that far from being linked to a single disease entity, each individual's melancholia is in a sense unique to them. As this encompassing catalogue reveals, melancholy is a *form* through which individuality is understood and expressed. In Shakespeare's play, Jacques uses this catalogue of melancholies to express his own sense of identity—he says that "it is a melancholy of mine own, compounded of many simples, extracted from many objects" (Shakespeare 1890, p. 211). What defines Jacques' self-identity is thus not so much his other dispositions and positions as his way of being melancholic. On this basis we might claim that melancholy in this context does not primarily function as a concept referring to a mental disorder. Rather, its primary function is to describe individuality and provide a form that makes it possible for individuals to address themselves as unique individuals. The uniqueness of being in melancholia is further supported by the reigning humoral theory—each individual has a unique constitution, as the number of different combinations of the four humors in the human body is potentially infinite. Variations in black bile were thought to shape bodily states, subjective experiences, and behavior in a way that explained both long-term behavioral dispositions and short-term episodic reactions to demanding circumstances in psychologically well-functioning individuals. This included short- and long-term traits, dispositions, and reactions in disturbed individuals. As becomes apparent in the work of the ancient Greek physician Galen, the general balance (and imbalance) of the humors and the associated qualities (warmth, cold, dryness, and moisture) shaped individual variation in temperament and character traits, such as the tendency toward a choleric, melancholic, or phlegmatic personality. Until the Elizabethan era, the humoral theories served to link normal dispositions and temperamental variation with states of apparent disorder and to support the assumption that brilliance and achievement were associated with melancholy (Radden 2000; Daly 2007).

Overall, there are good reasons for being skeptical about the continuity between melancholia and depression. In fact, it appears that there is very little basis for the thesis, given that it is hard to identify a single feature that unites the various experiences, traits, and behaviors that are linked to melancholia. It is not simply that melancholia is used as both a normal and functionally complex concept. Melancholia was a central cultural idea in western European history, but it was also a functionally complex concept that provided a *form* within the cultural horizon of social communities that significantly shaped reflections on individuality and its expression. Melancholia encompasses a broad range of states and dispositions, ranging from the normal to the pathological. Thus we might take seriously the claim made by Jean-Étienne-Dominique Esquirol in his *Treatise on Mental Maladies* that, since the term "melancholy" covers a number of quite different factors, including mental disorders, normal reactions, and even character traits, it "should be left exclusively to moralists and poets, who, in their expressions, are not obliged to employ so much precision as physicians" (Esquirol, 1845, p. 199). In other words, we seem to have good reason to follow Sena (1971) and rather speak of "a plurality of melancholies."

2. Melancholia as a pathological state: still a plurality?

Some of these difficulties could perhaps be removed by limiting the scope of the inquiry to melancholia as a *pathological* condition. As the aim is to shed light on the continuity or discontinuity of melancholia and contemporary depression, it seems appropriate to limit our investigation to accounts of melancholia and depression as they appear in medical traditions. However, even within this limited scope of investigation, due to the fundamental divergences, any attempt to link melancholia and depression results in the identification of a whole cluster of problems.

Early writers such as Timothie Bright and the Oxford scholar Robert Burton have acknowledged difficulty in finding consistency in the diverse plethora of symptoms that melancholia exhibited. The nineteenth-century physician James Cowles Prichard concluded that to be melancholic was simply "to be out of one's mind" (Prichard 1835, p. 27). As Ingram appears to maintain, a possible source of this problem could have been the synthesis of different medical traditions:

> Many [symptoms of melancholy] were inherited from classical sources and accepted, therefore, as unimpeachable marks of the melancholy temperament—causeless fear and sorrow, for example, and an association with genius and creativity. Many, too, were passed on from Burton: digestive problems, especially to do with wind and

> heaviness; wakefulness and insomnia; irritability, restlessness, resentment and the desire to be alone; suspicion and watchfulness, imagined slights and snubs; fear and anxiety; sadness and inertia; conviction of sin and the certainty of damnation and, its counterpart, belief in some kind of destiny or appointed role, especially when alternating with a sense of personal worthlessness; visions both pleasing and terrifying; and, ultimately, a weariness of all things human and divine. Equally, the different terms adopted during the period reflect partly, as Lawlor points out, changing trends and fashions both diagnostic and linguistic, but also the attempt to distinguish between shades of causes and effects: spleen and vapours, hypochondria and its manifold subdivisions.
>
> (Ingram 2011, pp. 180–181)

Given such a confusing picture, it is unsurprising that some authors reject the idea that ancient and early modern descriptions of melancholia refer to the same condition. As a consequence they also deny the existence of any continuity between melancholia and depression. For instance, Berrios (1988, p. 298) argues that historical examinations reveal that symptoms reflecting pathologically sad and depressed emotions and moods were not entirely a part of the concept of melancholia. Similarly, Berrios and Porter (1998) note that, up until the nineteenth century, melancholia was an opaque term that encompassed a range of mental illnesses in which low affect was not considered to be a defining symptom. They argue that up until the Napoleonic Wars, melancholia denoted a sizeable collection of mentally disturbed states, and the only feature that characterized all of these states was that they involved relatively few delusions. Indeed it is true that, in medical usage, the term "melancholia" referred to general states and disorders characterized by agitated, hallucinatory, paranoid, and demented states. Undoubtedly many psychiatrists today would regard such states as indicating forms of schizophrenia (Jackson 2008, p. 443). In support of such a view, Jones (1972) maintains that the term "melancholia" simply meant something akin to "nervous breakdown" before the nineteenth century. Therefore some authors maintain that the ancient diagnosis of melancholia simply has no accurate counterpart in modern psychiatric practice (Siegel 1973; Berrios and Porter 1998). Due to the confusing discrepancy and the obvious lack of a single encompassing definition of melancholia, they reject the notion of any continuity between melancholia and depression.

3. Interpretation and the horizon of texts

In the following account, the aim is to engage with philosophical hermeneutics in order to argue that the manifestations of melancholia might not be as unrelated and disparate as is often assumed. It will be shown that more similarities become apparent if we take into account both the content of the various descriptions *and* the underlying assumptions about human nature and the human body on which the explanations of melancholy were based. I shall proceed by presenting two such assumptions, one related to humoral theory and the other to a particular set of metaphysical assumptions. The claim is that if we take into consideration extra-textual factors and particularly the *cultural–historical embeddedness of the texts*, we might find some degree of unifying link between what at first might appear to be totally disparate aspects.

In *Truth and Method*, Gadamer (1989, p. 370) contends that any theory of interpretation needs to take into account the fact that understanding always and necessarily occurs within a larger historical context. His descriptive account of understanding (*Verstehen*) relies on Husserl's phenomenological concept of the "horizon" and Heidegger's account of the fundamental historicity of human beings. Understanding according to this view takes the form of "fusion of horizons" (Gadamer 1989, p. 306)—that is, a dialogic event, which is unlike the model of scientific theory. Importantly, the interpreter's horizon changes in a process in which it is extended to encompass the object of interpretation. While in this chapter the focus will be on textual interpretation, Gadamer is providing not only principles for the interpretation of texts, but also a model for all understanding.

To understand the meaning of a text it might be necessary to acquire its "horizon," which is made up of the background assumptions that underlie what is said. In order to understand the concept of "horizon," it is useful to remember that for Gadamer (and Heidegger), understanding and the circle of interpretation begin with the interpreter projecting a meaning for the text as a whole on the basis of some preconceived assumptions about it. These assumptions are sometimes referred to as "prejudice" or "tradition," but in order to avoid misunderstanding, Gadamer is keen to note that such pre-understanding is not something to be avoided. Rather, being embedded into a traditional culture of historical consciousness is the criterion for the interpreter being able to gain any understanding. Such embeddedness constitutes the historical horizon of human experience. The underlying idea is that language provides the speaker not only with a means of communication, but also with a standpoint from which to view the world—a "horizon" suggesting a view from a particular perspective. Acquiring a language is at the same time becoming culturally embedded in a "horizon" from which all understanding takes place. Language (which is always embedded in a culture) is more than a set of signs that are neutral with regard to the intelligibility of the world. Instead it is the "reservoir of tradition and the medium in and through which we exist and perceive our world" (Gadamer 1976, p. 29). Far from being unchanging and fixed, horizons evolve and change, or, in Gadamer's words, they are "something into which we move and which moves with us. Horizons change for a person who is moving" (Gadamer 1989, p. 304).[2]

Yet if horizons are an important element of understanding and they are at the same time significantly different depending on historical and cultural differences, how is it possible to understand ancient texts and speakers from other cultures? To be clear about this, Gadamer is realistic about the existence of contingent incommensurability. He would thus agree that understanding might sometimes be impossible because horizons might be too distant from each other. Importantly, however, such incommensurability between traditions is rare. Although important gaps and points of divergence do exist in communication between traditions, in most cases, there are also overlaps at some points. Thus, although understanding can sometimes fail, there is no particular reason why interpreters embedded in different traditions should not be able to find areas of convergence. Also, although the point is that we always understand the world through our being in a particular tradition, Gadamer is also a realist in the sense that he emphasizes that, although we may be from different traditions, our understanding is concerned with the same world, which we all share in common.

The text itself carries a certain tradition, representing aspects of an outlook that characterizes the historical situation in which the text originates. Both the interpreter and the interpreted always find themselves situated in a tradition that gives rise to a certain historical horizon—this is something that the interpreter needs to take into account. Therefore the interpreter should not regard understanding as a matter of casting meaning on a passive and lifeless object. Rather, understanding is a negotiation in which the present and past horizons should be productively brought together—something which is achievable as the horizon of the interpreter is in many ways interconnected with the past.[3]

4. Symbolic unities

One way of making use of the concept of horizon is to examine underlying metaphysical commitments that are revealed between the lines. Although

[2] As Charles Taylor notes, "Horizons identified by the agents whose worlds they circumscribe are always in movement. The horizons of A and B may thus be distinct at time t, and their mutual understanding very imperfect. But A and B by living together may come to have a single common horizon at t + n" (Taylor 2002, p. 136).

[3] Far from being locked into the past, within the horizon of an interpreter, the past always speaks through the present. Tradition is not rigid, but has a forward-looking element itself, and horizons are constituted by elements that draw upon the past and project into the future.

metaphysical commitments can be multifarious, we shall be particularly concerned with those that relate to the way in which reality is divided up and made intelligible. Drawing on the work of Michel Foucault, it will be demonstrated that such metaphysical commitments can be analyzed by the manner in which they create *symbolic unities* between events and objects. In the words of Foucault (2005, p. 118), such "symbolic unities" express underlying commitments that are not products of particular theories.[4]

First, if we want to explore the "horizons" of early texts on melancholia, it is important to emphasize the significance of humoral theory. Hippocrates famously rejected the ancient belief that mental illness was caused by supernatural possession and embraced a concept of health and disease based on a theory of humors. Humoral substances were assumed to be present in the body in the same way as phlegm and blood, while the spleen or the atrabiliary glands were regarded as the organs associated with black bile. The main assumption was that health is intrinsically linked to the equality or isonomic proportion of the humors, whereas disease is caused by an excess of one of the humors. According to this view, melancholia resulted from an imbalance of black bile in the body.[5] The black bile is described as cold and dry, and its being out of balance can lead to hemorrhoids, dysentery, and skin eruptions, while its excess disposes to sadness and to thinking horrid thoughts (Foucault 2005, p. 81). We begin to see why melancholia, as a certain disposition of the black bile, could refer to what we today would regard as a wide range of very dissimilar medical conditions.

However, the decisive issue in this context is the fact that humoral theory becomes embedded in a wider metaphysical view, establishing a *symbolic unity*. First, the four elements (water, earth, fire, and air) were associated with heat, cold, moisture, and dryness, and the four humors (yellow bile, blood, phlegm, and black bile) were also linked to these elements and qualities. In addition, the amount of black bile in the human body was linked to the astrological movements of the planet Saturn. Thus melancholia is associated or *symbolically united* with black bile due to the similarities of the dark mood, the eventually darkened skin color, and the dark smoky vapors from black bile. By affinity with other dark, cold, and dry elements, the melancholic is

4 It should be noted that although Foucault rejects the idea that symbolic unities are generated by theories, he argues that they are the products of "sensibility." However, it remains unclear what exactly this means. Overall, I interpret it as meaning that the idea of a "symbolic unity" is not only compatible with but also advances the inquiry presented in this chapter.

5 In ancient Greek, melancholia means "black bile" (*melas*, meaning "black," and *kholé*, meaning "bile").

identified as belonging to that order of things. It is by the same symbolic unity that melancholy is linked to Saturn.

In contrast to what we later came to understand as empirical methods, the affinities between coldness, blackness, dryness, and heaviness, shared by the particular humor, the melancholic, and Saturn, provided the unifying link. The coldness and dryness—believed to be common to the humor and the planet—provide the crucial link. Klibansky et al. (2001/1964) have shown that the astrological view of Saturn reflected the particular duality ascribed to melancholia. In other words, Saturn and the melancholic are imagined as sharing the qualities of being cold and dry and as being linked to lethargic and contemplative powers. Yet these powers are also depicted as ambiguous, since they both lead to fear, loneliness, and gloominess, and to extraordinarily inventive states of mind (Colby 1978; Klibansky et al. 2001, pp. 244–245; Johnsen 2009). Those who are under the astrological influences of ambivalent Saturn both suffer from diseases connected to the black bile and benefit from its intellectual vigor (Johnsen 2009, p. 79). With time, the references to black bile and Saturn diminished, but melancholy remained associated with insight well into the Romantic period.

What we see is that symbolic unities link what we would today consider to be dissimilar states, events, and objects, and they establish a link between disparate characteristics of melancholia and the natural world. This explains how descriptions of melancholia encompassed otherwise disparate entities just by sharing the same cluster of qualities. Taking into account this symbolic unity and the metaphysical assumptions that underlie its descriptions, melancholia seems to be less like a confusing cluster of disparate features. Furthermore, although humoral theory slowly lost its prominent place in medical explanations as it became increasingly incompatible with the emerging scientific world view, it is interesting to see that it was followed by another, albeit less comprehensive, symbolic unity.[6] The succeeding unity built on knowledge derived from seventeenth-century mechanistic science, which had an enormous impact on medical theories well into the nineteenth century. The human body was now pictured as a *machine* composed of different particles (Mead 1762; Hoffmann 1971; Jackson 1983), and pathology emphasized the role of

[6] For instance, in Philippe Pinel's account of melancholia, humoral theory no longer plays a crucial role (Pinel 1806). Other figures, such as Boerhaave, amended humoral theory and adapted it to emerging knowledge about the hydrodynamics of the circulation. For Boerhaave, the black bile was the pathogenetic by-product of certain mechanical or hydrodynamic processes (Jackson 1983, 1986). As a result, definitions of melancholia become narrower, since disparate forms of melancholia that were previously understood as different manifestations of the same state could no longer be held together.

the fluids and their circulation over the solids. Diseases were conceptualized as rooted in various forms of disordered flow or circulation—less lively blood gave rise to slowed blood flow in the brain, causing sad mood. In addition, as the body fluids became fixed, it was regarded as natural that the motions of the body would slow down (Jackson 1986, p. 130). Clearly, a less robust symbolic unity is at stake here. It is the slowness of the blood circulation and the slowness of the body in melancholia that provide the unifying link.

5. The continuity of melancholia and depression

Now that we have made more sense of what at first appeared to be disparate features of melancholia, we can return to the question of whether there is continuity between melancholia and depression. In particular, it is important to emphasize two features that seem to have remained relatively constant throughout the historical depictions. The first of these concerns a specific state bearing a particular affective signature. Jackson (1983, 1986, 2008) argues that, despite all of the differences in the signs of melancholia, essential affective aspects of the malady, such as fear and sadness, have remained the same.[7] In many ways the general picture that Jackson presents seems convincing. Galen had already noted that all melancholic patients exhibit fear and despondency. After the sixteenth century these affective states were increasingly described as occurring without any recognizable cause.[8] Thus, although increasing emphasis was placed on the clustering of sadness, gloom, and anxiety symptoms, it was also increasingly noted that these perturbations occur *without a reasonable cause*. During this period, philosophers and physicians continually emphasized the unreasonable nature of characteristic affective states in melancholia. In 1621, in *Anatomy of Melancholy*, Robert Burton defined melancholy by emphasizing emotional disturbance. For him, melancholy is "fear and sadness, without any apparent occasion" (Burton 1621/1850, p. 108). Timothy Bright, in his *Treatise on Melancholy* (Bright 1586), maintained that

[7] In an earlier paper (Varga 2013b, 2013c) I have argued that this requires clarification of whether fear and sadness are conceptualized in an intentional or non-intentional manner and, thus, whether or not they are directed toward a specific object—that is, whether such states are nebulous and all-pervasive moods that shape the cognitive content of experience.

[8] Such broad generalizations necessarily overlook the fact that, even if only rarely, such descriptions can also be found in earlier accounts. For example, in the second century, Aretaeus of Cappadocia notes that the melancholic suffers from a dejected mood "without any manifest cause" (Radden 2009, p. 77). Nevertheless, it is not until the sixteenth century that this aspect gradually evolves into a standard feature of descriptions (Jackson 2008, p. 446).

in melancholia, fear and sadness come without appropriate cause. Similarly, in *Leviathan*, Thomas Hobbes maintains that:

> Dejection subjects a man to causeless fears, which is a madness commonly called melancholy apparent also in diverse manners: as in haunting of solitudes and graves; in superstitious behaviour; and in fearing some one, some another, particular thing. In sum, all passions that produce strange and unusual behaviour are called by the general name of madness.
>
> (Hobbes 2006/1651, p. 41)

The second feature is linked to what we can interpret as an increasingly narrow concept of melancholia. The growing emphasis on the affective features in the first half of the nineteenth century is paired with a narrower concept of melancholia, in which the cognitive and delusional features of the disorder are increasingly distinguished from the affective ones (Jackson 1986). There is thus a departure from the view of Philippe Pinel and Samuel Johnson that melancholia is characterized by impaired thinking about a limited subject matter. Decisively for our inquiry here, the increasing focus on the affective aspect is also reflected in the change of vocabulary and the emergence of the term "depression." Whereas melancholia had previously referred to a wide range of conditions, including what would today be classified as delusional disorders, a narrower term, "depression," emerges that designates a cluster of symptoms in melancholia. Although "melancholia" is the preferred expression, the term "depression" nevertheless surfaces in medical writing as early as the seventeenth century in the context of mood disorder (Shorter 2005, p. 79), mostly as the "depression of spirits" or "depression of the passions."[9] Individuals can be "depressed into deep Sadness and Melancholy," in the words of Richard Blackmore (1725, p. 95), while for John Haslam (1809, p. 43) the melancholic suffers "depressive passions" (Jackson 2008). In 1765, Robert Whytt used the term "depression of mind" (Whytt 1768, p. 312), while in 1786, James M. Adair described the melancholic illness of Queen Anne as a "depression of spirits" (Shorter 2005, p. 78). Similarly, in 1812 the American psychiatrist Benjamin Rush referred to the "depression of mind" (Rush 1827, p. 44). In his notes on melancholy (which he regarded as a pathological variant of non-delusional melancholia) and melancholia in Tuke's *Dictionary of Psychological Medicine,* Mercier speaks of a characteristic "depression of feeling" or "mental depression" (Mercier 1892, p. 798). This tendency continues in the writings of William James, who uses the term "depression" (James

[9] It is worth noting that the term "depression" stems from the Latin terms *de* (meaning "down") and *premere* (meaning "press").

2002/1902, p. 116) to describe the characteristic emotional sign of melancholia. Although it had not yet acquired an acknowledged status as a genuine diagnostic term, there was a rapidly increasing use of the term "depression" in medical contexts in the nineteenth century to denote affect or mood melancholic disorders (Jackson 2008). Also in the nineteenth century the emphasis on depression in psychiatric classifications became even stronger, yet melancholia remained the fundamental diagnostic term for dejected states. Foreshadowing the developments of the twentieth century, in which depression became the primary term, in the early nineteenth century Samuel Tuke (1813, p. 216) took melancholia to mean all cases of mental disorder characterized by the "depression of mind."

So far, it appears that descriptions of affective states of sadness without appropriate cause are reliably present in the historical accounts of melancholia. There are also some clear parallels with the current understanding of clinical depression, especially if one takes into account the typical comorbidity of anxiety and depression. In addition, the emergence of the term "depression" is not just a more or less random change of terminology, but can be understood as a part of this development. The increasing emphasis on affect in the wake of the emerging term "depression" provides us with a useful link that connects melancholia and depression. However, as this tendency continues, the question of the relationship between affective and cognitive aspects becomes more pressing. Without a "symbolic unity," the question arises as to whether cognitive and affective aspects are disparate phenomena or merely different manifestations of the same thing. In the following account it is argued that this becomes clearer if we take into consideration a new symbolic unity that emerged together with a new idea of mind and disorder.

5.1. A new unity

An important change began to take place at the beginning of the twentieth century. While Kraepelin placed depression alongside melancholia in his influential textbook, in the fifth edition he abandoned melancholia in favor of depression (Radden 2000; Shorter 2005). At the same time, another unity, albeit a significantly less symbolic one, emerged together with a new picture of the human mind, cognition, and emotion. The mind was now thought of as a bundle of functionally autonomous modules in which the cognitive, emotional, and volitional modules of mental functions can become impaired independently of each other. This new picture had a decisive impact on the emerging field of psychiatry, and the appearance of "faculty psychology" sharpened the eighteenth-century distinction between the mental functions of cognition and affect. This divide was maintained in Kraepelin's influential division between disorders of affect (manic-depressive diseases and melancholia) and disorders of the cognitive faculties (dementia praecox).[10] Thus schizophrenia and paranoia became regarded as intellectual disturbances, depression and mania as affective disturbances, and psychopathic disorders as volitional disturbances (Berrios 1988).

It might at first appear curious that the relationship between affective and cognitive aspects is not really accounted for. Therefore the question might again arise as to whether we are dealing with disparate phenomena or merely different manifestations of the same thing. This becomes clearer if we take into account a new "symbolic unity" that links a new picture of the mind with biological explanations. Kraepelin, Mercier, and other influential figures became convinced that, analogous to organic disease, psychiatric symptom clusters and mental disorders could eventually be traced back to lesions in the brain. In Charles Mercier's article on melancholia in the influential *Dictionary of Psychological Medicine*, cognitive and emotional aspects are described as different manifestations of the same underlying biological condition caused by "change in nerve-tissue" (Mercier 1892, p. 790). It is important to bear in mind that this change cannot be attributed to robust empirical findings. Rather than being based on inferences from empirical findings, the unity emerged as a shift in thinking about mental disorder, which allowed biological explanations to unite cognitive and emotional features in melancholia.

It was noted earlier in this chapter that the mood states of apprehension and sadness without appropriate cause appear to be a relatively consistent theme throughout the historical accounts of melancholia. Again, however, it should be emphasized that such claims need to be qualified by taking into account symbolic unities that are tied to the horizons of the particular texts under scrutiny.

5.2. Sin and self-loathing

The last issue concerning the relationship between melancholia and depression to be addressed here is concerned with cognitive attitudes toward the

[10] This is not to say that Kraepelin was the first to make this distinction. Wyman and Griesinger had already suggested a corresponding division between "diseases of the intellect" and "diseases of the passions" (Berrios and Beer 1994).

self, such as self-loathing, self-accusations, and unreasonably negative thoughts about oneself in general. One might resist buying into a view that proposes the continuity of melancholia and depression by arguing that, at least until Freud, self-loathing and self-accusation were not continuously recognized as features of melancholia. This would contradict the contemporary view of depression, in which cognitive attitudes are granted a significant role. Contemporary approaches to the classification of depressive disorders in DSM-IV and *ICD-10* require a fundamental disturbance in mood, but also lowered self-esteem and ideas of guilt (*ICD-10*), or inappropriate or excessive guilt, with feelings of worthlessness (DSM-IV) as central diagnostic items (Gruenberg et al. 2005).

Although it initially appears that self-loathing and self-accusation were not continuously recognized as features of melancholia, it will be argued that we need to take a closer look at certain traditions. More precisely, the point will be made that we need to take into account the possibility that there might be culturally specific forms of suffering that are manifested in slightly different ways and which therefore might escape our attention.

We may start by noting that in certain periods in the history of (Protestant) Christianity, a somewhat similar type of suffering was rather common and had as its theme the consciousness of being separated from God by mortal sin such as pride (Moltmann 2002). The point that needs to be highlighted is that, in these accounts, we see melancholic attitudes of self-loathing, but they are disguised as descriptions of features associated with suffering from the conviction of damnation and sin. In a similar way to the features of melancholia already described, symptoms included despair, the idea of having committed an unforgivable sin, suicidal inclinations, fear of God's wrath, fear of eternal damnation, self-accusation amounting to a terror of conscience, and obsession with blasphemous thoughts. For example, Rubin notes that such feelings were conveyed by outcries such as "I am the vilest of sinners. There is no hope for me. I am lost. I am undone. I shall never obtain mercy" (Rubin 1993, p. 8).

> Religious melancholy, first identified by Robert Burton in *The Anatomy of Melancholy* in 1621, comprised three interrelated conditions: (1) the ontological status of humanity stained by innate depravity and sin engaged in the futility of worldly follies; (2) the crises of spiritual passage and conversion in which each penitent felt forsaken by God's love—the awakening and terror before God's law, the danger of damnation and the utter helplessness of each soul to engineer their own salvation through human agency; and (3) a distinctive psychopathology characteristic of evangelical Protestants.
>
> (Rubin 1993, p. 5)

From the seventeenth century to the nineteenth century, forms of religious melancholy were prevalent among Protestant groups, particularly among those who pursued a contemplative union with Christ and understood their self-identities as uniquely founded upon a personal relationship to God. As described by Bunyan, in many cases it was such individuals living lives pursuing the assurance of salvation, ascetic self-mastery, and systematic practice of piety who found themselves plunging into religious melancholy. Furthermore, expressions of hopelessness and despair in melancholia could be regarded as expressions of the sin of unbelief (Bunyan 1666/2007). As James (2002/1902, p. 104) commented, repentance and not giving in to melancholia was the proper way of getting away from the sin. On the contrary, succumbing to melancholia and letting oneself express despair would have been a sinful activity in itself.

Cognitive attitudes toward the self, such as self-loathing and self-accusation, became prominent in Freud's account. In *Mourning and Melancholia* (Freud 1969) he develops an elaborate parallel with mourning, which shares dejected mood, sadness, lethargy, and lack of interest. As Freud (1969/1917, p. 246) notes, the patient "represents his ego to us as worth-less, incapable of any achievement and morally despicable; he reproaches himself, vilifies himself and expects to be punished. He abases himself before everyone and commiserates with his own relatives for being connected with someone so unworthy." For Freud, the main similarities between mourning and melancholia are that they occur as a response to the experience of loss. This might be the reaction "to the loss of a loved person, or to the loss of some abstraction which has taken the place of one, such as one's country, liberty, an ideal, and so on" (Freud 1969/1917, p. 243). However, mourning is a constructive response to literal loss—it is a necessary part of a "working" process in which the mourner abandons affective bonds to the lost object or subject. In a second step, the mourner achieves a change by substituting the actual absence with an imaginary presence. Through the work of mourning, the mourner undoes the bond, which marks the end of the mourning. Importantly, whereas the mourning process allows the person to understand the significance and nature of the attachment to the lost object, the picture differs significantly in melancholia, in which the decisive aspect of object loss is hidden from comprehension and conscious awareness. There is an acute awareness of a loss that characterizes melancholia, but this sense of loss is undefined, mood-like, and without a clear object (Freud 1969/1917, p. 245). The melancholic cannot comprehend the loss, and, as Freud argues, the resentment of this objectless loss becomes directed toward the self. The puzzle of melancholia is that it is both a narcissistic disorder and at the same time involves a diminution of self-regard and the impoverishment of the ego. The characteristic self-accusation, which

Freud recognizes as a central characteristic of melancholia, reflects the objectless loss that is directed toward the self.[11]

For our purposes in this context, there is no need to cite further examples. The aim was merely to show that there might be reasons for believing that self-contempt as a part of melancholic suffering might in fact have a long history. Jackson (2008, p. 446) notes a similar tendency and maintains that, starting in the sixteenth century, references to self-accusation and guilt creep into descriptions of melancholia with increasing frequency. Indeed, the account of melancholia by Platter (1602) mentions themes of feeling guilty, damned, and fearing punishment. James (2002/1902, pp. 118–135) refers to forms of melancholia with religious themes that are concerned with the "conviction of sin," "loathing," and "self-contempt." Against this background, Jackson (1986) and Rubin (1993, pp. 3–9) describe religious melancholia as a culturally specific form of melancholia—a modality of the suffering that is peculiar to specific religious cultural milieus. In this case, the mental suffering is itself embedded in a culture that constitutes the specific directedness and meaning for the sufferer.

However, we should tread carefully here. In fact, any claim that the religious suffering in question is a form of melancholia must implicitly accept certain presuppositions. More to the point, it must accept the view that we have seen in the work of Kraepelin and Mercier. This is the "symbolic unity" that connects a new picture of the mind with biological explanations and understands mental disorders analogous to organic disease, as biological (or chemical) alterations of the brain that could result in culturally different manifestations. Clearly there is more evidence to support this view today than there was at the time of Kraepelin and Mercier. However, this does not alter the core claim that is being made here. The point is that whether or not we accept a continuity between this religious suffering and melancholia will depend not so much on the textual evidence itself as on our symbolic unities and metaphysical assumptions.

6. **Some conclusions and a complication**

This chapter commenced by stating that the gaining of a full understanding of a condition often requires historical inquiry and looking back on historical sources that might reveal crucial aspects. In the case of disorders, the

[11] Such a focus on cognitive attitudes is mirrored in contemporary approaches to the classification of depressive disorders in *DSM-IV* and *ICD-10*. Both require a fundamental disturbance in mood, reduced self-esteem, and ideas of guilt (*ICD-10*), or inappropriate or excessive guilt with feelings of worthlessness (*DSM-IV*), as central diagnostic items (see also Gruenberg et al. 2005).

gathering of historical "data" must rely on knowledge that is available in the form of historical artefacts, in most cases as written texts. In these cases, in order to produce the most robust and reliable interpretation of the text source, a thorough understanding of linguistic and cultural aspects is important. The task of gaining a historical understanding of mental disorders is even more challenging, as these disorders tend to take on special roles and gain different meanings in the cultural lives of historical communities—an aspect that increases the degree of ambiguity.

The engagement with philosophical hermeneutics helped to reveal the complex functional profile of melancholia, as referring not only to a disorder, but also to a part of the cultural framework through which a cultural–linguistic community interprets the world and shapes its ways of acting and thinking. Utilizing the concepts of *horizon* and *symbolic unity*, it was argued that, taking into consideration the *cultural–historical embeddedness of the texts*, we might find unifying links between what might at first seem to be totally disparate aspects. We also saw that although a certain continuity can be established between melancholia and depression, hermeneutics cautions us with regard to such claims. The question of continuity might in some cases be a question about the kind of metaphysical assumptions about disorder to which one subscribes.

Having focused on the exploration of challenges with regard to historical accounts, it may appear that such gaps between "horizons," which hinder a straightforward understanding, only open up when there is a certain historical distance between the interpreter and the text. However, there are also other situations in which this may occur. The remainder of this chapter deals with a type of challenge that is connected to contemporary texts. There is now a rich variety of autobiographical writing about mental illness available, which is beginning to inform psychiatric understanding. Researchers have started to make systematic use of autobiographical accounts in order to gain an understanding of experiential aspects that are not available in a clinical setting and cannot be found in third-person descriptions. Although one should appreciate this attention to autobiographical testimony, it also presents a unique methodological challenge that has not been dealt with in the literature (see Radden and Varga 2013). In other words, the question of continuity and discontinuity now arises between patient reports in clinical settings and rich descriptions in autobiographical writing.

7. Clinical reports and autobiographical writing

Over the course of the last five decades, in which modern hospitals and laboratories have implemented a wide variety of novel diagnostic procedures, many have lamented the way that paying attention to a patient's subjective experience and taking into account her comprehension of the meaning of disorder in her life has become neglected (Lawrence 1994; Bury 2001). Some bemoan the way that the traditional attempt to acquire a complete understanding of the patient's ailments has changed into merely accumulating evidence about symptoms that could be linked to specific underlying biological conditions. However, over the last couple of decades a tangible change has occurred, which can be traced back to several interrelated factors. The exponential development of information technologies has led to an enormous expansion of accessible information about disorders and to the development of patient organizations and self-help groups that collect and categorize this information. Rather unsurprisingly, this concentration of information that is accessible to patients has also led to the general weakening of medical authority. It is within such a setting that autobiographical accounts of physical disorders, disability, and mental disorders have become a public discourse that is generating enormous interest. Within a short period of time, large numbers of autobiographical accounts of mental disorder have become available (Sommer et al. 1998; Hornstein 2002). This must certainly be linked to a general cultural tendency manifested across a wide variety of media that fosters a focus on the private and personal lives of people. However, particularly in the case of mental disorders, many hold that the self-reflective work involved in the act of autobiographical writing is likely to have therapeutic potential and re-establish the sense of agency that has been affected in mental disorder (Kleinman 1988; Becker 1997; Frank 2000; Nelson 2001; Smorti et al. 2010).

An important factor that adds to the impetus of this change is the reaction of the medical establishment to these autobiographical accounts. Many prominent researchers in the field of psychopathology now explicitly cite autobiographical accounts, persuaded that they contain rich and detailed experiential information that is often lacking in patients' reports in a clinical setting (that is, the information that patients tell their doctors). Autobiographical accounts and patients' reports in clinical settings are now used *together*, complementing each other. Although the openness of psychiatric scholarship to autobiographical testimony is a positive development, a problem arises. The problem amounts to what could be called the *discontinuity between two types of discourses*. Unlike patient reports, memoirs are at the same time reports of experience *and* specific texts that are guided by the rules of a certain literary genre. Consequently there is a risk that using clinical reports by patients and descriptions in memoirs *side by side* assumes an unproblematic continuity that might lead to erroneous conclusions. The problem is that memoirs may reveal more about the standing of mental illness within the medium of literature than about the "pure" experience of symptoms and states. Thus, in order to assess how we are to understand the content of autobiographical depictions of experiential aspects, we need to understand the *epistemological status* of memoirs.

7.1. Autobiography

Autobiography was first classified as a distinct literary genre in the eighteenth-century Western world. Modern autobiography is defined as a narrative that is retrospectively created by an individual about important aspects of and development in their own life (Lejeune 1982; Anderson 2001). An important precondition of the emergence of this genre concerns the notion of individual subjects having developing personal identities that can be captured narratively (Eakin 1992). The author reveals certain episodes in their life while simultaneously reflecting upon the significance of these for their identity, while the reader assumes the identity of the protagonist (who undergoes the events that the author recalls), the narrator (who reflects on these experiences), and the author (who calls into life the narrator and the protagonist to publicly reveal something about their life) (Lejeune 1982; Wright 2006). Since the emergence of this genre, assessing the truth value of what is conveyed in autobiographical writing has been a source of conflict. Some have argued that autobiography should be understood as a species of biographical and historical writing, assuming that there is nothing inherently problematic about autobiographies providing direct and precise depictions of past experiences. Although there has been growing opposition to this understanding in the second half of the twentieth century, poststructuralist thinkers have taken the critique to the extreme. Rejecting the correspondence theory of reference, Paul De Man and Jacques Derrida have, to differing extents, argued that specifically literary and fictive features are present in autobiography, which means that this genre is just another kind of fiction.

To contemporary ears, the talk about there being no references outside the text, as well as comments about the autobiographical subject being "defaced" (De Man 1979) due to the reshaping of subjective content by the text, might sound odd. However, there is certainly some truth in Jacques Derrida's point that many of the laws and literary conventions that establish tacit norms for autobiographical writing are shared with fiction (Derrida 1980). The point is thus that experiences are depicted *within* specific literary laws that guide the deployment of dramatic and rhetorical devices and forms, such as closure and coherence. While taking this seriously, the position that I advocate here is more moderate, as I do not believe that there is any inference from the identification of fictional features to the attribution of fictionality to autobiographical narratives.

However, even according to this modest understanding, it seems justified to begin to suspect that there might be a *discontinuity* between experiences of mental disorder reported in a clinical setting and in memoirs. Also, in a specific sense, autobiographical descriptions of particular experiences might not be very dependable. It is not merely that the authors might avoid certain aspects, or that they might misrepresent them in order to enhance the dramatic flow of the text and live up to the guidelines of the editor. Rather, my point is that we should be cautious when interpreting, as the content might reasonably be expected to be affected by the particular literary medium within which it is situated. Without denying that autobiographical writing may sometimes accurately describe experiences, the point is that—in general—such texts are situated somewhere in between fact and fiction (Anderson 2001; Wright 2006). An inextricable fusion of phenomenal experience and cultural meanings is what we understand by normal subjective experience and what we find in all memoirs, which have been rightly recognized as being works of "faction" (Bury 2001).

7.2. The argument from autobiographical memory

However, some readers may resist these arguments that might seem to hinge on obsolete assumptions from literary and cultural theory. Fortunately, there is another manner in which such arguments can be further sustained by reflecting on the *nature of autobiographical memory*. Autobiographical memory focuses on the recollection of experienced past events in a way that combines personal experiences of self, objects, or others at a particular time and place with general knowledge about facts and the world. In other words, autobiographical memory involves both *episodic* and *semantic* knowledge of the past—whereas episodic memory makes possible the recollection of personal experiences that occurred at a particular time and place, semantic memory allows the retrieval of general knowledge and facts. Thus autobiographical memory contains both memories of first-person experiences of events and facts about oneself and the world (Schacter 2001).

The first aspect of interest for our purposes is the close connection between autobiographical memory and the sense of self-identity. As a general claim, the link between autobiographical memory and self-identity seems intuitively plausible—a sudden erasure of the autobiographical memory of a person (which might actually happen as a result of severe brain injury) will inevitably raise the question of whether we are dealing with the same person. However, what complicates self-understanding in an autobiographical context is that autobiographical memory and current sense of self-identity are dynamically intertwined. It is not just that the introspective activity of bringing the contents of our minds into consciousness is itself an active process that might affect the content of the relevant mental states. The recollection of past experiences often involves a two-step process. This can be explained by the fact that present mental states are more readily available upon introspection than past ones. Thus S's recollection of past mental state X starts with introspection about how S currently feels about X. From here there are two possibilities, depending on what kind of meta-belief S holds about her attitudes over time. Depending on whether S sees her attitude toward X as changed or stable over time, she will reconstruct past experience about X consistently with this belief. In other words, there is a process of evaluation, in which S assesses whether she has reason to suppose that her view of X has shifted over time. This process is itself a slippery one, as most people are biased toward assuming the stability of their attitudes and hence the continuity of their past and present attitudes. In contrast, people who expect change in their views might recollect the past according to whether they think that their attitudes have changed in a positive or negative way (Ross 1989).

Since there is wide agreement that the sense of personal identity necessitates some kind of narrative unity about oneself over time, one might intuitively think that people would be inclined to have meta-beliefs that confirm some kind of stability. Given such bias, one might expect that the recollection process in autobiographical memory could simply operate as an identity stabilizer, by increasing the sense of narrative unity. In support of such a thesis, Keyes and Ryff (2000) maintain that although changes over time may be rewarding, they tend to threaten a consistent self-identity. Although this might at first sound credible, Wilson and Ross (2003) have shown that people do not in general place an emphasis on such narrative consistency. Rather, they frequently highlight changes in their attitudes. However, these findings do not contradict the thesis that autobiographical memory may operate as an identity stabilizer. We might say instead that pointing out changes between current and past views can, under certain circumstances, be merely another—albeit more complicated—way of establishing narrative continuity.

When considering the identity function of autobiographical recollection, it is useful to look at the trajectory of the narrative. When the question is phrased broadly about past selves and self-identity, individuals tend to perceive their previous selves as inferior compared with how they think of their present identities (Wilson and Ross 2000, 2001). This bias can itself serve a specific function, and Wilson and Ross (2003, p. 139) argue that "people systematically devalue their distant former selves to create the illusion that they (or their relationships) have improved over time." Thus autobiographical memory may at least in part have the function of co-constructing the current sense of identity by establishing specific narrative patterns. In particular, the narrative of improvement seems to be more attractive and fulfilling than the narrative of stability. It seems likely that the current state is most appreciated if it is contrasted with a more negative past. In support of this thesis, Wilson and Ross (2003) maintain that people are more inclined to adopt a critical attitude when thinking about their past self.

Autobiographical memories are thus malleable and shaped by the current sense of self-identity. In fact this effect works in both directions—people's recollections may also help to alter their current self-regard. Thus, not only does autobiographical self-reflection involve the co-construction of what is recollected, establishing a link between the author's current view of himself and a set of past experiences, but also this process occurs in a loop-like, dynamic way—what is recollected influences the present self-understanding, yet the recollected material is itself influenced and altered on the basis of the present self-understanding. In other words, autobiographical self-understanding can be illustrated by calling into mind the hermeneutical circle—in the process of recollection, we co-construct what is remembered, establishing a dynamic circuit between our present selves and our past experiences. Our current self-understandings have an impact on the content of what is recollected, while in turn the recollected content influences our self-concepts. In addition, we might assume that the amount and degree of our co-construction increase in line with the time that has elapsed between the event and the autobiographical recollection—which is typically rather long in the case of memoirs compared with clinical reports.[12]

Overall, we have so far emphasized some of the challenges that are generated by the manner in which literary conventions and autobiographical memory work. An adequate interpretation of autobiographical writing in general needs to take these into account. While we have established that mental illness memoirs are something like a subgenre of autobiographical writing, we have not yet specified their particular characteristics. As we shall see, this is important because, in addition to the general ambiguities that are linked

[12] As Peter Goldie (2011) notes, a threefold "ironic" gap opens up in autobiographical memory. The gap can be *epistemic* (the author might now possess previously unavailable information), *evaluative* (the author now holds a different appraisal of the experience), and *emotional* (the author now feels differently about what happened). All of these aspects interfere with the remembered content, which further increases the ambiguity of the text.

to autobiographical writing, there are supplementary ambiguities that are unique to mental illness memoirs.

8. Memoirs of mental disorder

While caution is warranted with regard to the status of experiences depicted in autobiographical writing, even more care is needed when dealing with memoirs of mental disorder. These memoirs are organized around the author's experience of disorder, and they entail both a depiction of central experiential aspects and a reflection about the meaning of the disorder in the author's life (Hawkins 1993; Frank 2000; Wiltshire 2000; Conway 2007). In the following account, the inquiry will be limited to pointing out two additional sources of ambiguity with regard to memoirs of mental disorder.

The first source of ambiguity is partially linked to the particular *restorative function* that many attribute to mental illness memoirs (Hawkins 1993; Hyden 1997; Bury 2001). Thus the author really has a double task, in which the recounting of a disruptive experience and the restoration of some kind of coherence after the disruption are intertwined. In addition, the manner in which these pathological experiences can be molded into a coherent narrative is unavoidably shaped by the social or cultural meanings attached to that particular disorder. As Susan Sontag (1989) has shown, many medical conditions are in our collective imagination intrinsically connected to positively or negatively loaded images. While AIDS has long been linked to the image of hedonist transgression and perverse sexuality, cancer bears the connotation of warfare and is often described using military metaphors. Today at least some mental disorders also belong to a rather stigmatized category, so authors of mental disorder memoirs simultaneously engage with these negative connotations and must forge their experiences not only into a coherent narrative, but also into a coherent narrative of a *worthy* life. For instance, the narrating of experiences with schizophrenia is guided by different circumstances to the narrating of experiences with depression, because different meanings are attached to different mental disorders. However, sometimes different and even opposite meanings are attached to the same disorder. Depression still carries some of the connotations of melancholia linked to genius and ingenuity, but it also has connotations of overly sensitive and passive individuals who lack firm character (Radden 2000; Ussher 2011). The manner in which experiences are recounted will depend on how the author of the memoir deals with these (sometimes contradictory) connotations.

The second source of ambiguity is linked to the cognitive deficits that accompany many mental disorders. Empirical studies have revealed several forms of memory impairment in depressed patients, but it is the impaired recall patterns in autobiographical memory that are of particular interest in this context (Puffet et al. 1991; Burt et al. 1995; Kuyken and Dalgleish 1995). First, patients with depression have impaired access to emotionally positive memories, and they process positive material in a defective way (Werner-Seidler and Moulds 2011). Second, these patients have an over-general autobiographical memory. This refers to the fact that, when asked to recall a particular event, patients with depression are inclined to recollect a larger interval of their life and respond not so much to any particular event as to a whole class of related events. Both the over-general remembering and the impaired access to positive memories remain even after clinical improvement (Mackinger et al. 2000; Nandrino et al. 2002). These deficits related to memory are very likely to influence the descriptions in these patients' memoirs and have an impact on the co-construction of remembering.

Overall, it seems reasonable to assume that as well as exhibiting the ambiguities of autobiographical writing in general, mental disorder memoirs have their own unique ambiguity. Literary conventions and characteristic features of autobiographical memory generate some of the ambiguities in general autobiographical writing. The conclusion that we can draw from the background of this section is that the particular cultural meanings of mental disorders along with memory deficits linked to mental disorders render even more uncertain the kind of truth value that we should attach to disorder memoirs. These factors influence the way that the experience of the disorder is remembered and articulated, which should lead us to interpret such memoirs as being somewhere between reports of immediate experience (like those that patients present to their doctors in clinical settings) and cultural artefacts that carry different types of meaning. Importantly, none of the discussion that has been presented so far warrants the conclusion that researchers should abandon the reading of memoirs. The latter are indeed sources of relevant knowledge, but sources that may reveal just as much about conventions and the cultural meanings attached to disorders as they do about the "raw" experience of their authors. However, particular problems arise if researchers, implicitly assuming some kind of continuity between their sources, use descriptions of experience in memoirs side by side with patient reports from clinical settings. Therefore it is suggested that particular caution is needed when drawing conclusions based on these sources.

9. **Conclusion**

Knowledge of the historical aspects of disorders is often valuable, but in the case of mental disorders we must in most cases rely entirely on interpretations of textual evidence. This then leads to methodological reflections on how to engage with historical sources in a way that minimizes the ambiguities associated with the interpretation of the relevant texts. The challenges are considerable in the case of mental disorders, not because of the quality and representativity of the textual resources, but because the meaning of the mental disorder is essentially ambiguous in historical texts and different genres of contemporary texts. The development of reliable knowledge about mental disorders requires a comprehensive engagement that aims to unearth the meaning of the text in the light of the cultural horizons in which it was created.

This chapter has addressed two problems that are faced by current research involving historical and contemporary texts which describe mental disorders. The elaboration of these issues should be seen as an attempt to convey the extent to which knowledge of the *cultural–historical embeddedness of the text* and the *genre of the text* influences its meaning. To disregard such embeddedness might be to risk drawing erroneous conclusions about experiential aspects of mental disorders.

Chapter 4

Cognitivism, interpretation, and the therapeutic encounter

In the last chapter, it was argued that philosophical problems present themselves in a number of ways in psychiatry, but the focus was on methodological reflections about appropriate engagement with historical sources and with contemporary kinds of texts. In this chapter, the line of investigation that was followed in the first three chapters is continued, but the focus moves away from texts to processes in verbal therapeutic encounters. According to a broad definition, psychotherapy denotes the psychological treatment of various forms of mental and somatic conditions. Although psychotherapy is often associated with the psychoanalytic method that Freud developed, the practice of psychotherapy significantly pre-dates Freudian psychoanalysis. In fact, it can be traced back to the nineteenth-century practice of "moral treatment," and to various forms of "psychological healing" (Jackson 1999). Nevertheless, in general, psychological means of alleviating psychological and behavioral symptoms were relatively rare prior to the early twentieth century. Until then, most treatments of mental disorder reflected the medical community's strong commitment to the somatic paradigm (Cautin 2011). As the medical community adopted psychotherapy, psychoanalysis held a dominant position for a couple of decades. After the Second World War, the field of psychotherapy underwent intense growth and transformation, developing into a legitimate treatment for mental disorders. This was partly due to the fact that psychotherapy had been shown to be effective for treating a wide range of conditions, in that it led to significantly better outcomes than were observed in those who had not received psychotherapy (Lambert and Ogles 2004). In view of this background, it is not entirely surprising that psychotherapy has developed into an established practice, with over 10 million individuals receiving psychotherapy each year in the USA alone (Olfson et al. 2002; Wang et al. 2005). However, any account of the development of psychotherapy would be incomplete if it failed to mention the fact that psychotherapy has in many ways also become an integral part of Western culture (Cushman 1992). It now seems perfectly natural to individuals in Western societies to use "psychology discourses" to describe their identity and to explain personal traits and life challenges by referring to their psychological or psychiatric origin (Rose 1998). Thus, outside of the healthcare system, the widespread "culture of psychotherapy" is today clearly a significant force that shapes social practices.

Within the last couple of decades, the nature of the psychotherapeutic endeavor has changed considerably. One way to characterize the nature of this change is to say that psychotherapy has been "medicalized"—that is, it has been re-conceptualized in the healthcare system as resembling a medical treatment. One important factor in this change is certainly linked to modifications in the administrative practices of reimbursement by health insurance and maintenance organizations. In many mental healthcare settings the situation is now such that reimbursement of the therapist is largely dependent on whether the client has been assigned a particular diagnosis. Thus a patient who is experiencing severe problems with their life, marriage, work, etc. can now only be treated if she can be assigned a reimbursable diagnosis. One important aspect of this development was the shift in focus from the time-consuming approach to changing patterns in significant relationships to the relatively inexpensive alleviation of the symptoms (of the diagnosed disorder).

Alongside the growing medicalization of psychotherapy, in the course of the last couple of decades one particular cognitive approach to psychotherapy has become prominent and recognized as the most efficient therapy for many mental disorders. Building on the theoretical foundation of cognitive theory (CT), CT-informed therapy is today endorsed as the first choice of therapy for numerous mental disorders. The emergence of CT can be traced back to historical factors such as the "cognitive revolution" in psychology and the growing dissatisfaction with both psychoanalysis and behaviorist psychology (Dobson and Dozois 2010). Many argue that the rise of CT has been largely due to the increased emphasis on evidence-based practice and demands for accountability in the provision of health services (Herbert and Forman 2011). For a wide variety of disorders, CT-informed therapy is currently the preferred approach, because it has been found to be effective in randomized controlled trials and effectively translated to therapeutic manuals (Hollon and Beck 2004; Roth and Fonagy 2005; Epp et al. 2009).[1]

Despite such successes, an uneasy sense of inconsistency has been felt by many researchers and practitioners. This is because the general success of psychotherapy did not generate a profound knowledge of the nature of the

[1] However, we should note the increased number of critical debates about the effectiveness of this approach. In particular, a growing number of researchers are skeptical about protection against relapse and about long-term clinical improvement (Roth and Fonagy 2005; Brewin 2006).

communicative processes at stake in psychotherapy. In fact, what might seem to call into question the scientific status of psychotherapy is the combination of the wide variety of approaches available,[2] the relatively small amount of converging evidence for the effectiveness of a large proportion of these, and the lack of explanatory models that can be used to interpret the accumulation of facts. Large literature reviews and meta-analyses reveal that after controlling for various factors linked to experimental aspects and theoretical allegiances of therapy approaches, many of the different approaches turn out to be essentially equivalent (Wampold 2001; Lambert and Ogles 2004). In other words, although successful outcomes have been effectively measured, the exact nature of the processes and mechanisms responsible for such positive outcomes remains to a large extent unknown. However, it is acknowledged that the *therapeutic alliance*—that is, the cooperative relationship between therapist and patient—is not only indispensable for therapeutic effectiveness, but also the most obvious common factor for therapeutic success across a variety of psychotherapies (Wolfe and Goldfried 1988; Marmar et al. 1989; Salvio et al. 1992; Krupnick et al. 1999; Safran et al. 2009). The study by Krupnick et al. (1999) found that the therapeutic alliance had a substantial influence on the outcome not only of the therapeutic process, but also of pharmacological therapy. Put simply, it seems that the therapeutic alliance has created a type of trusting patient–therapist relationship in which the response to active and placebo pharmacotherapy is enhanced.

Although this chapter does not aim to shed new light on features of the processes that are linked to positive outcomes, it seems safe to assume that positive outcomes and the therapeutic alliance are somehow linked to successful understanding between patient and therapist. Therefore it does not seem implausible to suggest that clarification of some of the processes involved in a therapeutic encounter might also make a small contribution to a better understanding of the processes involved in positive outcomes. That said, the more focused aim of this chapter is to clarify two kinds of processes that appear to be crucial for an extensive understanding in a therapeutic setting, namely *self-interpretation* and *conversation*.

This task will be achieved in the form of a critical dialog with the influential cognitive theory (CT) and its philosophical assumptions.[3] This would appear to have a number of advantages. First, interweaving the clarification

[2] Several hundred approaches are available, which have been explained and analyzed in over 10,000 books (Wampold 2001).

[3] I have provided a detailed criticism of CT elsewhere (Varga 2014). My main objective in this chapter is to propose and clarify a hermeneutic position.

of interpretative processes with the critical exploration of CT provides a useful contextualization of the approach proposed here and makes it easier to understand. Second, it makes it possible to continue the investigation from the last chapter. While Chapter 3 argued against an overly literal understanding of texts, this chapter argues against an overly literal understanding of patient reports, which is characterized by a detached attitude and linked to the idea of objective observation. As will become clear, due to the lack of interpretative engagement, the CT-trained therapist is in many cases prone to misunderstanding the patient.

Before we start, it is worth clarifying this approach and considering a couple of obvious criticisms and limitations of such an endeavor. First, one could object that CT is diverse and based on a wide variety of assumptions that involve contrasting, and sometimes incompatible, emphases. Acknowledging this variety of versions of CT, we may agree that some of the critical points made in this chapter are directed at assumptions to which not all CT-based accounts subscribe. Obviously, such accounts will not be vulnerable to all of the concerns that I shall present here. That said, I also suggest that there are certain characteristic ideas that run across all the different strands of CT, the most central of these being a shared commitment to what we could call "cognitivism," namely the idea that disordered behavior and affect can be explained by unearthing cognitive contents and processes that decisively and directly influence and mediate them. CT has of course been altered over the last 40 years or so, but these changes have not affected its core principle, namely that mental disorder is essentially linked to impairments in cognition. Nevertheless, in order to limit the scope of the investigation, the focus will be on a canonical version of CT as defended by Aaron Beck and colleagues. There are several reasons why CT appears to be an obvious candidate for such an investigation. First, it is possibly the most popular approach to understanding mental processes in various forms of anxiety and depression. Alford and Beck (1997) claim that CT not only provides effective tools in practice but also explicates the factors responsible for psychopathology.

Before going further, we should consider a fundamental methodological objection to the whole endeavor of this chapter. What is the point of a philosophical investigation of CT that is obviously firmly based on scientific principles? To what extent is such an objection valid? In accordance with the scientific image of CT, leading figures have repeatedly emphasized the scientific basis of CT and openly critiqued other approaches as being of a more "philosophical" nature (Padesky and Beck 2003; Dryden et al. 2010). Thus the view is that CT's unique position in the field of psychotherapy is the result of its continuous commitment to a scientific perspective and to the fact that a large number of independent studies have evaluated the efficacy of CT-based interventions.

However, if we recall the discussion of "scientism" in Chapter 2, we can see that scientific method is not only embedded in a certain historical and social environment, but also to varying degrees based on philosophical assumptions that cannot be tested by the scientific method. Although they produce hypotheses that are testable, it is also the case that scientific theories develop within the framework of paradigms containing suppositions that are untestable.

The investigation in this chapter focuses on more specific assumptions that are related to the nature of human cognition and representation. CT relies on specific assumptions of a *philosophical nature* (McEachrane 2003; Lacewing 2004; Whiting 2006; Butera 2011). None of what is proposed here suggests that empirical studies are unable to demonstrate the particular cognitive propensities of mentally ill individuals, or to assess the efficacy of therapy. The point is merely that empirical analyses cannot be used to appraise the correctness of the underlying philosophical suppositions.

A final limitation of this approach that should be mentioned is related to the fact that approaches to psychotherapy could be studied in numerous ways. For instance, one could scrutinize the widespread acceptance of the view that the therapist is (or should be) a neutral observer undertaking a therapeutic endeavor that is objective and not significantly influenced by the cultural and historical embeddedness of the therapeutic process. Drawing on sources from the hermeneutic tradition, Cushman (1992) has maintained that we should doubt psychology's insistence that it is apolitical, neutral, and objective. He warns that to accept the supposedly neutral image of psychology is not only a philosophical mistake but may also be politically dangerous. This seems like a fruitful perspective which is in need of more contributions that demonstrate the cultural and historical embeddedness of psychotherapy and the way that it mirrors, reveals, and reproduces the historical and cultural context in which it is rooted. Although this is an important endeavor, and certainly one that would have to be included in order to map all of the interpretative processes that are involved in psychotherapy, a more limited approach will be adopted in this chapter. This will allow us to focus on the micro-level and to provide a more in-depth analysis of interpretation and self-interpretation.

1. **Cognitivism and CT**

The fact that CT has become the theoretical basis of cognitive therapy has not affected its core, as it is believed that this form of therapy consists of the "application" of CT (Beck and Alford 2009, p. 300).[4] In summary, CT holds

[4] Emphasizing the importance of CT, Beck maintains that "we do not believe that the therapy could be applied effectively without knowledge of the theory" (Beck et al. 1979, p. 4).

that emotional disturbances such as those in depression result from an inaccurate way of *thinking* about self and the world (Beck 1967, Wells 2008; Beck and Alford 2009). Distorted cognition is assigned a major causal role, and much of the bodily and emotional turbulence is traced back to "faulty information processing" or "distorted and dysfunctional beliefs" (Bracken and Thomas 2008, p. 86; Bracken 1999; Kuyken et al. 2005; DeRubeis et al. 2008). For instance, depression is understood as a "disorder of thought" (Beck and Alford 2009, pp. 208, 239), while its emotional dimensions are seen as the consequences of thoughts and beliefs. In other words, it is the activation of distinctive and reality-distorting cognitive configurations that is seen as the main cause of depression (Beck and Alford 2009, p. 243; Wells 2000). Accordingly, cognitive psychotherapy aspires to change such distorted cognitive processing, by contesting and altering the patient's beliefs and cognitive pattern, which is supposed to generate a positive affective and behavioral modification (Beck 1995; Clark et al. 1999; Beck and Alford 2009).

Perhaps the most important distinction in CT is that between "schemas" on the one hand and "automatic thoughts" on the other. Schemas are basically sets of interlocking beliefs that begin to develop in childhood and remain with us throughout our lives, constantly molding our experience of ourselves and the world (Beck and Alford 2009, p. 255; Williams et al. 1997). What is characteristic about the way we hold the beliefs involved is that we tend to think of them as unqualifiedly true. According to this view a schema is something like an accumulated body of knowledge comprising essential beliefs that are wholeheartedly accepted by the person as "just the way things 'are'" (Beck 1995, p. 16). Although (or perhaps because) these beliefs are so fundamental, in most cases individuals have profound difficulty in articulating them.

Importantly, some of these schemas are dysfunctional, and these are thought to cause the emergence, continuation, and recurrence of a wide range of mental disorders. The schemas are dysfunctional in terms of both their content and the way that they are held. For instance, the schemas of depression-prone individuals are considered to be dysfunctional because they contain beliefs about self and the world that are rigid and unrealistically negative (Kovacs and Beck 1978; Beck 1983; Hammen 1997; Blatt 2004; Epp et al. 2009). In depression, there is a particular cognitive configuration in which cognitive activity is focused on insignificance, worthlessness, lack of skill, or failure (Clark et al. 1989, 1990; Szentagotai et al. 2008). CT maintains that depressed individuals possess negatively biased cognitive schemas that reflect past experiences, and which organize and structure new experiences. In the case of numerous and significant early negative experiences, negatively biased schemas (e.g. "I am vulnerable," "I am worthless," or "The world is dangerous") may develop and come to influence the preferential style of information processing. Over time, these schemas often become unconditionally acknowledged as truths (Wells 2000), in the sense that they are not seen as contingent construals to which there are possible alternatives. It is against this background that Louis C. Charland (2006) has argued that depression assumes the "character of a cognitive module," adding that "a good theoretical formulation and defence of this hypothesis can be found in Aaron Beck's well-known cognitive theory of depression" (Charland 2006, p. 221).

The second crucial element of CT concerns a particular group of cognitive phenomena, referred to as "automatic thoughts." These are something like second-order thoughts which are activated by and express underlying schemas that are mostly not readily accessible to consciousness (Alford and Beck 1997, pp. 16–17). Automatic thoughts are the ones that just "pop up" in our heads following an event, generating behavioral and emotional responses. Overall, the relationship between core beliefs, automatic thoughts, and emotional distress is viewed in the following way. Experience is interpreted within the framework of schemas, which leads to specific automatic thoughts that in turn generate specific emotions. Although automatic thoughts can be either positively or negatively valenced, in a therapeutic setting the focus is on the negative thoughts. To illustrate the nature and frequency of such thoughts, J. S. Beck asks her readers to imagine a person who catches herself thinking "This is just too hard. I'm so dumb … I'll never make it as a therapist" (Beck 1995, p. 14) while reading a book on cognitive therapy. The way in which the nature of emotion-eliciting automatic thoughts is conceived is in accordance with basic "cognitivist" assumptions. Automatic thoughts are the situation-specific "actual words or images that go through a person's mind" (Beck 1995, p. 16). In other words, they are thought to consist of some kind of mental representation involving actual words; the authors also note that mental imagery can elicit the same effect. Importantly, however, such mental imagery is also thought of as being conceptually structured (e.g. Beck and Alford 2009, pp. 26, 37–38).

One of the chief therapeutic aims is to capture automatic thoughts in the moment, and then, by analyzing them, to explore the underlying, general belief schemas that these thoughts express. Over the course of therapy sessions, schemas become apparent to both the patient and the therapist as they identify the consistencies or themes that run through the patient's automatic thoughts. After the patient has been enabled by cognitive training to "catch" the emotion-eliciting automatic thoughts, an attempt is made to change the semantic information that the thoughts contain and to modify the content of basic schemas (Beck et al. 1979; Beck and Alford 2009). The patient is encouraged to logically challenge and test their thoughts against reality, both during the session and as homework in between sessions, and to create substitute representations that help to restore positive mood states. Within this framework, once the content of the maladaptive information-processing strategies has been determined, the correction has been made, and consistency with inter-subjectively valid standards has been achieved, these schemas can no longer trigger the unpleasant emotional disturbances.

2. Self-interpretation

Providing a better understanding of the cognitive, emotional, and volitional dimensions of the mind is central to most forms of psychotherapy. However, all such approaches must start by making assumptions about the kind of *access* that we have to our mental states and dispositions. CT is no different in this respect, and we may now proceed to analyze CT's understanding of the manner in which we gain *introspective access* to our thoughts.

To get a clearer idea of the nature of the CT account of introspection, it is helpful to bear in mind how much emphasis CT places on the need for patients to acquire the ability to "catch" the precise wording of their automatic thoughts. When the CT-trained therapist asks the patient (let us call him Tim) "What goes through your mind?", she not only assumes, implicitly or explicitly, that the "look inward" is possible, but she also assumes that Tim has a special authority when speaking about his own mind, due to some kind of *inner observation* that makes it possible for him to detect his inner states. Such an *observational account* is intuitively appealing, as it confirms the apparent asymmetry between first-person and third-person perspectives—most people would probably think that Tim is in a better position than anyone else in the world to speak with authority about his own states. He has the only epistemic access, or at least the most reliable access, to his mental states. In other words, the observational account of introspection in CT buys into two theses that Schwitzgebel (2010) refers to as *epistemic peculiarity* and *epistemic privilege*.

The epistemic peculiarity thesis refers to the belief that, in certain respects, introspection is different from other ways of knowing about the world. At first glance it appears that CT subscribes to a particular thesis of epistemic peculiarity and understands introspection as referring to a type of inner-directed observation (the words "*spicere*" and "*intra*" can be translated as "look" and "within"). The idea that we have some kind of ability to look inward upon conscious states is well known in philosophy. John Locke famously held that introspection is the perception of processes in our own minds that operates via a sense that has "nothing to do with external Objects; yet it is very like it, and might properly enough be call'd internal Sense" (Locke 1689/1975: II.1.iv). In this account, introspection involves a faculty somewhat like perception, but "looking inward," which provides one with a good view of mental states. The idea is that by introspection one can discover mental entities through a kind of "inner" perception, utilizing a perceptual faculty dedicated to the detection of mental states. Using more modern terminology, some philosophers speak about a kind of "self-scanning process" in the brain, in which the connection between the introspective state that does the scanning and the introspected state that is scanned is causal and contingent (Armstrong 1981). This model regards introspection as something that is fundamentally similar to perception by involving a monitoring and representative mechanism. Put simply, whereas outwardly directed perception provides us with information about current happenings in our body and environment, inwardly directed perception provides us with awareness about current happenings in our mental world (Armstrong 1968). The inwardly directed scanning device does not differ significantly from the way in which one discovers external objects through perception.

The epistemic privilege thesis means that Tim's judgments about his inner life are more reliable and immune from certain kinds of error compared with other ways of knowing about the world. Although CT concurs with this view of the particular nature of introspection, it does acknowledge that Tim can make important mistakes. More specifically, Tim might make mistakes if, instead of directly reporting on his states, he chooses to *interpret* them. It is for this reason that CT considers it absolutely crucial that the patient does not interpret but instead *directly reports* on the occurring (automatic) thoughts. CT theorists instruct practitioners to convey to their patients that it is of utmost importance to recognize and capture the "precise wording of their automatic thoughts" (Beck 1995, pp. 16, 88; Beck and Alford 2009, p. 311). Beck explicitly instructs patients not to interpret, but to simply observe introspectively and *report the actual words* that go through their minds. This is something that patients usually have to get used to, which is why therapists should be aware that "until they have learned to recognize these thoughts, many patients report *interpretations*, which may or may not reflect the actual thoughts" (Beck 1995, p. 88, emphasis as in the original).

Having outlined the observational account of introspection in CT and the particular manner in which it adopts the theses of epistemic peculiarity and epistemic privilege, we shall now consider two standard objections to such a view, regarding the relationship between perception and introspection, and pertaining to a possible vicious regress. First, one of the main assumptions of CT is that one's beliefs about inner states, dispositions, etc. are justified by inner observation which provides one with something like perceptual evidence. However, the objection might be raised that the claimed analogy between perception and introspection might be entirely misguided. If we admitted the existence of such an inner sense, could introspection be neatly modeled on externally oriented perception? To examine this further, consider that with regard to perception we usually speak of obtaining data about our surroundings via our sense organs, by tasting, hearing, seeing, touching, or smelling. Surely this is not the case when we are introspecting our mental states, so when we say that introspection is perceptual, it must denote something different from the way we use our sense organs. Of course, this does not mean that it is entirely wrong to think about introspection as perception-like. Recall that there are cases of perception that are significantly different from the standard examples that involve our sense organs. For instance, although proprioception is usually regarded as a case of perception, it makes perfect sense to say that Tim is perceptually aware that his left arm is raised without having to touch or see it. Thus perception does not appear to be dependent on use of the sense organs, but may simply refer to a way of acquiring information, in this case about ourselves. If this is correct, then introspection might indeed be perception-like, but inwardly directed. However, there are also significant differences that set introspection apart from perception. For instance, it is possible to lose a perceptual faculty such as vision, hearing, smell, or taste and continue living with diminished access to one's surroundings without damaging the self or its rationality. However, the loss of introspection would also involve suffering the loss of a constitutive element of personhood and agency that entails higher-order deliberation (Shoemaker 1968, 1994). In conclusion, then, there is nothing wrong in principle with CT's modeling of introspection on externally oriented perception, and there is no threatening regress.

Second, according to CT, it might at first glance seem that the awareness of a mental state is gained through an inwardly directed perceptive act. Often the impression is given that the thought that is the target of the introspection is itself unconscious, and that it is first brought to consciousness through the introspective process itself. However, this would pose a significant problem. It is important to bear in mind that not only the target state, but also the introspection itself constitutes a mental state. Thus we would be dealing with two states, one of them targeting the other and thereby making it conscious. However, if this is true, then the same procedure also has to apply to the second state—this is also a mental state that we must access and make conscious through another higher-order act of perception, and so on, leading to an infinite regress. However, on re-examination it is apparent that CT is proposing a picture of the nature of cognitive processes that shields the CT account of introspection from the charge of leading to an infinite regress. Apparently introspection brings into awareness some mental state with which one is already somehow acquainted. According to CT, introspection is a special type of second-order awareness of some pre-existing state of which one is—to some extent at least—already aware.[5]

2.1. Perception or self-interpretation?

So far none of the standard objections apply to the account of introspection that is proposed in CT. However, the analogy with perception generates another cluster of problems that have significant practical implications in therapy. Before addressing these, we should keep in mind that CT takes the perception-like nature of introspection very seriously. Recall that one of the most crucial instructions for therapists is that patients should learn to directly report on their thoughts *without interpreting them*. As I shall demonstrate in the following account, it is at this point that CT makes the mistake of neglecting the essential difference between perception and introspection. In order to maintain the model of inward observation, CT needs to posit a clear distinction between that which inspects and the object that is being inspected. However, this distinction is fuzzy and using it to model introspection obscures the special relationship that we have with our mental states and dispositions. In fact, such an *observational account* fails to acknowledge what we could call our *interpretative self-relation*. In other words, the *observational account* fails to acknowledge that human beings are "self-interpreting animals" and, thus, beings whose identity and mental life are at least partly constituted by their self-interpretations and self-descriptions (Taylor 1985a, 1985b).

2.2. Expert witnesses or self-interpreting agents?

Basically, according to the concept of introspection to which CT alludes, we are expert witnesses of our inner lives in the sense that we possess *access* to our thoughts. Although such access is introspective, the fact that it is direct

[5] We might also add a third point here. With John McDowell (1996), we might argue that any non-question-begging account of introspection has to assume that judgments warranted by introspection are rationally constrained. This does not seem to be a hurdle for CT. Due to the close modeling on perception, CT can maintain that just as perceptual judgments are rationally constrained by experiences of the outer world, so judgments about inner states are constrained by experiences of the "inner world."

means that it is *unmediated and non-interpretative*. The view is that, by introspection, human beings are able to gain awareness of their mental states in a direct way that is "undistorted" by additional interpretation. To avoid misunderstanding, CT does not claim that there are entirely "undistorted" thoughts, as it also holds that underlying schemas influence thoughts. Rather, the point is that the states of which introspection makes us aware are not "distorted" by any *supplementary* interpretation. Such a view appears plausible, partly because it allows us to hold on to our ideas about some kind of intimate epistemological relationship to ourselves. Yet the problem is that this account neglects the constitutive agency that we have with regard to our mental life. That is, we are more than spectators, as our self-relation is to a significant extent characterized by terms of agency.

As a first step, we might consider an analysis of introspection that was proposed by John McDowell. He models his view of introspection on perception, clearly advocating the viewing of "inner sense" in parallel with "outer sense" "to the fullest extent that is possible" (McDowell 1996, p. 22). Importantly, however, McDowell's distinction between inner sense and outer sense emphasizes that whereas the objects of outer sense have an independent existence, the objects of inner sense cannot exist independently of our awareness of them (McDowell 1996, p. 21). For instance, if he does not have some awareness of his pain, Tim cannot be said to be in pain. Therefore in such cases we cannot make a clear distinction between the inner impression and what it is an impression of. Accordingly, McDowell notes that in many cases the object of inner experience "has no existence independently of the awareness that the experience constitutes" (McDowell 1996, p. 36). The important conclusion is that, unlike the "outer sense," in some cases the awareness of mental states to a certain extent constitutes the states in question.

Admittedly, pain might be a very specific example, and the result might not be generalized without further argument. Nonetheless, McDowell's account is useful in that it begins to indicate that in some cases we have special authority over our mental states. Sometimes our introspective awareness of a mental state is constitutive of it. This is in contrast to the CT account of introspection, which assumes that introspection brings into consciousness an independently existing state of mind.[6] However, we might take this one step further. In many cases, in the process of becoming aware of aspects of our mental

[6] We might add that there are also instances in which we acquire knowledge of our inner life and make self-ascriptions not by looking inward, but rather by looking at the world. To use an example provided by Garret Evans (1982, p. 225), consider how you would answer if someone asked you "Do you think there is going to be a Third World War?"

life, we are far from being the neutral expert witnesses that CT assumes. Instead, the distinctiveness of the mental state that we bring into consciousness depends upon our interpretation of it, in which we apply conceptual resources. As Richard Moran notes, bringing mental life to consciousness involves a "stance of agency beyond that of being a kind of expert witness to one's internal states" (Moran 2001, p. 4). Answering the question "What do you think?" does not often involve acquiring knowledge of our inner life through the perception-like and neutral epistemic task of an expert witness. Rather, the process has specific, formative consequences for the object of introspective retrieval. In such a process, we do not merely report, but rather we shape and sometimes co-constitute the state in question. Thus in those instances in which answering the question "Do you think that P?" involves an introspective process, the introspection shapes and alters the content in question (Moran 2001, p. 40).

According to the observational account of CT, one is justified in ascribing a thought to oneself whenever one is reporting on a pre-existing mental state observed via introspection. Thus introspection grants one a privileged perspective from which one can observe thoughts, and this privileged position also explains the special first-person authority that one entertains vis-à-vis one's mental life. Many authors have expressed doubt that we have any robust evidence for the existence of such an inwardly directed introspective faculty, but in that case the problem that such an observational approach faces is that it cannot account for any special first-person authority or immediacy of our self-knowledge. To solve this impasse, philosophers such as Moran argue that we have a special authority when we make self-ascriptions, but this authority stems from the fact that we have the capacity to play a constitutive or at least a co-constitutive role when we bring our mental life to consciousness. Sometimes our "introspective" retrieval of a mental state is at least co-constituted by the very process of "retrieval."

The point is that, in this situation, in answering the question, you would have to attend to an outward phenomenon, and answer in the same way as you would answer the question "Will there be a Third World War?" Thus, in order to be able to decide whether one holds the belief that X, one must also, to a certain extent, attempt to decide whether the case really is X, and this involves "looking outward" and examining the evidence regarding X. The belief that X involved here is open or "transparent" to external evidence with regard to X. Thus we not only discover our inner states but in addition to a certain extent we constitute them by a process that also involves looking "outward," focusing our attention not on the belief itself as the object of knowledge, but on the state of affairs in the external world.

Against this background we may begin to doubt the adequateness of CT's observational account of mental states. In contrast to what CT claims, mental states are not necessarily independently occurring and stable entities that await introspective discovery. Rather they are "distorted" by introspection as our mental states are dynamically intertwined with our first-person agency. In accordance with this view, Peter Carruthers (2009) has argued that if one prompts people to identify the specific thoughts that go through their minds, they will engage in self-interpretation instead of introspection. Of course the CT theorist might claim that with adequate psychoeducation, patients eventually learn to introspect and report instead of interpreting. However, the point that Carruthers is trying to convey is that making sense of thoughts that are in the periphery of our awareness inevitably involves some kind of interpretation. In other words, what the CT account of introspection seems to neglect is that acquiring knowledge about our inner lives ordinarily involves a process of self-interpretation. The objects of introspection are not stable objects that can be brought to awareness without being shaped by self-interpretation.

3. Conversation

So far, the focus of this chapter has been on processes in a psychotherapeutic setting that concern self-interpretation. However, it is obvious that psychotherapy is not only about the self-interpretation of the client, but also to a considerable extent about the interpretation of the client's utterances by the therapist. In fact there is a heavy interpretative burden on the therapist, who has to combine, analyze, and understand the meaning of the patient's utterances. It is quite clear that psychotherapy involves interpersonal understanding through interpretation in conversation. But what is interpersonal understanding in this context? As I shall argue, Gadamer's work can provide a helpful perspective here. Not only does Gadamer develop a rich account of the processes in conversation, but also he regards it as one of his main contributions to relocate "the idea of conversation to the very centre of hermeneutics" (Gadamer 2001, p. 39).

To start with, it is important to point out that the observational paradigm of CT wants to limit interpretation in order to eliminate as many sources of misunderstanding as possible. When the CT-trained therapist asks Tim "What do you think?" or "What goes through your mind?", she expects that Tim will introspectively identify the conscious mental representation of the thought that occurred to him. By this point in the therapeutic conversation the therapist is already primarily interested in limiting the interpretative conversation (and the number of possible interpretations). However, as will be demonstrated shortly, this approach is problematic and runs the risk of overlooking the wide variety of meanings that the patient might attempt to convey.[7] I shall then go on to suggest a corrective, arguing that the therapist needs much more interpretative sensibility in order to uphold what Gadamer refers to as the "openness" of the conversation. Otherwise there is clearly a risk that even if the patient flawlessly identifies automatic thoughts involving words, CT would be unable to make adequate inferences to underlying schemas.

Let us start by demonstrating how the hasty termination of the dialog that the CT-trained therapist might execute in many instances wrongly infers the existence of corresponding internally represented propositional content and seriously misunderstands the *meaning* of the patient's report. Suppose that Tim is somehow uncomfortable with the session, and he answers the therapist's question with the rather brief statement "I think this is awkward." What is the therapist justified in concluding in this situation? In accordance with CT, the therapist assumes that the formula "I thought that P" is reducible to the formula "the thought that P occurred to me," and therefore concludes that Tim has introspectively identified a conscious mental representation of the thought "I think this is awkward" that occurred to him. However, this is far from necessarily (or even reliably) being the case. We have to bear in mind the crucial difference between "thinking" and "having thoughts" (see Malcolm 1972; Davidson 1987; McEachrane 2003; Varga 2014). The fact that we sometimes use the verb "think" in a transitive manner, thus implying that it has a propositional object, seems to mislead the CT-trained therapist into believing that "thinking" involves the representation of a propositional content. However, in everyday language, saying that a person "thought that P" does not imply that he thought *of* P, or that P occurred to him in his thoughts. Tim might very well be aware of the situation being awkward without the thought "This is awkward" actually occurring in his mind. He might often shift position in his chair, expressing his unease, clearly having some kind of cognitive awareness of the awkwardness of the situation, but without the thought "This is awkward" necessarily coming into his mind. The talk of "thinking" does not necessarily entail the representation of propositional content. Of course, sometimes thinking that "This is awkward" might involve the thought "This is awkward" actually occurring to Tim. However, assuming that this is generally the case, and that "thinking" always entails "having thoughts," makes the

[7] Although I earlier argued that we cannot assume with CT that the patient is able to reliably identify automatic thoughts involving words, I now ask the reader to suspend any disbelief for a moment. This is useful, as it is only in this way that we can discern another hermeneutic complication that CT faces.

mistake of taking grammatical form to be the index of psychological reality. The same would be true if the therapist observed Tim's bodily expressions and attributed the thought "You think this is awkward" to him. In this case, too, the therapist might use the sentence "You think this is awkward" without necessarily having to hold that for this statement to be true, the mentally represented thought "This is awkward" must have occurred in Tim's mind. In fact, properly understood, the therapist's observation need not involve positing the existence of any particular representation going through Tim's mind. Rather, in saying "You think this is awkward," the therapist is attributing thoughts to Tim, making use of the term "think" to describe and explain the situation in a way that makes sense of Tim's behavior.

We can thus see an emerging variety of meanings that can be linked to a very simple utterance, such as "This is awkward." It is already clear that more interpretation is needed in order to know whether we are actually dealing with a mental representation, which is the precondition for a warranted inference to an underlying schema. However, the variety of possible meanings does not stop here. To complicate matters further, there are other ways of understanding Tim's simple statement "This is awkward." Let us imagine that when Tim gets home he discusses with his wife the psychotherapeutic session that he has just experienced. His wife might ask him what went through his head as the session started, to which Tim might reply "I thought it was awkward." Now so far we have seen that nothing Tim reports necessarily supports the conclusion that the mentally represented thought "This is awkward" actually occurred to him. But what is Tim really reporting on? It is quite possible that Tim's statement "I thought it was awkward" is not in fact reporting on a particular cognitive phenomenon, but rather it is expressing his confusing affective experience. His utterance might very well convey the manner in which he experienced being in what he thought of as an embarrassing and helpless situation. In general, we might say that a thought or a belief need not be constitutive of an emotion, but might simply be *expressive* of it. What here could easily be mistaken for an internally represented thought is in fact better understood as an expression of a tacit affective experience of self and environment. With his utterance, Tim could be expressing what it felt like to undergo an affective experience which had a certain atmospheric quality to it, shaping the horizon of possible experiences and meaningful practical possibilities.

The same is true for situations in which the therapist seeks to change the "vocabulary" and reduce the patient's utterance "This is awkward" to some kind of belief. CT teaches practitioners that clients should be corrected when they describe their experiences by using the phrase "I feel" (Beck et al. 1979, p. 37). Therapists are instructed to help patients to "translate" the phrase

"I feel" into "I think" or "I believe" (Beck et al. 1979; Beck 1995; Beck and Alford 2009).[8] It seems that such a translation comes at the cost of losing important aspects of a complex experience. "This is awkward" might harbor a much more complex relationship to self and the world than certain beliefs about the state of things. Referring to feelings might just be the most adequate means of expressing the transformation in the overall sense of being in the world. We have to bear in mind that such alteration encompasses a range of subtly different predicaments, and it might be difficult to convey it in other terms. Thus, whereas CT would attempt to reduce the utterance "This is awkward" to a thought, the same utterance might figure as a useful characterization of the altered background structure of experience. A nuanced understanding of such utterances may also help to make the first step toward the patient working with the background of the experience instead of focusing on cognitions.

What this inquiry is beginning to reveal is that there is a need for an interpretative sensitivity on the therapist's part. If one is interested in concluding the dialog and quickly making inferences to the underlying schema, one runs the risk of misinterpreting the patient. Carrying some of these assumptions into a therapeutic dialog might jeopardize a precise understanding of the patient's report. However, we may ask how far this critique reaches and to what extent we need interpretation in such cases. To address this question, let us consider a case that is apparently so clear-cut that we might be tempted to suggest that no further interpretation is necessary. Putting aside many previous considerations, we should ask ourselves what the situation would be if we assumed that the patient had a clear, internally represented, and resounding thought.

Consider the following example, closely modeled on Varga (2014). Tim is a rather disorganized man, who often forgets to lock the door of his car despite knowing that there are exceptionally high rates of car theft in the city in which he lives. Both his wife and his employer have tried warning him several times that if he continues this forgetful habit, it will only be a matter of time until his car is stolen. One day, returning to the parking lot from his lunch break, he finds that his unlocked car has disappeared. The first thought that enters his

[8] For example, the patient might say: "So, during the course of the day, driving into work, being at work, I was just in a nervous state. Not in extreme panic, but just in a nervous state. A feeling of, like, 'I don't know if I want to stay here or if I want to go'" (Scott et al. 1991, p. 18). The therapist answers and "translates" the patient's report into a cognitive vocabulary: "You had automatic thoughts like 'I don't know if I want to go or stay at work'?" (Scott et al. 1991, p. 18).

mind is "I had that coming." Surely it would appear that, in this case, there is no need for further interpretation—the CT-informed therapist might proceed to make inferences to an underlying schema. However, even in such an apparently clear-cut case further interpretation is necessary.

The difficulties start to arise when we ask ourselves whether we can be sure that the proposition involved (the resounding words "I had that coming") can be said to *constitute* the client's thinking. Although this is what CT assumes, it is far from obvious that the resounding words *constitute* Tim's thinking. We can envisage two scenarios here. First, when Tim "hears" himself inwardly uttering "I had that coming" we cannot even unequivocally assume that he is aware of a genuine mental episode of thinking. A comparison of inwardly and outwardly uttered sentences may be helpful here. Alex Byrne argues that the "outer utterance is not itself an episode of thinking, but something produced by such an episode; likewise, if there were ... an inner utterance it wouldn't be an episode of thinking either" (Byrne 2011, p. 115). Thus we could argue that what Tim is really aware of when he "hears" himself inwardly uttering "I had that coming" is not the thinking process itself but rather its *product*. In other words, without further arguments or evidence, we cannot assume that the inwardly uttered "I had that coming" constitutes his thinking. In such situations, words resound in our heads, and the words in question are only accompanying our thinking, rather than constituting it.[9]

Second, there is another reason why we cannot simply assume any constitutive relationship. Recall that internal dialogs with others often occur "in our heads" while we think through specific scenarios. Therefore it is not entirely implausible to assume that at the moment when the thought resounds, Tim is imagining describing the episode to his wife or employer. However, if that was the case, would we still think that the resounding words "I had that coming" are the indispensable and constitutive aspects of his thought? It does not appear to be so. Instead, it would be much more plausible to say that the resounding words have an *accompanying* role. Perhaps the resounding words add a meta-level to his thinking, which would be consistent with the view that words and language are not necessary for thought, but only for meta-level thought (Davies 1998; Smith 1998).

So why is this important? Indeed, a CT theorist might argue that it does not really matter whether the resounding thought constitutes or merely accompanies thinking. She might remind us that what really matters is that these

[9] It is important not to confuse the view that thinking does not necessarily involve words with the view that not all thinking may involve concepts. Jose Bermúdez (2003) has argued in favor of non-conceptual processes of representation.

thoughts are generated by a (negative) schema, and they can be used to detect that schema. However, this objection is not entirely convincing. If one assumes that the resounding thought in question merely accompanies thinking, then it is doubtful whether it would necessarily or even reliably reveal underlying schemas. We shall now consider why this is so.

Let us imagine that Tim felt depressed and consulted a CT-informed therapist. When Tim is talking about the episode when his car was stolen, the therapist asks him "What went through your mind?", to which Tim replies "I had that coming." Now let us suppose that the words in question (we are assuming that they resound) play a merely accompanying role, not a constitutive one. The difficulty we then face is as follows. If the resounding thought only accompanies thinking—for example, if Tim is thinking by imagining himself speaking about the episode—then this is an instance of thinking that is located at a "higher" level of thought, and the connection to an underlying schema becomes more uncertain. In other words, it is no longer plausible to think that the thought necessarily (or even reliably) reveals or reflects an underlying schema. Therefore in order to avoid potential misunderstanding, and to maximize the reliability of the CT therapist's judgment, it is safer if the therapist only makes inferences to an underlying schema in cases in which the resounding thought has a constitutive role.

The conclusion is that even in such seemingly clear-cut cases, further interpretation and sensitivity are needed to disentangle the relevant meanings. Inferences to underlying schemas would be far too premature, and misinterpretation of the patient would be highly likely. To be clear, the claim is not that it cannot be clarified whether a resounding thought has an accompanying or constitutive role. Rather, the point is that it would take a great deal of interpretative effort, of exactly the kind that CT is keen to avoid.

3.1. **Interpretation and openness**

As has already been mentioned, the hermeneutical tradition focuses on human expression, the conditions under which different types of interpretation can occur, and it deals with the understanding of meanings rather than the understanding of facts. We have seen that in numerous cases the CT-trained therapist might wrongly infer some internally represented propositional content and seriously misunderstand the *meaning* of the patient's utterance. In such cases, the framework of CT appears to be a barrier to comprehensive understanding, not only because of the nature of its theoretical commitments, but also because it seems to promote an attitude that favors quickly identifying the inference with an underlying schema and thus ending the dialog. As we have seen, there are good reasons for believing that many important meanings will to a large extent first become intelligible by further interpretations and questions. Therefore one rather obvious corrective that CT could accommodate is to put more emphasis on interpretative skills and reduce the focus on thoughts as mental representations.

However, there is another, more radical idea that would be useful to draw on in order to promote understanding in a therapeutic setting. Admittedly, this idea is indisputably more difficult to implement. The idea is not only that the conversation in a therapeutic setting should not primarily focus on mentally represented thoughts. It is also that the therapeutic conversation should not be merely (or at least not primarily) about getting the interpretation right, but rather it should be about establishing and maintaining a genuine dialog. The creation and maintenance of such a therapeutic dialog is crucially dependent on whether the therapist is able to ensure the continuous *openness* of the dialog.[10] The understanding of meaning in a dialogical situation is always an understanding from within the pre-theoretical horizon of the person's historical situation. Therefore, as Gadamer has continuously argued, understanding is a dynamic process that "goes continually beyond what can be brought to the understanding of the other person's words by methodological effort and critical self-control" (Gadamer 1976, p. xxii). In that case, the establishment of a genuine dialog starts with the acknowledgment that no single interpretation can be completely exhaustive. According to this view, the acknowledgment of the open-endedness of interpretation should lead to a certain *ethos* and *sensitivity* in the interpreter, which is characterized by an uncompromising openness to the possibility of constantly evolving understandings:

> The hermeneutical consciousness culminates not in methodological sureness of itself, but in the same readiness for experience that distinguishes the experienced man from the man captivated by dogma.
>
> (Gadamer 1989, p. 362)

[10] Interestingly, Gadamer (1972/2006, p. 357) speaks of a particular type of conversation, which he calls "curative conversation," that he sees in the practice of psychoanalysis. He notes that "the incapacity for conversation is almost the starting point from which the reacquisition of conversation presents itself as the process of healing." The point seems to be that the patient in psychotherapy is prevented from taking part in a genuine conversation. This might not seem to sit well with my effort here to use Gadamer's notion of conversation to explain hermeneutical processes in psychotherapy. However, we should note that Gadamer is concerned with individuals suffering from pathological disturbances with delusional features. As he notes, "The patient is so mired in these delusions that he can no longer really hear what the other says, and instead just feeds on his own diseased delusions" (Gadamer 1972/2006, p. 357).

In the following account it is argued that there are two sides to such an "ethos of openness," both of which are of great relevance to our endeavor in this chapter. At this point we may distinguish between the *openness of the subject matter* and the *openness of the stance* of the interlocutor. First, the issue of the openness of the subject matter is closely tied to the insight about the prejudiced character of understanding. This insight is supposed to lead to further openness and to a constant effort to revise anticipations of understanding in the light of a better and more cogent understanding of the whole. Clearly such an attitude involves a willingness to leave things open and, in many cases, to simply tolerate a plurality of possible interpretations. Therefore we can say that openness in this sense refers to the subject matter—to what is in question. As Gadamer has stated:

> The openness of what is in question consists in the fact that the answer is not settled. It must still be undetermined, awaiting a decisive answer. The significance of questioning consists in revealing the questionability of what is questioned. It has to be brought into this state of indeterminacy.
>
> (Gadamer 1989, p. 371)

One side of the openness thus consists of the unsettled state of the answer. It is not difficult to see the conflict with the view that CT endorses. CT propagates a type of interpersonal relationship that promotes a "scientific," disinterested interpretation and a way of relating to a person as something that is subject to predictable laws that can be fully uncovered. As we have seen, in some cases the process of grasping the meaning of what the patient says does not lead to genuine openness, as it rigidly isolates what the interpreter takes to be the answer to the important question. Instead, maintaining the openness of the conversation would involve the therapist being provoked by the patient's answer to question them further in the direction that the answer indicates. Such questioning would mean keeping open possibilities to counteract the alleged conclusiveness of the current opinions of both the patient and the therapist. This would be a good match with the nature of the subject matter that psychotherapeutic endeavor attempts to unearth. Given that our inner lives are, at least in part, constituted through our self-interpretations, and given that these self-interpretations are dynamic and cannot be understood in absolute terms (Taylor 1985a, 1985b), we should not expect patients' reports to be immune to further questioning and reinterpretation. Some of these interpretations are attempts to articulate the agent's sense of self-identity and are provisional, occurring against a background of a collective horizon of intelligibility that is never fully transparent to any individual.

Second, the issue of the *openness of the stance* is connected to a view about the nature of understanding. From a hermeneutical perspective, interpersonal understanding is not so much about achieving the correct interpretation of what has been uttered (although that is important), as it is about maintaining a certain quality of the intersubjective relationship in a conversation. This certain quality of the conversation is something Gadamer often refers to as the "openness" of the conversation. For Gadamer, the primary issue is not the knowledge that is gained by concluding the process of interpretation, but the openness with which we encounter the other. In this sense, openness has two intertwined roles, functioning as both the culmination of the interpretative process and its precondition. In a sense, the peak point of interpersonal understanding is not some kind of a conclusion, but more like a new door that opens up toward further understanding and insight. Genuine dialog arises not by applying a certain technique of interpretation, but by upholding an attitude of openness and thereby creating what Gadamer calls "a genuine human bond," which he links to the highest type of hermeneutical experience:

> In human relations the important thing is, as we have seen, to experience the Thou truly as a Thou—i.e., not to overlook his claim but to let him really say something to us. Here is where openness belongs. ... Without such openness to one another there is no genuine human bond. ... Openness to the other, then, involves recognizing that I myself must accept some things that are against me, even though no one else forces me to do.
>
> (Gadamer 1989, p. 355)

An important part of the openness of the conversation is enabled by way of questions and answers, and to illustrate this point Gadamer draws on the Platonic conception of dialog. What Gadamer emphasizes as being of central importance for the openness of the dialog is the "primacy of questioning." It is through proper questioning that the appropriate relationship for understanding is upheld. As he notes, the crux of the question is simply to unearth and keep open possibilities. The questioning would allow constantly exceeding the historically situated horizon of the patient and its fusion with the horizon of the therapist.

From this perspective, to understand is not just to refrain from interrupting the dialog the first time the patient says something that fits with the therapist's theoretical expectations. It also involves the capacity to ask further questions in a manner that involves the questioner herself being questioned by what the patient says. In other words, the interpersonal relationship in a genuine dialog is characterized by the fundamental openness of our own stance. According to Gadamer, participating in a genuinely open dialog involves not only questioning, but also the experience of being questioned (possibly in unsettling ways) and, thus, the readiness to permit oneself to be challenged by the other. Therefore one should not strive to "conduct" a conversation:

> We say that we "conduct" a conversation, but the more genuine a conversation is, the less its conduct lies within the will of either partner. Thus a genuine conversation is never the one that we wanted to conduct. Rather, it is generally more correct to say that we fall into conversation, or even that we become involved in it. The way one word follows another, with the conversation taking its own twists and reaching its own conclusion, may well be conducted in some way, but the partners conversing are far less the leaders of it than the led. No one knows in advance what will "come out" of a conversation. Understanding or its failure is like an event that happens to us. Thus we can say that something was a good conversation or that it was ill fated. All this shows that a conversation has a spirit of its own, and that the language in which it is conducted bears its own truth within it—i.e., that it allows something to "emerge" which henceforth exists.
>
> (Gadamer 1989, p. 385)

Instead of thinking in terms of conducting a conversation and correcting the patient's vocabulary (by translating it into cognitive terms), it might be more appropriate to think in terms of "falling" into conversation, emphasizing the point that anyone who enters a genuine dialog must be willing to undergo radical questioning. It is not difficult to see that such an openness might help to generate the trust and mutual involvement, which is for Gadamer the zenith of the encounter and which might be essential for a successful therapeutic alliance. The idea of the openness of the conversation takes into account the ontological nature of the hermeneutic circle, which means that it is not some shortcoming that can be overcome one day, but rather a constitutive element of understanding.

4. Conclusion

While Chapter 3 dealt with problems with textual sources that present themselves in psychiatry, the focus in this chapter was on interpretative processes in therapeutic encounters. We started out by noting that although there is general recognition of the success of psychotherapy, the characteristics of the communicative processes involved in successful outcomes are not adequately understood. In this chapter, the main aim was to clarify the role of some of the processes that are involved in a therapeutic encounter. A critical dialog was initiated with the influential CT, which constitutes the predominant paradigm in the understanding of affective disorders and psychotherapy. CT promotes a particular project, which manifests itself in two ways, both resulting in what we could understand as two sides of an *observational stance*. First, it promotes an observational stance toward the patient—an attitude of engagement that is characterized by a detached attitude, which, as has been shown, is often not adequate for understanding the meaning of the patient's utterances. Second, it also promotes an observational stance of the patient in relation to himself. Overly focusing on the content of mental representations (and not on interpretation) not only strengthens a particular attitude toward the patient's reports, but, given that the therapist explicitly educates the patient to consent to this theory, it also promotes a form of self-understanding that views mental states as a matter of passive observation rather than active interpretation. Of course, none of this is to deny that the cognitive conceptualization of emotions and affective disorders has led to a variety of theoretical, empirical, and therapeutic advances. However, it is to be expected that CT's intention to identify automatic thoughts and to correct and "translate" affective utterances into a cognitive vocabulary can lead to a variety of serious misunderstandings, which can be assumed to have a negative impact on the therapeutic outcome. Integration of a hermeneutical perspective would have several advantages and could provide the basis for a more precise understanding of the patient's utterances in the therapeutic encounter.

Opposing such an observational picture, two kinds of processes were emphasized, which both appear to be crucial for a thorough understanding in a therapeutic setting. These are connected to *self-interpretation* and *conversation*. In other words, the corrective suggested that it would be appropriate for the therapist to adopt a hermeneutical–participatory stance toward the patient and to encourage the patient to adopt a hermeneutical–participatory stance toward herself. Such a stance would involve acknowledging that we are "self-interpreting animals," and thus not constituted by individuated mental entities that exist entirely independently of our self-interpretations. In many cases, understanding can only be established via a process that requires a stance such as interpretive engagement.

To conclude, let us briefly return to the issue of the therapeutic alliance that we considered at the beginning of this chapter. As we have noted, there is a mismatch between solid evidence for the successful outcomes in psychotherapy on the one hand, and ignorance about the nature of the processes responsible for such positive outcomes on the other. What is relatively certain is that the *therapeutic alliance* between therapist and patient is a factor responsible for the effectiveness of psychotherapy. In the light of the material that has been discussed in this chapter, and the theses that have been introduced, it seems timely to reflect on the following issue. Would what we could call "the ethos of openness" and the suggested openness of the conversation promote the creation of the conditions under which a strong therapeutic alliance is generated? Although this is not the place to argue for this thesis, it seems likely that it would, if only because it promotes an engaged relationship instead of one in which the therapist is a detached, neutral observer.

Part 2

The concept of mental disorder

Chapter 5

Introduction to Part 2: two types of criticism

Hermeneutics has in the last two centuries developed into a philosophical enterprise that aims to go beyond dealing with prescriptive questions in textual interpretation and with situations that require interpretative effort. Philosophers have increasingly explored the nature and structure of interpretation, claiming that all understanding is profoundly embedded in historically and linguistically constituted horizons. Opposing the idea of strictly differentiated realms of comprehension, they have highlighted the fundamental "historicity" (*Geschichtlichkeit*) of all understanding. It is relatively straightforward to survey and comprehend the implications of this view when dealing with texts and utterances in interpersonal communication. Part I of this book dealt with the consequences for psychiatric practice and research, showing how a hermeneutically informed perspective might be fruitful for a more adequate understanding of certain subjects.

Part II continues the inquiry into issues pertaining to psychiatry, further sustaining the view developed in Part I that, given its unique position, psychiatric practice and research faces unique methodological challenges, some of them philosophical in nature. In Part II, the fundamental "historicity" of all understanding is taken seriously, which means that our self-understanding as human beings is no exception to this rule. As we are thoroughly historical beings, understanding our own situation cannot be sharply delineated from understanding ourselves. Far from being reducible to some core, what we are is itself affected by the "historicity" of understanding by our being "thrown" into a particular historical situation and social community. From such a general perspective, Part II will attempt to continue the investigation of psychiatric issues, now addressing the concept of mental disorder. Admittedly at this point it is far from clear what our self-interpretations as human beings have to do with the concept of mental disorder. Briefly, the main goal of Part II of this book is to argue that the concept of mental disorder is to a large extent connected to processes of self-understanding.

In accordance with the general approach that was adopted in Part I, this task will be achieved by means of a critical dialog involving different "naturalist" positions on the concept of mental disorder. Thus the engagement with "naturalism" and its philosophical assumptions will interlink the clarification of interpretative processes with the critical exploration of claims put forward by naturalist approaches. A "naturalist" approach denotes in this context a number of approaches that aim to provide an *objective and value-free* concept of mental disorder, and a connected classificatory system that picks out differences between types of mental disorder that are objective and theoretically significant. To demonstrate what this means, consider the case of past mental disorders such as drapetomania (used to describe slaves who wished to escape), sluggish schizophrenia (used to describe political dissidents in Soviet psychiatry), and masturbation. While some have viewed such examples as evidence for the historical and cultural relativity of mental disorders, naturalists hold that these are simply discomforting examples of bad science, which has been corrected not by moral progress but by genuine scientific progress (Woolfolk 1999). The opponents are those naturalists who, often referring to classificatory systems in chemistry and biology, maintain that mental disorder can be defined solely on the basis of "pure" facts.

1. The concept of mental disorder

So far, much of what has been said hinges on the assumption that the concept of mental disorder is important for psychiatric research and practice and has substantial implications for diagnosis and interventions. Familiar from medicine, the concept of disorder is crucial to many important issues—it guides judgments about whether a condition is classified as pathological, and it has a multiplicity of implications for diagnosis and treatment. Whether an individual has a disorder often determines whether they have a moral claim on others for assistance, and it governs the responsibilities of physicians and public health officials. If the condition of an individual is classified as a disorder, it might lead to certain rights and benefits (such as health insurance coverage), or to certain constraints (which might even include confinement). Similarly, the way in which disorders are defined will have an impact on research. With regard to ethical issues, a variety of implications arise. For instance, if a person exhibits strange and antisocial behavioral patterns, he will probably be labeled as a morally bad person, but if a connection is established between his behavior and a disorder, his actions will be judged in a completely different manner. An offender may thus be legally or morally excused for otherwise unacceptable and punishable behavior.

However, we may ask why the concept of mental disorder constitutes a philosophical problem, or at least a problem that philosophers might be able to assist with. Acknowledging that present-day criteria are subject to ongoing revision, and that there is no "gold-standard" biomarker or laboratory test for mental disorders, it might be objected that we actually have diagnostic criteria laid down in the DSM and ICD, which function as authorities to which we may turn in order to establish whether or not a condition warrants the label of disorder. In addition, we have at our disposal tests of validity, such as co-occurrence of symptoms, family history, statistical and taxometric analysis, genetic factors, response to medication, etc. However, using the criteria and techniques for identifying disorders to pick out mental disorder itself relies on assumptions about the concept of disorder (Wakefield 2010). This means that conceptually these tests cannot have any final authority—although they are able to distinguish between constructs, they are not capable of making distinctions between disorders and non-disorders, partly because they are satisfied by a range of normal and disordered conditions. That is, tests of validity cannot draw the boundaries of mental disorder without, in a circular manner, appealing to an independently supposed notion of disorder. Thus empirical approaches can only be successful in picking out mental disorders if they are combined with solid conceptual work.

Despite its crucial importance, providing an adequate definition of disorder has proved to be a notoriously problematic issue. While the question of where to draw the boundaries between health and disease can be difficult to answer in medicine, it is even more difficult in relation to mental health. For the psychiatrist, in Gadamer's words, "the category of illness … is not simply given in the same way as it is for other forms of medical diagnosis" (Gadamer 1996, p. 168). In addition to having to deal with diagnostic uncertainty, psychiatry is further removed than other medical subdisciplines from the type of knowledge that characterizes the domain of the natural sciences. Psychiatry is unique due to its connection to socio-political and philosophical issues. The well-known realism versus anti-realism debate in philosophy has an additional normative implication and is linked to a number of ethical and policy issues. Some of these aspects have contributed to the fact that no other medical subspecialty has faced so much criticism for being unscientific on the one hand (for lacking a unified account of mental disorder, as well as a diagnostic classification system with reliable biological criteria), and for being little more than a manifestation of normalizing socio-political forces on the other (Szasz 1965, 2000; Horwitz and Wakefield 2007).

2. The extent of the criticism of psychiatry

Despite the importance of mental disorder, it was not until the publication of the DSM-III that a coordinated effort was made to define it. Since then a general consensus has developed that a persuasive definition of mental disorder is important. This change in attitude coincided with the political climate that the American Psychiatric Association (APA) faced during the 1970s (Kutchins and Kirk 1997; Cooper 2005). The APA encountered fierce criticism relating to a number of issues. On the one hand, there were intense debates about the issue of whether homosexuality should be classified as a mental disorder as the DSM-II had suggested. Due to growing discontentment and critique by organizations, this classification was becoming increasingly untenable. On the other hand, support groups had campaigned for the recognition of mental disorder as a disease like other medical diseases (such as diseases of the brain) for several reasons. Recognizing that the diagnosis of mental disorder had a more stigmatizing effect than a diagnosis of physical disease, many hoped that recognizing mental disorder as fundamentally similar to physical diseases would eventually weaken the stigmatization. It was also hoped that recognition of this similarity by the medical establishment would lead to a political change and, ultimately, that the same benefits would be granted to the mentally ill as to the physically ill.

However, the most powerful and comprehensive criticism was launched by what later became known as the "anti-psychiatry movement." Due to this unique position, all of the critical questions that arise in other medical subspecialties arise even more forcefully in psychiatry. Furthermore, adding to its ambiguities, psychiatry is the only subdiscipline that has exclusive power to exercise preventive and therapeutic measures that include denying individuals the right to their liberty—the right that the Declaration of Independence describes as "unalienable" and conceives of as securing protection from despotism. In the words of the famous critic Thomas Szasz, "Incarceration of law-abiding individuals in an insane asylum … constitutes the backbone of psychiatry" (Szasz 2012, p. 349). It is thus not surprising that psychiatry has been the target of more and harsher criticism than other scientific disciplines or medical subspecialties. Nevertheless, the criticism leveled at psychiatry is remarkable, not only in its austerity, but also in terms of its fundamental nature and the variety of critical voices from a wide range of professional backgrounds. Like no other scientific discipline, psychiatry has had its very foundation attacked by a wide range of opponents from diverse backgrounds, including philosophers, sociologists, psychiatrists, feminists, psychologists, social workers, and political scientists. The critique has very often been of a fundamental nature, because its target was the very concept of "mental disorder" that lies at the core of psychiatry. More to the point, the tenor of the criticism is that rather than picking out real entities in the world, psychiatry in fact pathologizes in different ways—it transforms normal suffering, "problems in living," and deviant behavior into psychiatric conditions.

Instead of attempting to incorporate all of the different strands of critical thought about psychiatry, the focus of this chapter will be on *two prototypical versions of criticism*. Although the proponents in the two camps approach problems related to psychiatry from very different perspectives, most scholars (although for a notable exception see Bracken and Thomas 2010) have tended to lump them together under the label "anti-psychiatry."[1] Here, however, it will be suggested that there is a need to distinguish between *categorical* and *dimensional* types of critique, both of which level criticism at the concept of mental disorder. Briefly, whereas the *categorical criticism* radically argues that the whole concept of mental disorder is a misnomer, the *dimensional criticism* opposes the manner in which certain diagnostic boundaries are placed. Whereas the categorical criticism questions the scientific legitimacy of psychiatry as a whole, the dimensional criticism mainly seeks to correct the course that psychiatry has taken with regard to certain diagnoses.

As well as attempting to correct the tendency to lump together these quite disparate criticisms, the distinction introduced here will highlight how the various critical analyses lead to different answers to the questions posed. In addition, such division of the criticism into two types is useful in that it gives us a more precise picture of the challenges that definitions of mental disorder, including naturalistic ones, will have to face.

2.1. The categorical criticism

Whereas the dimensional criticism opposes the manner in which a diagnostic boundary is placed, the categorical criticism is more radical and argues that mental disorders do not exist in the world—a view that is reflected in the title of Thomas Szasz' popular book, *The Myth of Mental Illness* (Szasz 1961). Szasz, who has perhaps contested the theory and practice of psychiatry and mental health more than anyone else (Williams and Caplan 2012), claimed that psychiatry is exercising social power by transforming "problems in living" and deviant behavior into psychiatric conditions. The Szaszian categorical criticism maintains that, instead of diseases, psychiatric patients suffer from problems in living, while psychiatric classification is really an exertion

[1] David Cooper's book, *Psychiatry and Anti-Psychiatry* (Cooper 1967), is often referred to as the origin of the term "anti-psychiatry."

of social power that identifies the sufferers as social misfits. According to this view, mental disorder is little more than a label that justifies and masks the use of power against socially unacceptable behavior. Szasz has more recently restated his position, arguing that:

> psychiatrists and their allies have succeeded in persuading the scientific community, courts, media, and general public that the conditions they call mental disorders are diseases.
>
> (Szasz 2000, p. 31)

Proponents of this line of reasoning were expressing fundamental doubts about the scientific nature and legitimacy of psychiatry. Highlighting the differences between mental and physical illness, they argued that psychiatry is not a genuine branch of medicine. As long as no objective, physico-chemical processes can be causally related to mental disorders, the assertion that they are "real" conditions that warrant psychiatric care is unsubstantiated. According to this view, in the absence of clear-cut (biological) boundaries, the identification of psychiatric disorders is an illegitimate process of exclusion that simply reflects value judgments about undesirable beliefs and behavior. What we see here is that the categorical criticism argues from two particular conceptual premises.

First, this categorical criticism relies on the assumption that only "physical" diseases can be regarded as genuine diseases. As Szasz (2004) notes, diseases are malfunctions of the human body and its organs, such as the heart or the brain. According to this view, the very concept of mental disorder is suspect, leaving little room for psychiatry. If mental disorders were real biological conditions, they would fall under the purview of other medical specialists, such as neurologists. Thus what really confuses those who want to hold on to the concept of mental disorder is that they fail to see that psychiatry is merely parasitically using medical terms to describe "problems in living," behavior, and experiences that are regarded as deviant from certain socially constructed standards.

Second, categorical criticism is dependent on the assumption that disorders (diseases) can be objectively defined in terms of their representing departures from objective norms. Physical illness is a deviation from an anatomically and physiologically demarcated norm linked to the "the structural and functional integrity of the human body" (Szasz 1960, p. 114). Both such norms of functional integrity, and also health itself, "can be stated in anatomical and physiological terms" (Szasz 1960, p. 114).

Overall, while espousing a naturalist position, the categorical criticism accuses psychiatry of being infected with *conventionalism*—that is, fundamental principles that define mental disorder as a kind are grounded on explicit or implicit socio-political constellations, rather than on "external" reality, as in "nature's joints." Szasz thus maintains that the only legitimate psychiatric kind that justifies therapeutic attention is a *natural kind*—a term that refers to a class or composition of entities that have natural boundaries independent of human interests. This means that a disorder has to have clear-cut boundaries that are independent of our classifications. The assumption is thus that the conditions medical science treats are natural kinds, and that diagnostic boundaries should follow "naturally" occurring underlying discontinuities.

Szasz's unbending critical attitude toward research and practice in psychiatry had an undeniable effect on the course of the field. His influence is partly due to the fact that libertarian intellectuals welcomed his critical thoughts and used them as a source of inspiration in their campaign for individualism and anti-paternalism. His work played a role in discussions in influential law journals about civil commitment and the insanity defense—debates that proved influential in informing particular decisions and reforms of a legal and judicial nature. It is important to emphasize to what extent the categorical criticism has contributed to the delegitimization of psychiatry as a scientific–medical discipline. For our purposes in this chapter, we may distinguish two ways in which the categorical criticism has functioned as a decisive factor in changing the course of psychiatric practice and research. First, on the legal side, one change involved a significant part of the supervisory control for mental health patient care being taken from psychiatrists and given to lawyers and lawmakers:[2]

> Szasz first criticised "mental illness" as a legal term in a 1958 issue of the *Columbia Law Review*. At the time of publication, five U.S. states restricted involuntary commitment of people with mental illness to those deemed "dangerous." The other states generally permitted commitment for anyone with mental illness who had a "need for treatment." By the end of the 1970s, every state had either changed its statute or interpreted its pre-existing statute to narrow criteria in the direction Szasz first advocated. The number of patients in public psychiatric hospitals or "asylums" fell from an all-time high of more than 550 000 in the mid-1950s to fewer than 150 000 by the end of the 1970s.
>
> (Williams and Caplan 2012, p. 1380)

Second, and most significant for our purposes, such profound criticism was one of the motivations behind a development in which many psychiatrists

2 These changes were met with severe criticism. In 1979, Paul Appelbaum and Thomas Gutheil published a critical piece with the telling title "Rotting with their rights on."

began to more insistently seek to identify the underlying biological, chemical, genetic, and physiological bases of mental disorders and to think of the concept of mental disorder in naturalistic terms. In other words, the categorical criticism propelled a move toward an intellectual climate in which there was a general orientation toward naturalism.

2.2. The dimensional criticism

Although Foucault is often labeled as an "anti-psychiatrist," his project about the history of madness is best seen as a subtle attempt to develop a different sensibility toward mental illness.[3] The aim is neither to abolish psychiatry, nor to eliminate the notion of mental disorder, nor to make the case in favor of a specific notion of mental illness. Rather, the project is best seen as aiming to demonstrate that our modern concept of "mental disorder" has a particularly complex history, in which contingent historical events have significantly shaped its contemporary meaning. The hallmark of the approach is the focus on the peculiar liaison between certain (discursive) disciplines and the objects that they study and classify. Foucault's analyses are led by a puzzle over the more or less taken for granted ontological systems behind our classifications:

> When we establish a considered classification, when we say that a cat and a dog resemble each other less than two greyhounds do, even if both are tame or embalmed, even if both are frenzied, even if both have just broken the water pitcher, what is the ground on which we are able to establish the validity of this classification with complete certainty? On what "table," according to what grid of identities, similitudes, analogies, have we become accustomed to sort out so many different and similar things? What is this coherence which, as is immediately apparent, is neither determined by an a priori and necessary concatenation, nor imposed on us by immediately perceptible contents?
>
> (Foucault 1970, p. xviii)

Foucault's point is that although it is often taken for granted, similarity is far from being a logically robust and incontestable category of analysis. The nominalist tendency of his thinking manifests itself in a determined skepticism about the idea that systems of classification are unmediated and hence directly refer to the world. Rather, he argues that it is through the capacity of abstraction of human minds in linguistic and cultural practices that different

[3] *Madness and Civilization* (Foucault 1967) builds on a characteristic method of historical inquiry, which Foucault lays out in *The Order of Things* (Foucault 1970). It should be noted that two different versions of Foucault's work on the history of mental illness are available. The classical version is shorter than the more recently published *History of Madness* (Foucault 2006).

things become similar enough to be grouped into kinds. To put this in more contemporary terms, the different orders that underlie classificatory systems are socio-culturally constructed. Behind them there is a "hidden network" that determines the way in which objects appear in relation to each other.[4]

A corresponding line of thought provides the foundation for the critique of psychiatry. The aim is to show that mental disorder, far from being a natural kind, is an unstable and historically contingent category, heavily shaped by diverse power relationships throughout history. In contrast to the categorical criticism, Foucault takes a middle position, depicting mental disorder as a genuine occurrence in the world, but not one that we can discover in the way that we supposedly discover natural kinds. At the same time, he also leaves open the possibility that some of the specific conditions that we understand as instances of mental disorder do not exist independent of psychiatric theories and institutional practices. Although many historians have criticized Foucault's sometimes hasty generalizations and inaccurate historical facts (for example, the "ships of fools" never existed), the general point is an interesting and valid one. It is a contingent matter of fact that from the Enlightenment period we began to conceptualize madness as the "other" of reason, no longer as strange but as *ill* and, hence, to be treated by physicians. The previously "undifferentiated experience" (Foucault 2005, p. ix) of madness became systematized and classified in terms of mental disorder, no longer thought of as a moral or spiritual problem, but rather as an essentially medical one. This marks the emergence of "that other form of madness, by which men, in an act of sovereign reason, confine their neighbors" (Foucault 2005, p. ix).

One of the most unique aspects of Foucault's analysis lies in the fact that he links the emergence of psychiatric classification with specific constellations of socio-cultural powers and interests. For instance, the insane were confined together with the "delinquent," "the poor," and the "idle" during a period in which cities were concerned with ridding themselves of beggars, solving labor problems, and protecting themselves against unrest or revolt. This coincided with the redefinition of "normality" in terms of willingness and potential to be economically productive. Idleness then became thought of as the source of both delinquency and mental illness (Foucault 2005, p. 46). The confinement

[4] Foucault's "archaeological" approach to knowledge, truth, and classification seeks to detect hidden patterns of thought and show the fundamental *arbitrariness* of our systems and categories. In its more radical formulations, Foucault denies that truth is essentially a relationship between concepts and objects and holds instead that it is a relationship between discursive patterns in a specific historical period.

had its own rationality, providing some kind of solution to the economic crisis. The confined were put to work, which was conceptualized as therapy, but which also provided a source of valuable cheap labor. The overall attitude of Foucault's approach can be described as combining "archaeology" with a "hermeneutics of suspicion." The reason why some systems of truths emerge, and why classifications and connected practices become accepted as normal, might be linked to the fact that the classifications of individuals, be it as delinquent or insane, further the solidification of specific social orders. According to this view, mental disorder reflects not so much specific and unchanging realities in the world, but rather a certain cultural "space of exclusion" within society that is determined by the changing constellations of power in socio-cultural and economic structures.

Foucault's critique of psychiatry can thus be seen as a form of *dimensional criticism,* which does not deny the existence of mental disorder, but resists the idea that there should be a categorical difference between "normal" experience and mental disorder. In addition to seeing a continuum between these poles, Foucault refrains from making a normative judgment about the correct point on this continuum at which to fix the boundaries of mental disorder. Rather, a major point is that we should be aware of the fact that wherever we place those boundaries, they will always be "muddled" by the power relations inherent in social orders.

While Foucault's work is probably the most well known, other authors have also put forward similar forms of dimensional criticism. In recent work by Horwitz and Wakefield (2005, 2007) that mainly focuses on depression, we find a critical account of mental disorder that is in many ways comparable to that of Foucault, although it is less complex. In their book, *The Loss of Sadness* (Horwitz and Wakefield 2007), they defend the thesis that the then contemporary DSM-IV definition of depression is too broad and tends to include a number of individuals who suffer from nothing more than states of sadness that are normal responses to life events. According to this criticism, due to the broadness of definitions, psychiatry tends to pathologize everyday problems in living and relabels a normal form of distress or misery as depressive disorder. Just like Foucault, Horwitz and Wakefield do not aim to abandon the concept of mental disorder and understand "normal" experience as continuous with that in mental disorder. We may also say that there is a certain suspicion in their work, which mainly targets the powers of the pharmaceutical industry.

> We argue that the recent explosion of putative depressive disorder, in fact, does not stem primarily from a real rise in this condition. Instead, it is largely a product of conflating the two conceptually distinct categories of normal sadness and depressive

> disorder and thus classifying many instances of normal sadness as mental disorders. The current "epidemic," although the result of many social factors, has been made possible by a changed psychiatric definition of depressive disorder that often allows the classification of sadness as disease, even when it is not.
>
> (Horwitz and Wakefield 2007, p. 6)

In other words, the criticism is dimensional, as its target is the position of a diagnostic distinction on the continuum between mental disorder and normal experience. In principle, such criticism can go both ways—it is possible to criticize a definition for being too broad (with the risk of including individuals who are merely experiencing transitory distress) or too narrow (with the risk of overlooking individuals who would benefit from clinical awareness of their condition).

The fundamental difference between the path chosen by Foucault and that chosen by Horwitz and Wakefield is linked to their normative aspirations. Horwitz and Wakefield aim to solve the challenge by developing a certain prescriptive account of how we should use the concept of mental disorder. What makes their critique different is that they do formulate a judgment about the boundaries of mental disorder:

> The most plausible demarcation point between human normality and disorder in the medical sense is, we believe, that between biologically "designed" functioning (i.e., the result of natural selection) and the failure of such functioning, that is, dysfunction.
>
> (Horwitz and Wakefield 2007, p. 15)

Although they argue that the current diagnostic boundaries of depression are "muddled" by the power relations inherent in social orders, they nevertheless think that it is in principle possible to "discover" where the boundaries of mental disorders are located.

3. **Toward "naturalism"**

In reaction to forms of dimensional and categorical criticism and to the pressure from support groups pushing for recognition that mental disorders are diseases of the brain (and therefore just like somatic diseases), in 1973 the American Psychiatric Association created a special Task Force. Their task was to elaborate an adequate definition of mental disorder that would satisfy the support groups and defuse the criticism (Barton 1973; Spitzer et al. 1977; Cooper 2005). The outcome was a definition in the DSM-III, which emphasized that a condition only qualifies as a mental disorder if it gives rise to some kind of distress or disability. In order to qualify as a mental disorder, a condition has to be "a clinically significant behavioral or psychological syndrome or pattern that occurs in an individual and that is typically associated with either a painful symptom (distress) or impairment in one or more areas of functioning (disability)" (American Psychiatric Association 1980, p. 6). On the basis of this definition, homosexuality was no longer considered to be a mental disorder, unless the sexual orientation caused significant distress for the homosexual individual. Homosexuality was abandoned as a disorder in favor of "Sexual Orientation Disorder," which did not include homosexual individuals who did not experience distress about their sexual orientation. Such a definition, which granted the subjective experience of distress a prominent position, differs from a more medical approach according to which someone who does not experience distress while being infected could still be considered to have a disease. Homosexuality was effectively eliminated as a mental disorder, and we may also add a couple of other positive developments—the stigmatization of the mentally ill has significantly decreased, and there has been a movement toward a fairer balance between benefits granted to the mentally ill and those granted to the physically ill.

However, such changes clearly did not solve the issues relating to the objectivity and scientific status of psychiatry that had been raised by categorical and dimensional forms of criticism. Therefore, at the same time as these changes were implemented, considerable efforts were made to strengthen the position of psychiatry as a legitimate branch of medicine (Spitzer et al. 1977; Cooper 2005). Efforts to support the notion that mental disorders are fundamentally similar to physical diseases were coordinated by the time DSM-IV was published. Of course, as we have seen in Chapter 2, these efforts were hindered by the fact that research failed to provide solid evidence for underlying biological conditions that could be causally linked to mental disorders. Nevertheless, one step in this direction was to eliminate formulations that could be understood as implying some kind of dissimilarity between mental and physical disorders. In an influential paper with the telling title "Now is the time to retire the term 'organic mental disorders'," Spitzer et al. (1992, p. 240) argued that DSM-IV should eliminate the term "organic," because it implies "an outmoded functional/structural, psychological/biological, and mind/body dualism." The authors also feared that the term implied that some psychiatric disorders do not have a biological contribution.

3.1. Varieties of naturalism

In such an intellectual climate, where psychiatry was under pressure to prove its legitimacy as a genuine medico-scientific discipline, it is not entirely surprising that opinion began to favor a scientific, naturalized, and value-free concept of mental disorder and a linked classificatory system, akin to those in chemistry and biology, that picks out theoretically significant and objective differences between mental disorders. Kendell (1986) maintains that:

> the most fundamental issue, and also the most contentious one, is whether disease and illness are normative concepts based on value judgments, or whether they are value-free scientific terms; in other words, whether they are biomedical terms or socio-political ones.
>
> (Kendell 1986, p. 25)

The idea is that if it turned out that mental disorder could successfully be defined solely on the basis of "pure" facts, then psychiatry would be shielded against both forms of criticism. As Woolfolk (1999) has noted, many scientists and clinicians have endorsed the naturalist position, proclaiming that mental disorder is objective in the sense that it is not determined by the values of a particular historical period.

Although naturalism holds that mental disorder results from failures that can be fully described in objective and scientific terminology, it occurs in several forms. In Part II of this book, the focus is on critically engaging with several variants of naturalism with regard to the concept of mental disorder. Two versions of naturalism will be distinguished, which are dealt with in Chapters 6 and 7, respectively. First, Chapter 6 explores a version of naturalism which argues that mental disorders are *natural kinds* (referring to the kinds studied by the natural sciences). Chapter 7 then describes the second version of naturalism, which maintains that mental disorders involve a deviation from the proper functioning of the human organism. Both Christopher Boorse and Jerome Wakefield maintain that their aim of providing a naturalist account of disease is partly motivated by the desire to clarify mental health controversies and to contribute to discussions that followed upon the proliferation of forms of categorical and dimensional criticism.

Whereas Chapter 6 and 7 critically assess the arguments in support of naturalism, Chapter 8 deals with a less strict version of naturalism. Thornton (2007) and Graham (2010, 2013) have opted for what is referred to as a "having it both ways" account, accepting that the concept of mental disorder is value laden, while simultaneously maintaining that there are objective truths with regard to mental disorder attributions. This leads on to Chapter 9, which aims to explain the failure of both naturalist and (quasi-)value theorist accounts and set out a position that is situated *between* naturalism and relativism.

Chapter 6

Natural kinds

The two types of criticism noted earlier have contributed to strengthening a naturalist orientation in psychiatry that looks back on a long history in the discipline. Founding figures such as Griesinger, Bleuler, and Kraepelin were persuaded that ultimately it would be possible to explain mental disorders in terms of brain diseases. Toward the beginning of the twentieth century, this reasoning was also supported by empirical successes. The etiology of the mental disorder *general paresis* (symptoms of which included defective speech, forms of delusions, paralysis, and dementia) was determined in laboratory studies. It was discovered that the condition is related to damaged brain tissue caused by syphilitic infection. With the identification of the biological etiology of this mental disorder, a biological treatment became possible. Particularly in the last four decades, there was growing popularity of the "disease" model of mental disorder and a particular psychiatric classification, which rely on the assumption that mental disorders are fundamentally similar and in all important respects equivalent to physical diseases treated in general medicine (Kiesler 1999, pp. 16–17; see Perring 2007). Often the bottom-line position is that mental disorders should be understood in biological terms because they are reducible to biological abnormalities (primarily in the brain). Such a view has been put forward by prominent figures such as Guze (1989), who in an editorial with the title "Biological psychiatry: is there any other kind?" argues that mental disorder is the manifestation of disturbed processes in brain systems mediating psychological functions.

At the same time, on many accounts, these biological abnormalities are conceptualized as *natural kinds*. In philosophy, discussions about natural kinds are often connected to questions about what makes an individual thing belong to a certain kind, the same kind as other particular things. Importantly, it is often held that by scientifically dividing entities into distinct kinds, we are in fact disclosing facts about nature. Thus, while philosophers reflect on what it is for a thing to be a member of a kind, scientists discover what kinds and properties there actually are—for instance, the discovery that the essence of water is that it is composed of H_2O (Dupre 2011). Although the term "natural kind" does not often explicitly surface, Zachar (2000) notes that mental health professionals often use related concepts to evaluate classification systems.

Considering the pressure on psychiatry, it is not difficult to see why such a naturalist understanding of mental disorder as a biological natural kind appears to be an advantageous option. By adopting such a strategy, psychiatry could defend itself by maintaining that psychiatric classification tracks "real" diseases in the world that do not involve value judgments. Yet how accurate is such a view? This chapter starts out with a critical assessment of the view that we should conceptualize psychiatric disorders as natural kinds. After a short introduction, it is demonstrated that the essentialist view of natural kinds conflicts with our knowledge about a number of biological entities. Then, accounts are explored that recognize the inadequacies of essentialism about natural kinds, while trying to salvage the idea that the special sciences investigate natural kinds in their respective domains. Such views relax naturalism, incorporate conventionalist elements, and present less strict accounts of natural kinds. While rescuing the idea of mental disorders as natural kinds (consistent with a scientific picture), these accounts aim to maintain that it is possible for our psychiatric taxonomies to track natural kinds individuated by properties that exist independently of us.

1. Natural kinds

Many exemplary scientific disciplines seek to develop scientific theories that formulate generalizations in terms of "natural kinds," which separate and categorize their subjects of inquiry, just as chemistry classifies individual substances and categorizes them via their structure at the molecular level. Unsurprisingly, the topic of natural kinds is of interest not only to scientists, but also to those who work in metaphysics and the philosophy of science. It was John Stuart Mill who first spoke of "real Kinds," in contrast with kinds established by convention. He wrote that:

> [if a] natural classification is grounded on real Kinds, its groups are certainly not conventional; it is perfectly true that they do not depend upon an arbitrary choice of the naturalist.
>
> (Mill 1843, p. 720)[1]

Since natural kinds have "truly" existing boundaries in the world (as opposed to boundaries created by conventions), an adequate scientific classification should match these actual boundaries in nature. The underlying metaphysical

[1] For a historical survey, see Hacking (2007).

view is that there are natural divisions between natural kinds, which are essential building blocks of the world, individuated by their intrinsic properties.

Although there is a multitude of ways in which natural kinds can be defined (see Bird 2009), we shall first be concerned with a specific, *essentialist understanding* of natural kinds, which claims that natural kinds fulfill criteria such as being regular and internally consistent from one instance to the next. As Boyd notes, according to an essentialist understanding of natural kinds, the members exhibit "definitional essences that define them in terms of necessary and sufficient, intrinsic, unchanging, ahistorical properties" (Boyd 1999, p. 146; Ereshefsky 2007; Bird and Tobin 2008). Natural kinds possess properties that are both necessary and sufficient to label something as an instance of the kind and that causally constitute that kind (Wilkins 2003). According to the essentialist understanding, natural kinds thus pick out entities that:

(C1) have common intrinsic properties that are necessary and sufficient conditions for a particular's being a member of the kind,

(C2) support inductive inferences, and

(C3) are bounded and categorically distinct.

Take the standard example of gold. (C1) is fulfilled, as being made out of atoms that have 79 protons is the intrinsic property that is necessary and sufficient in order to fulfill kind membership (see Ellis 2005). Thus, since this is a defining property, any element that fulfills this criterion is gold, even if it does not have other usual characteristics of gold, such as the typical color. As well as determining membership of the kind, such essential defining properties are also taken to determine the other properties exhibited by kind members (Ellis 2001; Lowe 1998). It is against such a background that J. S. Mill argued that natural kinds provide us with a solid basis for inductive inferences (C2). For example, a lawful result of having an atomic number of 79 is that a certain piece of gold will be metal and melt at exactly the same temperature as other members of the kind "gold" (see Quine 1969; Nagel 1979). While (C1) to (C3) ensure that natural kinds are correctly distinguished from groups of entities that merely share a property, (C3) guarantees "naturalness." The borderline between kinds is drawn by nature without the possibility of transitional entities between them (Ellis 2001).

As each and every member of a natural kind behaves correspondingly, natural kinds are of obvious interest to science. For instance, measuring the conductivity of a certain sample of gold will simultaneously reveal information about the conductivity of all samples of that kind. In this manner, natural kinds provide a system for classification, which can be used to predict and explain the behavior of the classified entities (Daly 1998).

As noted previously, many exemplary scientific disciplines pursue the categorization of the subjects of their inquiry into natural kinds that match the structure of the world and develop scientific theories that formulate generalizations in terms of "natural kinds." It is usually assumed that respectable sciences "get it right"—they are able to successfully discover natural kinds and construct scientific taxonomies that are consistent with the mind-independent structure of the world. In Chapter 2 it was indicated that psychiatry has, since its beginnings, aimed to gain recognition as a scientific, medical subspecialty on an equal footing with any other subspecialties. From this perspective, the motivation underlying the attempts to understand mental disorders as natural kinds is quite understandable. That is, if mental disorders are natural kinds and their domain and structure can be discovered by empirical research, then psychiatry is indisputably scientific. Psychiatry would then be a respected scientific discipline that is capable of generating solid inductive inferences. Similarly, psychiatric taxonomy would then track bounded categories in the world that are exhaustively defined with reference to inherent properties and provide a classification on the basis of necessary and sufficient internal conditions and essential properties that determine kind membership. In addition, psychiatry would be shielded from various anti-psychiatric arguments that accuse it of unavoidably relying on (questionable) values. Against such a background, it is not surprising that some believe that psychiatric nosologies can "carve nature at its joints" (see Ghaemi 2007, p. 99; Zachar 2000; Zachar and Kendler 2007) and track kinds that exist independently of our classifications.

Nevertheless, there are important aspects that speak against adopting the natural kind approach to mental disorders. In the following account, it is argued that their biological nature, dimensionality, and historicity are all aspects that make it doubtful that mental disorders are natural kinds.

2. **Biological kinds and mental disorders**

Whereas natural kinds might be useful when identifying and classifying substances such as gold, when we move into the terrain of biological entities the classificatory value of natural kinds appears uncertain. Aristotle believed that there were certain biological entities such as species that could justifiably be labeled as natural kinds. Although this view of species having sharp boundaries in nature had a significant influence on our thinking, opinion has changed to viewing species as statistical abstractions (Hull 1989). Contrary to (C1), post-Darwinian biology no longer subscribes to Aristotle's idea of species as natural kinds—what constitutes a species is partly model dependent. Rather than individuals sharing a common essence, Darwin regarded species in terms of populations of unique individuals (Dupree 2000; Beebee and Sabbarton-Leary 2010). Instead of being natural kinds, species are better described with recourse to prototypes—that is, particular members that accurately exemplify the kind. Attempts to classify biological entities such as species as having necessary and sufficient internal conditions for their identification have failed. Biological species change as they adapt to specific environments that transform over time. If this is true, then it more or less follows for (C2) that induction on the basis of the relevant (natural kind) properties will be problematic for causal explanation and prediction—environmental changeability and adoption introduce a dynamic that cannot be accounted for in terms of natural kinds. With regard to (C3), as early as 1689, Locke had expressed some skepticism about the metaphysical thesis that nature is made up of discretely occurring, bounded categories with sharp boundaries. In the case of species, there is now broad agreement about the existence of interforms between them. A certain form of pluralism has become widely accepted, acknowledging that different taxonomic systems result in different classifications of species. For instance, a particular model that groups organisms on the basis of mathematical analysis of outward appearances includes mountain zebras in the species zebra, whereas another model that groups organisms according to their common ancestors classifies zebras as horses.

Overall, a deeper understanding of biological entities such as species—especially in the light of evolution—has cast doubt on the claim that species are to be regarded as natural kinds in the essentialist sense (Bird 2009; Beebee and Sabbarton-Leary 2010). In the case of gold, it may be said that "if you have seen one, you have seen them all"—whatever differences there may be, these will typically turn out to be ignorable differences in the course of scientific exploration. However, this is not the case with biological kinds. The differences between the individual instances may have an important explanatory function.

2.1. Diseases and mental disorders

If biological kinds such as species are not natural kinds in the essentialist sense, the question is whether diseases and mental disorders could turn out to be natural kinds. Here the essentialist might maintain that a single causal agent (e.g. a microorganism) may be able to define each kind of disease. According to this view, conditions such as tuberculosis (caused by *Mycobacterium tuberculosis*) are assumed to be paradigm cases, but they can also be applied to other conditions (Carter 2003; Kendler et al. 2011). However, it is questionable whether tuberculosis or infectious diseases could be natural kinds in the essentialist sense. In these cases, it seems that the disease cannot be reduced to an inherent property, but rather it results from a *specific interaction* between infection and host (Wallace 1994). The disease is characterized not by an inherent property, but by a relational one, since the bacterium or virus is necessary but not sufficient for the development of the disease. In other words, even these diseases cannot properly be identified with respect to inherent properties. Identification must make recourse to external criteria, such as the criteria of a specific, pathological interaction.

In addition, the idea of a single etiological factor has proved to be flawed in countless cases in which the onset of the disease is connected to a broad range of factors, including environmental, genetic, social, and behavioral factors. Many diseases can be distinguished from each other on the basis of numerous causally and dynamically intertwined factors, which indicates that it is highly unlikely that they could qualify as natural kinds in the essentialist sense. Moreover, it is also apparent that some chronic diseases, such as hypertension and hypotension, do not qualify as natural kinds. They can neither be said to mark discrete bounded categories, nor even to represent qualitative alterations of biological processes. Rather, in many cases they merely mark two extremes on a continuum that unites them with "normal" biological processes.

If at least a number of diseases do not fulfill the criteria set by the essentialist account of natural kinds, then we have convincing reasons for suspecting that mental disorders do not qualify as natural kinds. To an even greater extent than bodily diseases, mental disorders can be individuated on the basis of numerous causally and dynamically intertwined factors. Many, if not most, mental disorders share the characteristics that disqualify diseases from being natural kinds. For example, consider the issue of continuity. Whether the underlying structure of mental disorders is taxonic (categorical) or dimensional (continuous) is a fundamental issue in psychiatric nosology (McHugh and Slavney 1998). Some researchers argue that an adequate classification should make room for continuous variation, but asssume that as a rule a *categorical approach* is appropriate (Haslam 2003). Others argue that a *dimensional approach* to classification should be introduced to make it clear that mental disorders exist along a continuum with normality, and to acknowledge that they are of a pragmatic nature (Jablensky 1999; Zachar 2000). For instance, in the case of depression, the question would be whether there is a qualitative or "just" quantitative difference between mild depressive symptoms and those in major depression as a syndrome. A commitment to the continuity view of depression would entail maintaining a quantitative difference between mild and severe forms of depression. In contrast, a commitment to the discontinuity view, which characterizes natural kind accounts of mental disorder, would entail addressing major depression as a distinct entity.

In favor of the continuity view, recent taxometric analyses have consistently failed to find evidence of a latent category that would support a categorical approach (Ruscio and Ruscio 2000, 2002; Franklin et al. 2002; Beach and Amir 2003). For example, Ruscio and Ruscio (2000) have found that major depression represents the end point along a continuum of depressive symptomatology, rather than a structurally discrete entity. All in all, the contemporary taxometric research tends to favor a continuum view of depression, maintaining that depression is located on a continuum, with normal forms of distress differing only quantitatively from it in the intensity, depth, or durability of the distress. In addition, Kendler and Gardner (1998) have evaluated two divergent theories about the boundaries of major depression, asking whether the then current criteria (DSM-IV) manage to "carve nature at its joints," or whether they identify a point on a continuum. One important outcome was that they were unable to find evidence for a discontinuity. Furthermore, in empirical research it is common practice to separate samples into "depressed" and "non-depressed" groups on the basis of standard cut-off scores on the Beck Depression Inventory (Beck et al. 1996). Here again the boundary is approximate—the result of a complex score on the inventory is imposed at a particular point on the continuum.

The same picture is found in the DSM-IV criteria for major depression. In order to warrant a diagnosis, the patient must exhibit five (or more) symptoms (that indicate a change from previous functioning) for a period of at least two weeks. In addition, at least one symptom has to be of an affective nature, such as low mood, or loss of the ability to take pleasure in activities. The main point to be emphasized here is that the threshold of five symptoms is not the result of the identification of a discrete category but of *practical* concern. Similarly, the criteria for major depressive disorder in the DSM-IV include an exclusion criterion for uncomplicated bereavement. This means that following the death of someone close, up to two months of depressive symptoms are not regarded as warranting the diagnosis of depression. However, also arguing against the natural kind view, there is no neutral norm that could establish whether "up to two months" is the "natural" time interval. Rather, it is a statistical abstraction that reflects the reaction pattern displayed by the majority of the population. In other words, rather than reflecting natural independent boundaries, "up to two months" marks the boundary of a disorder that is established on practical grounds. It is against such a background that some argue that mental disorders are really something like "practical kinds" (Zachar 2000). This term is meant to convey that practical reasons might play a decisive but also completely legitimate role in defining categories of mental disorder.

All in all, recent taxometric research favors a dimensional approach, and this view is also supported by the structure of psychometric scales and clinical instruments. Most mental disorders lie on a continuum between pathological conditions and normal ones (Radden 2009, pp. 81–82). However, there are two additional aspects which characterize some mental disorders and that make it even less likely that they could be understood as natural kinds.

2.2. **Historicity**

Young (1995) has provided a telling example of how particular mental disorders emerge as a result of complex interactions between historical constellations, technologies, and interests. Young maintains that the history of post-traumatic stress disorder (PTSD) sheds light on the role of societal factors and forces in the process of inventing rather than discovering a disorder. He describes how, on returning from Vietnam, some military personnel experienced serious problems in readjusting to their peacetime roles and displayed antisocial behavior and a range of psychiatric disturbances. The veterans were first diagnosed as suffering from a wide range of disorders, such as anxiety, depression, personality disorder, or schizophrenia. Later, as a result of lobbying, the veterans were given specialized psychiatric therapy informed by the new diagnosis, which shifted the focus from the individual background to the pathogenic nature of war. By way of socio-historical analysis, Young shows that the disorder is neither timeless, nor characterized by an intrinsic unity, but "glued together by the practices, technologies, and narratives" that reflect "various interests, institutions, and moral arguments" (Young 1995, p. 5). The important issue here is that if the disorder has emerged from the interface of historical situations and forces, and if the disease entity has been even partly socially constructed, one cannot reasonably claim that it is a natural kind. However, this raises the following question: what kind of kinds are mental disorders?

2.3. **Interactive kinds**

In the framework of his discussion of contemporary philosophy of science, Ian Hacking (1999) has put forward a stimulating thesis concerning psychiatric classifications that might advance our attempts to adequately describe the kinds involved in mental disorder. Hacking maintains that, in contrast to the natural sciences, the classifications in social sciences are distinctive—natural sciences study and classify natural kinds (which Hacking terms "indifferent kinds"), whereas human sciences classify "human kinds" (Hacking 1999,

p. 108). Importantly, whereas "natural kinds" (and classifications in the natural sciences) are indifferent to their being classified, human kinds are essentially "interactive kinds" that interact with what they classify:

> when known by people or those around them, and put to work in institutions, [classifications, SV] change the ways in which individuals experience themselves—and may even lead people to evolve their feelings and behavior in part because they are so classified.
>
> (Hacking 1999, pp. 103–104)

For instance, depression is an interactive kind because it enters into interaction with and influences what it classifies. In contrast to interactive kinds, a natural or indifferent kind such as gold is classified, but that classification does not interact with or affect what it classifies. As Hacking would say, when the natural scientist classifies a piece of metal as "gold," it makes no difference to the gold, and it does not change anything about the object under study. Also, since such classifications are independent of their objects, once they have been classified the objects do not produce "feedback" that leads to changes in the classification. In contrast to this, with interactive kinds the act of classifying the object of study interacts with the object in a two-way process that might change that object. The act of classification interacts with the classified object, and the interaction results in a phenomenon that Hacking calls a "looping effect"—that is, a kind of feedback wherein the classification, such as "depression," influences the behavior of those who are classified as depressive, who then might start to act in accordance (or in discordance) with the expectations fostered by that classification. Classified individuals might be motivated to make an effort to alter the ways in which they behave, think, and feel, and with such changes, for Hacking, the kind in question also changes. Hacking argues that such looping effects prove that human kinds are qualitatively different from natural kinds. They are, in a sense, "moving targets."

One could initially object that psychiatric conditions such as childhood autism could pose a challenge for Hacking's position, simply because an autistic child might not be fully aware of his or her classification. Given the possible lack of such awareness, it might be wrong to claim that the classification "autism" interacts with autistic children. Hacking notices this problem and makes his account of interaction more clear:

> by interaction I do not mean only the self-conscious reaction of a single individual to how she is classified. I mean the consequences of being so classified for the whole class of individuals and other people with whom they are intimately connected.
>
> (Hacking 1999, p. 115)

In other words, looping is not limited to the direct effects that result from being conscious of being classified in a certain way, but it also includes those more indirect effects that result from the expectations of parents, teachers, doctors, and others who interact with the classified person.

The examples that Hacking uses one-sidedly emphasize a specific interaction pattern, in which classified individuals self-ascribe aspects of the classification and increasingly modify their behavior based on their understanding of that classification. As a result, their behavior comes to conform to norms and practices associated with the classification. However, interactions might take a more complex path. In an earlier text, Hacking (1995) demonstrated that as a result of autistic individuals responding to being classified, some symptoms typical of autism have changed. This is further supported by other examples. For instance, consider the classification "depressed." It comes bundled with certain norms and expectations about the individuals who are bound together by the classification. It is possible that the classified individuals come to learn about the ways in which experts classify them—for instance, a tendency to act aggressively. It seems natural to assume that there is a possibility that they will react negatively to this information—they might respond by consciously cultivating non-aggressive behavior. As the classified individuals change their behavior and practices in reaction to the classification, the very nature of the classification changes, or at least it affects the way we understand the original classification. Such examples demonstrate more clearly the fact that sometimes interaction is two-sided, with interaction flowing from the "objects" of classification to those who perform the classificatory work.

2.4. **Toward conventionalism**

Viewed from an essentialist perspective, many of the kinds to which psychiatry devotes itself do not qualify as natural kinds. The biological nature, the dimensionality, and the historicity of mental disorders support this conclusion. Even if biological psychiatry could discover the "pathology P" underlying a specific cluster of syndromes, it is still doubtful whether that entity would qualify as a natural kind and whether the relevant classifications would be able to pick out natural kinds in the sense required by essentialism. Within the framework of an essentialist perspective, it is difficult to conceive of biological kinds that would qualify as natural kinds—perhaps only those in physics and chemistry would qualify.

In this case, the question is how to navigate the failure of an essentialist understanding without sliding into a full-blown conventionalism of the questionable kind, which tends to focus on the social context and disregard potentially helpful knowledge about genetic and physiological elements that often co-occur in particular cases of mental disorder. Such a scenario creates several possibilities for psychiatric research.

2.4.1. Practical kinds

Some authors have argued that any use of the term "natural kind" and its metaphysical baggage should be dropped. In his most recent work, Hacking argues in favor of this and makes the radical suggestion that we should "delete every mention of natural kinds" (Hacking 2007, p. 229). In this vein, some prefer to embrace a purely "practical" orientation. This reflects a practical view of scientific inquiry and classification, in which it is more important to achieve certain goals than to achieve classifications that perfectly correspond to a mind-independent reality. In other words, this option would give up the metaphysical commitment behind the essentialist view and accept the plurality of taxonomies. According to this view, the best classification is relative to the given purposes of the scientific inquiry. If a classification yields robust diagnostic and predictive results, and helps to select the treatment that improves the condition, then the question of its connection to a mind-independent reality does not really matter. In such a "practical kinds" approach to psychiatric disorders (Zachar 2000, 2008), classification is determined by its pragmatic benefits, which again depend on shifting scientific or medical goals.

For those who defend the idea of practical kinds, the lack of a clear underlying discontinuity does not make a diagnostic boundary arbitrary. The point is that there are legitimate practical grounds that determine the positioning of the boundary. If the decisive boundaries are too broad, the disorder will include too many of those who normally would not be recognized as being sick enough to warrant treatment. On the other hand, if the decisive boundaries are too narrow, individuals who are in need of clinical attention might be excluded. To take two familiar examples, hypertension and hypotension are not qualitative alterations of biological processes with decisive boundaries like natural kinds. However, even if it appears to be continuous with normal variation, for pragmatic reasons a categorical distinction is drawn at a position where the serious health risks increase rapidly, and therefore appropriate clinical attention and eventual treatment appear to be defensible. Therefore, although there is no inherent categorical discontinuity to justify the boundaries, pragmatic (e.g. socio-political, scientific, ethical) reasons that are external to the structure of the entity might legitimately play a decisive role in defining it. The same can be said of depression. As we have seen, the contemporary taxometric research favors a continuum view of depression, maintaining that this disorder differs only quantitatively from and falls on a continuum with normal forms of distress. Nevertheless, for pragmatic reasons a boundary is introduced at a largely arbitrary position on the continuum—for example, where health risks such as suicide risk increase rapidly. In both cases, the boundaries of the disorder are provisional and can be corrected if new evidence about the link to serious health risks emerges. This means that, according to this view, the fact that mental disorder is not a natural kind does not justify the conclusion proposed by Szasz. The underlying supposition, according to which, other than natural kinds there can be no legitimate kinds that justify therapeutic attention, is erroneous.

Although this "practical" position has a clear conventionalist dimension, it seems compatible with different branches of conventionalism, and much will depend on whether it embraces a weak or strong version. For instance, the practical approach is first compatible with the view that our current classifications do not pick out natural kinds because the level of sophistication of current science does not allow this. Second, it is compatible with the view that there are no natural divisions to track, as facts about the world are not mind dependent. Third, it is compatible with the view there cannot be an objective justification for classification, because justification will always be relative to pragmatic interests.

From the point of view of the dimensional and categorical criticism launched against psychiatry, depending on the degree of conventionalism, there is a sense in which the account of practical kinds appears to be begging the question. The dimensional critic could ask why a diagnostic boundary is placed at a certain, largely arbitrary, position on the continuum. They could point out that there is a risk either of pathologizing everyday "problems in living," and thus relabeling a normal form of distress as disorder, or of overlooking individuals who would benefit from clinical awareness. Those who defend the practical kind view could emphasize the ethical aspect of the approach and counter that the diagnostic categories are not random (although they do not "carve nature at its joints"), but serve the *moral* purpose of reducing the amount of suffering among those who seek psychiatric help.

However, this answer is inadequate. The fundamental question that is left unanswered is whether the particular case of human suffering that the clinician encounters is what we would regard as a "normal" part of life or something that should be treated as a disorder and given proper clinical attention. Furthermore, the Szaszian categorical critique would surely not be satisfied with this type of answer. He could argue that the lack of clear, "natural" boundaries makes possible the labeling of socially unacceptable behavior, the medicalization of "problems in living," and the exertion of social power. In fact, both the dimensional and categorical critiques might hold that to conceive of mental disorders as practical kinds is to leave too many important questions unanswered. Unconvinced by a purely practical approach, they might think that it fails to say anything about the nature of the *right* goals in psychiatry.

If one rejects the account of psychiatric disorders as practical kinds, there is another possibility. This is to attempt to keep the notion of natural kinds in connection to mental disorders but to opt for a less essentialist understanding. The motivation is to recognize the inadequacies of essentialism with regard to natural kinds, while salvaging the idea that special sciences investigate natural kinds in their respective domains. With respect to biological species, Dupre (2011) argues that entities might be regarded as natural kinds in a relaxed sense, for instance, if the properties possessed by the members of a particular kind are lawfully linked—a characteristic that would allow inductive inferences to be made across the kind. In the realm of psychiatry, Rachel Cooper has proposed a particular understanding of natural kinds and argued that some types of mental disorder are natural kinds (Cooper 2005, p. 47). In a different manner, in his earlier work, Hacking (1999) also argued that underlying parts of mental disorders could be regarded as natural kinds. In the following sections, we shall turn our attention to these accounts that attempt to salvage the idea that psychiatry investigates natural kinds.

2.4.2. Hacking's relaxed account of natural kinds

In "practical" approaches to mental disorder, the influence flows exclusively from the classification to the classified object. In this regard, the account of human kinds and "looping effects" that Hacking proposes is complex and able to account for the influence that sometimes flows from the object to the classification. Although this two-way interaction provides important insights, it might be unclear how radical this claim really is. Does it mean that disorders of the interactive kind are interaction-like "all the way down," thus affecting and changing potential underlying biological conditions? For instance, let us assume that autism has a clear-cut underlying biological cause. Then the question would be whether the classification really enters into interaction with the underlying biological entity. Hacking seems to avoid this issue, and in developing his account he makes room for the "indifference" of such a possible underlying biological entity. He examines childhood autism as an example of a *both indifferent and interactive* kind. We might suppose that there is a basic biological disorder that produces the symptoms we currently classify as autistic. Scientists might announce the discovery of the genetic, neurological, chemical, or other abnormality P that causes autism:

> Let us posit that there is a pathology P, no matter how it will be identified. By hypothesis the pathology P will be an indifferent kind. The neuro-geno-biochemical state P is not aware of what we find out. … In more traditional jargon, P would be a natural kind.
>
> (Hacking 1999, p. 116)

Hacking continues:

> childhood autism is (is identical to) a certain biological pathology P, and so is a 'natural' kind or an indifferent kind. At the same time, we want to say that childhood autism is an interactive kind, interacting with autistic children, evolving and changing as the children change.
>
> (Hacking 1999, p. 119)

In trying to reconcile the emerging dilemma of something being both indifferent and interactive, he draws on the ideas of Putnam and Kripke (Putnam 1975; Kripke 1980) to propose a "semantic resolution." According to Putnam, the meaning of a term is constituted by a stereotype, syntactic and semantic markers, and the extension. For example, "gold" is a natural kind term. The stereotype is a type of metal with a certain color, and this is what needs to be known in order to understand the term. The extension denotes the whole class of entities to which the term applies, which in the case of gold is all samples of entities with the atomic number 79. When applied to psychiatric classifications, this means that the referent of a classification is pathology P, while its stereotype is the collection of beliefs, theories, and typical examples currently correlated with the classification. Thus Hacking's "semantic resolution" to the problem of how an entity can be both an interactive kind and an indifferent kind is to argue that the referent P is an indifferent kind, while its stereotype is an interactive kind. In this way, Hacking's account appears to be helpful in accounting for psychiatric conditions, as it makes room for both predictable biological entities and simultaneously accounts for the looping effects of classifications. Hacking's account advances the discussion by capturing a specific phenomenon that arises in the case of mental disorders and by accommodating the interaction that flows from the object to the classification—an aspect that might have some explanatory relevance. However, there are a number of issues that can be raised against significant parts of his account. One concern is that Hacking collapses the difference between natural kinds and indifferent kinds. The problem is that there are kinds that are at the same time "indifferent," while falling on a continuum with other kinds that differ only quantitatively from them.

A more substantial concern is Hacking's argument that the underlying "pathology P" could be a natural kind. In the following account, this view is scrutinized, and it is argued that the underlying "pathology P" can both be a practical kind *and* an interactive kind. The first question is why we should accept that "pathology P" is a natural kind. The defining threshold of such a "pathology P" might very well be a matter of a practical ground. For example, it is widely held that the typical low affect in depression is caused by the hypoactivity of certain monoamine neurotransmitters. However, one then has to ask at what point this hypoactivity that constitutes "pathology P" would qualify as a natural or indifferent kind. Hacking's account does not provide us with reasons for thinking that there is one particular threshold at which the pathological hypoactivity starts. In other words, there are no inherent properties that would give us grounds for positioning the threshold at a particular position on the continuum. Rather, it seems that in this case the thresholds and boundaries would be justified by pragmatic reasons, and thus by recourse to factors that are external to the structure of the entity. If this is true, then we may say that the underlying "pathology P" is not a natural kind, but a practical kind.

The second concern is connected to Hacking's idea that we can hold on to a notion of natural kinds since feedback does not interact with the underlying biological entity ("pathology P"). According to Hacking, such feedback might interfere with our ideas and behavior with regard to the kind, but not with the underlying biological pathology itself. Recall that the difference between natural and interactive kinds is that natural kinds such as the "pathology P" are unaffected by the looping effects. This is how it is possible for Hacking to maintain that "pathology P" can be a natural kind. However, this is not entirely convincing. Take the case of the pandemic H1N1 virus to be the underlying "pathology P." There is now considerable success in treatment of this virus with antiviral drugs (oseltamivir and zanamivir), leading to an improved clinical outcome in patients. However, one characteristic of influenza viruses is their ability to mutate, and the World Health Organization (WHO) urges practitioners to be vigilant in cases that might contribute to the development of resistant H1N1 viruses. Of course, resistance to antiviral drugs can occur spontaneously, during the course of antiviral exposure or antiviral treatment. Nonetheless, resistant forms of a virus may in particular develop in patients who show evidence of persistent viral replication despite prolonged treatment with medication (possibly due to a weakened immune system). In such cases, the WHO suggests that laboratory investigations should be conducted to determine whether there is a resistant H1N1 virus, and appropriate measures should be implemented to prevent the spread of the resistant virus. For similar reasons, the WHO discourages the use of antiviral drugs for prophylactic purposes, in the hope that such measures will ensure that any future increase in the number of resistant viruses (currently 28) is kept to a minimum.[2]

This example is useful as it demonstrates that it is indeed possible that a certain mutation of the H1N1 virus emerged as a result of human interference (in the course of prolonged medication). There are no clear reasons why such a case should not be regarded as exhibiting a Hacking-style looping effect. The virus interacts with the medication, which is the consequence of our classification of the H1N1. This interaction has specific consequences for the kind, which has to be redescribed in order to accommodate the new medicament-resistant mutations. In addition, prediction and explanatory patterns linked to the virus must also be changed. Thus, in human interaction with the kind, there is a looping effect and the boundaries and regularities of the supposed natural kind ("pathology P") change.

However, if this is correct, and at least in some cases feedback does interact with the underlying biological entity ("pathology P"), then we might begin to think that Hacking's point is flawed. In that case, according to Hacking's own definition, "pathology P" cannot be assumed to be a natural kind. Rather, "pathology P" itself can constitute an *interactive kind* (although it is of course not the case that it is the virus's becoming aware of the classification that starts the loop). Therefore, rather than collapsing the distinction between natural and indifferent kinds, and rather than suggesting that "pathology P" is a natural or indifferent kind, a more fitting suggestion seems to be to think of "pathology P" "at the bottom" as a practical or interactive kind. Thus, according to the view proposed here, a mental disorder such as depression might be composed of a practical kind *and* an interactive kind. Against this background, there seems to be potential for further research on an approach to define mental disorders that is open and dynamic both "at the top" and "at the bottom." This means that at the top it can accommodate looping effects and the shaping power of cultural frameworks, which renders it compatible with the findings of cultural psychiatry. At the bottom the openness of a definition means that while it does not exclude the possibility of the discovery of causal factors (biological, genetic, social, political, and psychological classifications), it does not have to state that natural or indifferent kinds are involved at this level. If this aspect was also to be taken into account on this level, then dimensionality would no longer pose a problem.

[2] World Health Organization (2009) Antiviral use and the risk of drug resistance. www.who.int/csr/disease/swineflu/notes/h1n1_antiviral_use_20090925/en/index.html Retrieved November 2012.

2.4.3. Cooper's relaxed account of natural kinds

Exploring a different path, Cooper rejects an essentialist understanding while aiming to salvage the idea that some mental disorders are natural kinds and have boundaries between them that exist in the real world. She proposes a relaxed account of natural kinds that closely builds on the work of Dupree, and she suggests that members of a natural kind have similar, central properties that determine numerous other properties that members of the kind exhibit. In contrast to an essentialist account, in Cooper's view it is enough for the *determining properties* of kind members to be similar (given the constancy of environmental factors). They need not be identical (Cooper 2005, p. 51). What this means is that different domains will require focusing on different determining properties:

> For chemical isotopes, for example, the necessary dimensions would plausibly be atomic number and neutron number. For biological species it is plausible that dimensions corresponding to various genetic properties would be required (or even more probably dimensions corresponding to particular genetic properties plus whatever environmental factors are important in determining how they are expressed).
>
> (Cooper 2005, p. 51)

Thus the determining properties need not be microstructural (e.g. a particular atomic number), but could for instance in the case of species be evolutionary pressures, if they reliably explain observable properties. Hence Cooper rejects the first criterion of natural kinds (C1). Instead of claiming that members of a natural kind possess *common intrinsic properties,* her claim is merely that members of a natural kind have *similar determining properties.* This leads to further reflections linked to both the notion of "similarity" and "determining property." As similarity occurs to various degrees, Cooper accepts the occurrence of "borderline natural kinds whose members possess determining properties that are quite, but not very, similar" (Cooper 2005, p. 52). However, it is also indeterminate when a property can be considered to be sufficiently significant to be regarded as a determining property. Again Cooper must here admit some indeterminacy and accept that, according to her account, there will be "borderline natural kinds" in which the members are held together by *relatively* important properties.

Accordingly, Cooper also rejects (C3), arguing that natural kinds are not necessarily discrete, divided by natural boundaries that do not allow intermediate forms:

> I claim that natural kinds do not need to be discrete. In order to count as co-members of a natural kind, entities just need similar determining properties, and whether or not kinds are discrete makes no difference to their ability to fulfill this criterion.

> As a consequence, I think that debates as to whether mental disorders are separated by "zones of rarity" (that is, whether there are gaps between them in quality space) are not relevant to the question of whether they are natural kinds. It might well be the case that types of depression and of anxiety disorder merge into each other, for example. Conceivably this might occur because the genetic bases of both depression and anxiety disorders are similar, if not identical, and similar environmental stressors are risk factors in both cases. In such a situation, when plotted in a multi-dimensional determining-property space, cases of the disorders would not form distinct clusters. Still, cases of depression could form a natural kind in my sense—all cases might be fundamentally similar, and this might also be the case for anxiety disorders.
>
> (Cooper 2005, p. 53)[3]

Overall, Cooper's account of natural kinds can be summarized by the following characteristics. Natural kinds pick out entities that:

(D1) have similar determining properties and

(D2) support inductive inferences.

It is useful to focus on Cooper's reasons for making this step. She argues that there is no reason for holding on to the claim that natural kinds must be discrete, as:

> On my account, the determining properties do all the work when it comes to making inductive inferences and grounding explanations. It is because members of a natural kind all have similar determining properties, and the determining properties determine the other properties of the entities, that we can predict that all members of a natural kind will behave similarly. The "gaps" between natural kinds, where there are any, do no work. Thus there seems to be no reason to claim that natural kinds must be discrete, and abandoning this claim has the advantage that kinds that are not discrete, such as alloys, can be accommodated within a natural kind account.
>
> (Cooper 2005, p. 53)

She thus rejects (C3) by arguing that the determining properties "do all the work," where this work is defined in terms of *explanation*. She accepts that there might be gaps in the relevant domains, but sees this metaphysical "deficit" as counterbalanced by epistemological and explanatory advantages. In addition, she rejects dimensional models and argues that a classificatory system that is categorical is better for everyday practical reasons—it is simply easier to use (Cooper 2005, pp. 54, 74). In addition, Cooper argues that a classification system is case relative—sometimes it is best that it reflects the

[3] Some researchers, such as Kendell and Jablensky, propose less rigid criteria, but tend to emphasize (C3) when attempting to delimit valid psychiatric disorders. They maintain that valid disorders are *bounded, categorically distinct* entities that are disconnected from normal conditions and other disorders by a gap—a "zone of rarity."

natural structure of a domain, while in other cases it uses categories that do not reflect natural boundaries (Cooper 2005, p. 74).

However, there is a rather fundamental shift occurring when Cooper simultaneously rejects essentialism and, focusing on (C2), understands natural kinds as serving a particular investigative or explanatory goal. According to her account, natural kinds can be discriminated from other groupings based on their fulfilling an explanatory task. Thus her concern is not so much whether our classification "carves nature at its joints," as whether it groups together entities that are similar to each other to a degree that allows for sound inferences in an explanatory inquiry:

> Similarly, we should primarily worry whether categories, such as "schizophrenia," group together cases that are actually similar to each other at a fundamental level, or whether we are lumping together cases that are fundamentally radically different. If schizophrenia fades into some other category, such as schizotypal personality disorder, then it will of course be as well to know this, but so long as cases of schizophrenia are fundamentally similar, schizophrenia is still a natural kind on my account. Even if schizophrenia fails to be discrete, knowing that someone suffers from schizophrenia could still be used as the basis of inductive inferences and function as an explanation.
>
> (Cooper 2005, pp. 73–74)

In order to salvage the notion of natural kinds, Cooper abandons metaphysical commitments and focuses instead on explanatory virtues; she redefines natural kinds as to some extent relative to the goals of the explanatory inquiry. In order to manage the ambiguities that arise when picking out the relevant "determining property" and the right grade of "similarity," the researcher should be guided by her explanatory goals.

Now in principle there is nothing wrong with this strategy. However, there are several aspects that make Cooper's account more problematic than might initially be supposed. First, although she emphasizes the legitimacy of taking into consideration practical reasons, it is not entirely clear how practically useful her relaxed account of natural kinds is. In practice, given the very limited understanding of mental disorders that is available for current theorizing, it is extremely difficult to adjudicate both the determining properties of instances of the disorder and their grade of similarity.

Second, it seems somewhat uncertain whether there are any good reasons for Cooper's account to retain the label "natural kind." Her account is very broad, and it eliminates the metaphysical aspects traditionally linked to the idea of natural kinds in favor of explanatory and practical usefulness. Due to these characteristics, her relaxed account also admits a *significant degree of conventionalism*—she agrees that what a "determining property" is and what the right grade of "similarity" is are underdetermined. This is why she is able to maintain that it is acceptable for researchers to pick out the relevant "determining properties" and determine the right grade of "similarity" guided by their explanatory goals.

Third, while keeping in mind this last point, recall Cooper's point that it is "perfectly consistent" to maintain that some entities form distinct natural kinds while holding that certain differences between these entities are created by social powers (Cooper 2005, pp. 75–76). When we take these two issues together, we see that Cooper's account allows for precisely the possibility that naturalist accounts of mental disorder wanted to exclude. It is possible, on the basis of Cooper's account, that our decision as to what counts as a "determining property" and the right grade of "similarity" with regard to a mental disorder might pick out properties that are produced by socio-political currents and value-laden judgments. However, we might recall that—at least in part—the reason why the concept of natural kinds seemed attractive to psychiatrists was precisely because it avoided this possibility. The problem is that Cooper's account of mental disorders as natural kinds does not shield against the categorical and dimensional criticism that the boundaries established by mental disorders are artificial. Instead of "carving nature at its joints," the categorical critique would be justified in saying that Cooper's account might result in a taxonomy that could simply be reproducing value judgments and political currents.

In addition, compared with other accounts, such as that of Boyd, Cooper's account does not necessitate some mechanism behind the simultaneous manifestation of the relevant properties (Cooper 2005, p. 55). Her aim is that the relevant taxonomy informed by her account of natural kinds can pick out similarities, where similarity becomes relevant to the particular explanatory undertakings. However, it is then difficult for such taxonomy to arbitrate, for instance, between the biologist who maintains that lilies are onions and the landscaper who argues that they are flowers.

Overall, then, Cooper's view of natural kinds in psychiatry is not only too weak to arbitrate between competing ideas about psychiatric taxonomies, but also cannot defend against the anti-psychiatric (categorical) criticism that mental disorders do not pick out properties "in the world," but reflect socio-political tendencies. However, we then might ask what the additional classification as a natural kind adds to anything. If the account is so liberal that it no longer conveys a metaphysical thesis but is only governed by explanatory and practical purposes, then holding on to the notion of natural kinds seems unwarranted. Instead of some epistemic gain emerging from the use of this terminology, it might just create more confusion. It seems that once the metaphysical aspirations are given up and natural kind classifications are simply seen as those exhibiting robust explanatorily and predictively success, we lack good reasons for using the term. In the case of mental disorders, the suspicion might be that the chief reason for using the term "natural kind" is that it confers on the class some rhetorical pedigree.[4]

2.4.4. Boyd's homeostatic property cluster (HPC)

Boyd proposes an interesting account that is less liberal then those of Cooper and Hacking, as he assumes the metaphysical thesis that the joints of nature are situated at the boundaries of mechanisms (Craver 2009). Boyd's account of *homeostatic property* clusters (*HPC*), which views biological kinds as natural kinds, was developed with an eye to biological species (Boyd 1991, 1999). Also here the motivation is to recognize the inadequacies of essentialism about natural kinds, while salvaging the idea that the special sciences investigate natural kinds in their respective domains (Bird 2007). The HPC view opposes conventionalism and maintains that natural kinds reflect real boundaries in the structure of the world. Hence the HPC explores a promising third way between essentialism and conventionalism, by relaxing strong naturalism but salvaging the idea that it is possible for our scientific taxonomies to track natural kinds individuated by properties that exist independently of us. As Wilson argues, the HPC:

> claims that there are natural kinds in the world individuated by properties existing independently of us, and that our schemes of categorization in science track these natural kinds. ... The view is a loosening of traditional realism, not an abandonment of its realist core.
>
> (Wilson 2005, pp. 111–112)

Boyd (1991, p. 128) aims to "defend the enthusiasm for natural kinds" while acknowledging important philosophical and methodological dissimilarities between kinds that are defined by necessary and sufficient conditions and kinds that are defined by property clusters. Instead of necessary and sufficient conditions, Boyd's "natural kinds" are defined by "a 'homeostatically' sustained clustering of those properties or relations" (Boyd 1991; Boyd 1999, p. 141). Boyd's rejection of essentialism about natural kinds entails conceding that, due to external circumstances (e.g. environmental changes), over time all of the properties in the cluster associated with a kind might change—there

[4] Although he is not explicit about his correction of his earlier view, in a recent paper Hacking (2007) seems to abandon all the talk about natural kinds and expresses the suspicion that the term "natural kind" is mostly only useful for conferring a rhetorical pedigree on the class.

is often no fact of the matter that we could appeal to in order to decide whether some particular entity is a kind member. To put it another way, HPC natural kinds are multiply realizable. Furthermore, it is not necessary for members of a kind to exhibit overlapping traits, but only for members to be clustered together due to the same causal mechanisms (be they evolutionary, environmental, physiological, or developmental). Boyd's HPC account replaces the essential properties in the essentialist account of natural kinds with homeostatic mechanisms (Griffiths 1999).

Due to the nature of these mechanisms, Boyd's account can accommodate the occurrence of hybrids, as it relaxes the divergence between natural kinds and otherwise constituted categories of entities. While he argues that the cluster of co-occurring properties associated with a natural kind allows inductive inference as required in scientific explanation, he allows for some conventionalist elements to enter the account. One central idea is that natural kinds are to be described as co-occurring clusters of properties, where they co-occur not because they tend to be clustered together by conventions, but because of the functioning of certain homeostatic mechanism related to the property cluster. These mechanisms are thus responsible for generating similarity and the simultaneous occurrence of properties in the cluster. Therefore, in Boyd's view, a classification informed by HPC natural kinds is adequate if the kinds in that classification track mechanisms that belong to the causal structure of the world. Boyd thus makes room for some conventionalism while still claiming that the HPC view of natural kinds might inform classifications that "carve nature at its joints."

Importantly, the reason why Boyd can claim that HPC natural kinds carve nature at its joints is because *he takes nature's joints to be situated at the boundaries of mechanisms* (Craver 2009). At this point, we see both that Boyd's account is less liberal than those of Cooper and Hacking, and it assumes a particular metaphysical thesis about the joints of nature being situated at the boundaries of mechanisms. This is how the HPC view is able to oppose full-blown conventionalism and maintain that natural kinds reflect real boundaries in the structure of the world. Just like conventionalism, the HPC view emphasizes the practical usefulness of taxonomies, but claims that the practical usefulness in terms of predictive and explanatory advantages emerges because the HPC kinds are maintained by genuine mechanisms. Following Boyd (1991, 1999), natural kinds are characterized by:

(E1) a regularly co-occurring cluster of properties explained by the functioning of

(E2) a (homeostatic) mechanism.

Boyd thus explores a promising third way between natural-kind essentialism and conventionalism, which might be why his account has recently been discovered by researchers working on psychiatric taxonomy. Researchers in this field, such as Kendler et al. (2011) and Beebee and Sabbarton-Leary (2010), have argued that psychiatric kinds can in principle be viewed as natural kinds according to the HPC account. The popularity of the HPC account might be at least partly explained by the connected hope that psychiatric classification informed by HPC would be immune to both the dimensional and the categorical critique of the conventionalism of psychiatric classification. If psychiatric classification "carves nature at its joints" and tracks mechanisms belonging to the causal structure of the world, then it could no longer be accused of simply labeling socially unacceptable behavior or medicalization of "problems in living." However, a closer look at Boyd's account reveals that it contains more conventionalism than was first assumed. In view of this, it is likely to turn out that the HPC account informing psychiatric classification will not be able to provide full protection against the dimensional and categorical critiques of the conventionalism of psychiatric classification.

The first issue to note is that some property clusters are maintained by homeostatic mechanisms, but carry no predictive or otherwise practical value. There is a wide variety of regularly co-occurring effects that constitute a property cluster and that can be traced back to the same causal mechanism. For instance, consider the previously discussed example involving the pandemic outbreak of the H1N1 virus. To name just some of the regularly co-occurring effects that can be traced back to the outbreak of the H1N1 virus, we may say that individuals in the affected regions typically suffer from fever, cough, sore throat, runny nose, headache, loss on investments due to a decline in stock-market indexes, negative consumer behavior, falling value of their pension investments, a drop in the gross domestic product, negative impact on insurance claims, reduced opportunity for access to capital (as investors favor short-term bills and markets risk freezing in), rising airfares, a reduced social life due to the suspension of public activities, and closures of universities and schools. Clearly we cannot want *all* such commonly co-occurring effects to become a part of the cluster that makes up the natural kind, even if they are explained by the functioning of the same mechanism. The term would simply lose its meaning, as far too many clusters would qualify. Thus properties that are part of the cluster sustained by a mechanism but that carry no practical value must be eliminated. At this point the elimination occurs by the introduction of conventionalism (perspective relevance), much as we have seen in Cooper's account—whether a particular group of properties counts as genuine cluster properties will to a certain degree depend on particular explanatory goals. In Boyd's account, this step toward conventionalism is still consistent with naturalism (realism), as the underlying mechanism still binds them together with a causal structure that is a genuine part of the world. However, when we look closer at the nature of mechanisms, we see that Boyd concedes more to conventionalism than this.

2.4.5. Interpretation: splitting and lumping

The point can be formulated more precisely if we recall the goal of the HPC, namely to provide a scientific classification that reflects the mechanistic configuration of the world. We see that it is consistent with two common strategies in the sciences—splitting and lumping. These strategies are relevant whenever (a) a cluster of properties linked to a putatively distinct kind is explained by several mechanisms, or (b) several presumably distinct kinds are explained by the same mechanism.

(a) To avoid heterogeneous kinds, a cluster should be *split* into subset clusters, in case each of them can be explained by a single mechanism. As these particular mechanisms can be expected to be altered independently, splitting will yield a taxonomy with predictive or explanatory value, as it better reflects causal structures.

(b) To avoid heterogeneous kinds, whenever several putatively distinct kinds (groups of phenomena previously considered as separate) are explained by the same mechanism, they should be *lumped* together. As it avoids generating differences without distinctions, lumping will yield a taxonomy with predictive or explanatory value, as it better reflects causal structures.

What we see here is that the crucial strategies of splitting and lumping depend on the adequate individuation and prioritizing of mechanisms. However, at exactly this point, two dilemmas appear, linked to (1) prioritizing and (2) individuation. In both cases, the elimination of the dilemma occurs at the price of *steps toward conventionalism*.

(1) *Prioritizing.* The problem is that a multitude of mechanisms are causally active in the case of most putative kinds. For instance, consider the multiplicity of explanations in recourse to mechanisms that can be given for the same behavioral pattern of an organism. Many of them are simultaneously explainable by etiological, developmental, and evolutionary mechanisms. Now if multiple, mechanism-based explanatory pathways terminate in the same property cluster, we are faced with a dilemma as to whether we should split or lump. As Craver (2009, p. 583) notes, the problem is "that one can be led to lump or split the same putative kind in different ways depending on which mechanism one consults in accommodating the taxonomy to the mechanistic structure of the world." It may

be that if one focuses on the etiological mechanism, one should split, while if one focuses on the other mechanism, one should lump. The dilemma is that while one must prioritize one mechanism over the others in order to arrive at a classification, the choice will be one that is not warranted by the causal organization of the world. Rather, in such cases, the choice of strategy will be *contingent on the particular explanatory undertaking.* Crucially, the elimination of the dilemma occurs at the price of another step toward conventionalism.

(2) *Individuation.* Craver (2009) highlights an additional source of ambiguity that is linked to determining when mechanisms are of the same kind. First, there is no fact of the matter that could arbitrate whether one is using the appropriate degree of abstraction when characterizing the "kind" constituted by mechanism. Nevertheless, this is important, since an overly abstract description would leave out sub-kinds, while an overly detailed description would turn each individual mechanism into a kind. Again, no facts about the world's causal structure can be used to determine the right degree of abstraction. Rather, the positions at which the boundaries of mechanisms will be drawn are *contingent on a preceding demarcation that is guided by what we find relevant to the property cluster (explanandum) that we seek to illuminate.* Again, the elimination of the dilemma occurs at the price of another step towards conventionalism.

With these conventionalist elements in mind, let us now recall that the original motivation behind the HCP was to recognize the inadequacies of the essentialist understanding of natural kinds, while salvaging the idea that the special sciences investigate natural kinds in their respective domains. This means relaxing naturalism while keeping its core—that is, salvaging the idea that it is possible for our scientific taxonomies to track natural kinds individuated by properties existing independently of us and grounding taxonomies in hard facts regarding the world's mechanistic structure. To save the notion of "natural kind" as scientifically useful, the relaxation that the HPC view has embraced was necessary. However, the conventionalist aspects in the HPC should make us doubt whether the project of finding a third way is successful, at least in its current shape. As noted previously, the reason why Boyd can claim that HPC natural kinds carve nature at its joints is because he takes nature's joints to be situated at the boundaries of mechanisms. Nonetheless, it seems that there is no independent fact of the matter that could help us to understand the adequate boundaries of mechanisms themselves, or how to prioritize them. Rather, *the boundaries and priorities are determined by the choice of explanandum and the aims of the particular scientific inquiry.* With this, values enter into the picture, and it becomes difficult to see how the HPC could argue that these conventionalist aspects are compatible with the naturalist core that the HPC aims to salvage.

Now this suggests that, given the distinct mechanisms associated with kinds, we should accept a pluralistic view of natural kinds. What a legitimate scientific kind is will be contingent on the parameters and interests of the particular scientific enterprise. However, pluralism also means that HPC-informed accounts will not be able to arbitrate competing taxonomies. While this might be regarded satisfactory with regard to a great deal of the special sciences, it does not live up to the naturalist ambitions pursued in psychiatry.

3. **Conclusion**

This chapter started out by noting that in psychiatric nosology there is a tendency to approach and understand mental disorder as a natural kind. Espousing a naturalist view, some hold that psychological disorders are conceptualized as entities that are qualitatively distinct from normal functioning (Guze 1992), while others maintain that the underlying biological "disorder P" is a natural kind, and thus something bounded and qualitatively different from normal functioning (Hacking 1995). It seems understandable why accounts operating with a natural-kind notion of mental disorder appear attractive to some. If mental disorder is a natural kind, relying solely on pure biological facts, then psychiatry could be easily defended against forms of categorical and dimensional criticism. Psychiatry would then be concerned with "real" diseases and not merely categories that involve value judgments.

This chapter examined several naturalist accounts of mental disorder. First, it was established that an essentialist understanding of mental disorder as a natural kind is a non-starter. While the essentialist use of the term "natural kind" might be useful for identifying natural substances, it is not an adequate means of conceptualizing psychiatric disorders. Even a discovery of the biological "pathology P" underlying a specific cluster of syndromes and a matching classification would leave open the question of whether the classification picks out natural kinds in the sense required by essentialism. Within the framework of an essentialist understanding, it is difficult to conceive of biological kinds that would qualify as natural kinds—perhaps only those in physics and chemistry would do so. Importantly, this would not warrant the conclusion that, although they provide predictively and explanatorily robust accounts, biology—and psychiatry for that matter—are not genuinely scientific disciplines, or they somehow fail to aim for goals that are adequate for scientific inquiry. Rather than casting doubt on the scientific standing of biology or psychiatry, the conclusion must be that not every scientific discipline should aim at an essentialist natural kind classification.

The failure of an essentialist-naturalist understanding need not mean that we have to embrace a full-blown conventionalism, which discounts the genetic and physiological elements that often co-occur in mental disorders. One possibility is to embrace a purely practical orientation—to give up the metaphysical commitment behind the essentialist view and be agnostic about the question of whether our classifications correspond perfectly to a mind-independent reality. According to this view, the mere lack of such a correspondence does not make a diagnostic boundary arbitrary, as long as there are legitimate practical grounds that determine the positioning of the boundary (identify individuals who seek and require treatment, entitlement to insurance coverage, rights or benefits, etc.). The metaphysical question can be set aside if a classification yields robust diagnostic and predictive results and helps to select the treatment that improves the condition. Thus the view is not only that the best classification is relative to the given purposes of the scientific inquiry, but also that classification is determined by its pragmatic benefits, which depend on goals that can be of a scientific, medical, and even socio-political nature. As was argued earlier, one major problem with this account is that it may be overly permissive. If it allows interests and goals of a socio-political nature to play a decisive role in defining the boundaries of mental disorder, then it is susceptible to critique from both camps.

Another possibility that has been explored is to acknowledge the inadequacies of essentialism about natural kinds, but to salvage the naturalist idea of mental disorders as natural kinds. The point is that by relaxing naturalism and incorporating certain conventionalist elements, it is possible to maintain that psychiatric taxonomies track natural kinds individuated by properties that exist independently of us. In different ways, both Cooper and Boyd have put forward such accounts.

Cooper shifts the focus from metaphysical commitments to explanatory virtues and adopts a degree of conventionalism by acknowledging that natural kinds are to some extent *relative to the goals of the explanation*. In addition, Cooper accepts that some entities form distinct natural kinds, even if some dissimilarities between them are caused by social forces (Cooper 2005, pp. 75–76). However, it is then possible according to Cooper's account that our decision as to what counts as "determining property" and the right grade of "similarity" with regard to a mental disorder might pick out properties that are produced by socio-political currents. Also, since the boundaries of certain disorders are sensitive to practical grounds, and since practical grounds are themselves context dependent and therefore likely to change over time,

Cooper's account must acknowledge that the boundaries of a mental disorder are likely to be revised when new practical grounds emerge. Conventionality then enters the picture again in yet another manner—what we take to be a convincing practical ground is dependent on socio-political currents. These issues render the account vulnerable to both dimensional and categorical criticism. The critic could claim that, according to Cooper's account, it is possible that the boundaries of mental disorders are artificial, in the sense that they reproduce value judgments and socio-political currents. In the light of the degree of conventionality that Cooper admits, it is difficult to ascertain whether using the term "natural kind" actually plays any useful role.

Boyd's HPC view also presents a relaxed form of naturalism, but he proceeds differently and aims to ground taxonomies in facts about mechanistic structures. This is how Boyd can claim that HPC natural kinds carve nature at its joints. However, his account depends on the adequacy of the unsupported metaphysical assumption that nature's joints are situated at the boundaries of mechanisms. Without a qualified defense of this metaphysical claim, the account fails to exhibit a satisfactory degree of robustness.

As matters now stand, we might have to accept the fact that when we use the term "mental disorder" we are referring to a range of conditions that does not correspond to any "natural" class of entities "out there." It might very well be that the boundaries of psychiatric kinds are fixed by verdicts about how convenient a specific kind is for the objectives of the researcher, for the goal of explanation or prediction. Whether a kind matches causal structures in the world is secondary, at best. In any case, it appears that there are no good reasons to believe that clinging on to the notion of natural kinds would make any difference. If there is nothing that prevents conventions and socio-politically informed practical reasons from playing a decisive role in determining what should count as a psychiatric kind, then adhering to the terminology of natural kinds is confusing and may only confer a misleading rhetorical pedigree. If natural-kind classifications are simply seen as those that exhibit robust explanatory and predictive success, and a kind is only "natural" *relative to* a specified enquiry, then we do not have sufficient reasons to justify the use of the term.

Some may not be satisfied with this conclusion and may object that any conventionalist account will be susceptible to the kinds of criticism that dimensional and categorical critiques have put forward. In some ways this seems unavoidable. However, we have to bear in mind that this criticism is founded upon the idea that the only legitimate psychiatric kind that justifies therapeutic attention must be a natural kind, with clear-cut boundaries, independent of our classifications. This claim is unsubstantiated. The world in which we live displays a degree of complexity and an overwhelming multiplicity of joints, so it seems futile to suggest that a single enquiry can carve it up along all of the joints at once. However, if different enquiries require carving along different joints, then we need to accept the plurality of taxonomies. The most sensible solution seems to be to adopt a kind of agnosticism—the world may or may not have a proper structure with joints to be carved, and we simply lack the capacities to identify and carve them correctly. Rather than adopting either naturalism or conventionalism in their entirety, this position emphasizes that there is a fundamental and unsolvable discrepancy between metaphysics and epistemology.

Chapter 7

Naturalizing biological function

A different version of the naturalist view does not claim that some underlying biological disorder is a natural kind, but rather that diseases in general (and also mental disorders) involve a deviation from the proper physiological or psychological functioning of parts of the human organism. Such views maintain that the core of mental disorder is the malfunction of some mechanism that is part of the human organism. The naturalist inclination of this position becomes clear when we turn our attention to its underlying descriptive claims. The point is that, according to this view, bodily disease and mental disorder can be construed *descriptively* as a failure of function, while the malfunctioning can be distinguished from proper functioning by a scientific, value-neutral investigation. Accordingly, disease is a theoretical concept in medicine that is non-evaluative, and hence value-laden evaluations are not necessary to identify a dysfunction. Christopher Boorse, one of the most prominent proponents of this view, argues that whether something can be identified as a disease is "a matter of natural science, not evaluative decision" (Boorse 1977, p. 543). Evidently, given that mechanisms in an organism can be regarded as having several functions, any concept of disease as a malfunction can only be understood in the context of a certain conceptualization of the nature of proper functioning. To identify a particular condition objectively as a disorder, advocates of this approach invoke the idea of *natural functions*. In the course of this chapter, the goal will be to explore this version of naturalism, which we may call *natural function naturalism* (see Varga 2011a). As was pointed out in the introduction to Part II of this book, it is important to note that the aim of *natural function naturalism* is to help to render the discussion of health and disease more scientific by proposing an objective, value-free definition.

This position has a number of variants, in which the "natural" quality of functions is understood in different ways. In the first part of the chapter, the views of two prominent proponents of natural function naturalism, who nevertheless approach this matter in significantly different ways, are explored. First, the "biostatistical" account proposed by Christopher Boorse (Boorse 1977, 1997, 2014), which combines a certain understanding of statistical normality with biological function, is discussed. Much of Boorse's work from the 1970s and 1980s is well known, but he has recently put forward a qualified defense of this view (Boorse 2014), to which special attention is given. In the closing part of this section, a modification of Boorse's theory by Manesh Ananth (Ananth 2008) is scrutinized. In the second part of the chapter, the focus is on the merits of a natural function naturalism approach originally developed by Jerome Wakefield. While accepting "harm" as a value-laden element, Wakefield embraces an objective understanding of natural function that is informed by evolutionary theory. The point is that since the physiological and psychological sub-parts that constitute a human being were naturally selected to perform certain functions, natural functions are objectively discoverable.

Overall, then, the goal of this chapter is to critically engage with the arguments that support natural function naturalism. After highlighting the unique perspectives that such a view provides and some flaws that might undermine their utility, the chapter closes by considering the scope of evolutionary explanations.

1. Boorse's biostatistical theory (BST)

Among the influential naturalist approaches to defining "health" and "disease" (Kendell 1975; Boorse 1976, 1977, 1997, 2014; Scadding 1990), Boorse's work is probably the most prominent and well developed. In a series of articles that span more than four decades (Boorse 1975, 1976, 1977, 1987, 1997, 2014), he has proposed a complex account of disease that is in accordance with the basic perception that health is the absence of disease. Although he often considers somatic disorders, he also claims that his account applies equally to mental disorders (Boorse 1997, 2014). His biostatistical theory (BST) is currently one of the most influential naturalistic accounts of disease, which is not only well known in the philosophy of science, but also informs debates on ethical aspects of healthcare and distributive justice (Amundson 2000). Before proceeding to inspect the details of the BST, it is helpful to have an understanding of Boorse's motivation. Linked to the discussion in the introduction to Part II of this book, Boorse maintains that his motivation to analyze various notions of health and to provide a naturalist account of disease was in part due to a desire to clarify what he calls the "morass of mental-health controversies" (Boorse 1977, p. 543). In other words, his work may at least to some extent be regarded as driven by the discussions that followed upon the proliferation of forms of categorical and dimensional criticism. Boorse notes that the basic perceptions underlying his account of health and disease are simple ("It is that the normal is the natural"; Boorse 1977, p. 554), and health represents normality (Boorse 1975, p. 50). It is from such relatively simple intuitions that he develops the idea that health is connected to the normal causal contributions of (biological) functions to an organism's survival and reproduction.

Prior to Boorse's work, there had been partially related but less sophisticated attempts to unravel the idea that disease must be related to the lack of (statistical) normality and biological disadvantage. Robert Kendell has put forward a comparable account of disease informed by biostatistics, in which he argues that it is appropriate to classify schizophrenia and manic depression as diseases, because it can be demonstrated that they inflict biological disadvantages on sufferers. Those with such conditions have a shorter life expectancy and fewer children than the general population. Glenis J. Scadding (1967) has maintained that disease is the sum of the abnormal phenomena by which the diseased individual differs from a species norm, resulting in a biological disadvantage. More recently, Peter Tyrer and Derek Steinberg have argued in favor of a definition of mental disorder that involves both statistically significant deviance and biological disadvantage (Tyrer and Steinberg 2003, p. 8). In this way, it is claimed, a definition could avoid value judgments and might help to limit the increasing medicalization of "problems in living." As Tyrer and Steinberg note, the use of such a model in psychiatry "helps to decide which of these conditions is beyond its scope and unsuitable for mental health interventions" (Tyrer and Steinberg 2003, p. 8). They emphasize that such an account would impose important boundaries, ensuring that conditions such as "late luteal dysphoric disorder" (premenstrual tension) would be excluded, although they might represent deviations from a norm.

The view that Boorse proposes is in many ways significantly more sophisticated, and it does not depend on the problematic claim that disorders are statistically infrequent conditions that decrease fertility and life expectancy. If these were necessary and jointly sufficient conditions for a disease, we would have to accept that being a mercenary, which is both statistically rare and probably reduces life expectancy, warrants the label of disease (Cooper 2005). Boorse's account steers clear of such problems, while holding on to the basic idea that the definition of disease (and mental disorder) in general can indeed be scientific and objective. Boorse focuses on biological function and statistical means, arguing that the objectivity and neutrality of a taxonomy can be preserved if guided by the characteristics of biological design. It is against such a background that Boorse claims "If diseases are deviations from the species biological design, their recognition is a matter of natural science, not evaluative decision" (Boorse 1977, p. 543). Boorse has since reiterated this view a number of times, arguing that "disease is only statistically species-subnormal biological part-function; therefore, the classification of human states as healthy or diseased is an objective matter, to be read off the biological facts of nature without need of value judgments" (Boorse 1997, p. 4; Boorse 2014).

According to this view, disease should be understood in a broad sense, in which health is the absence of disease, and disease refers to conditions that medicine views as "inconsistent with perfect health" (Boorse 1977, p. 7). Boorse understands the human organism (body and mind) as a goal-directed system that aims to maintain survival and reproductive ability, composed of numerous subsystems (organs, the nervous system, cognitive subsystems such as memory, etc.) that each have at least one function. The proper function of a subsystem is revealed when we understand how it contributes to achieving the goal of the system. Thus Boorse understands functions in terms of their physiological and psychological causal contributions to the survival and reproduction of an organism. In addition, he associates health with normal species functioning and defines the latter as the statistically representative subsystemic contribution to the survival and reproduction of the organism.[1] The unit of comparison with respect to which the statistical typicality of a contribution is determined is the "reference class"—a unit consisting of the total number of individuals who belong to the same gender and age group (Boorse 1977, p. 555; Boorse 2014, p. 684).

(1) The reference class is a natural class of organisms of uniform functional design; specifically, an age group of a sex of a species.
(2) A normal function of a part or process within members of the reference class is a statistically typical contribution by it to their individual survival and reproduction.
(3) Health in a member of the reference class is normal functional ability: the readiness of each internal part to perform all its normal functions on typical occasions with at least typical efficiency.
(4) A disease is a type of internal state which impairs health, i.e., reduces one or more functional abilities below typical efficiency.

Boorse (1997) later introduced several changes, mainly with regard to the last two points:

[1] It should be noted that Boorse (2014) now recognizes that identifying the goals of organisms as survival *and* reproduction might be problematic. Instead, he suggests that they should be survival *or* reproduction.

(1) The reference class is a natural class of organisms of uniform functional design; specifically, an age group of a sex of a species.

(2) A normal function of a part or process within members of the reference class is a statistically typical contribution by it to their individual survival and reproduction.

(3) A disease is a type of internal state which is either an impairment of normal functional ability, i.e., a reduction of one or more functional abilities below typical efficiency, or a limitation on functional ability caused by the environment.

(4) Health is the absence of disease (Boorse 1997, pp. 7–8).

Quite appealingly from a naturalistic perspective, Boorse advocates understanding health in terms of normal functioning. In other words, organism X is healthy if it is functioning normally, which means that there is a statistically typical contribution of X's parts to X's general aims—reproduction and survival. In contrast, organism X is diseased if there is a discernible statistically significant deviation with respect to the ability of X's parts or processes to fulfill their species-typical contribution to X's overall aims. We should remember that Boorse is not concerned with illness (a value-laden term involved in the applications of medical theory in medical practice), but with disease, which he simply takes to mean a statistically significant departure from the norms of functioning that are characteristic of the species. While acknowledging that values play a role in medical practice, Boorse claims that medical theory operates within a completely different conceptual framework. He argues that, while talking about "illness" with its associated negative evaluations characterizes medical practice, the term "disease" used by medical theory is neutral and descriptive:

> But behind this conceptual framework of medical practice stands an autonomous framework of medical theory, a body of doctrine that describes the functioning of a healthy body, classifies various deviations from such functioning as diseases, predicts their behaviour under various forms of treatment, etc. This theoretical corpus looks in every way continuous with theory in biology and the other natural sciences, and I believe it to be value-free.
>
> (Boorse 1975, p. 55)

The introduction of a reference class, with respect to which a contribution can be seen as statistically typical, offers a solution to the difficulties to which less sophisticated accounts, such as that of Scadding, are susceptible. Boorse realizes that, given the enormous variability in functioning, reference classes need to be a part of the definition. In most cases it is not possible to pinpoint characteristics that are statistically representative for the *whole* species. For instance, depending on the age and gender of the person, identical concentrations of certain hormones could indicate either healthy or diseased conditions. In addition, reference classes must be kept above a certain size. This becomes apparent if we imagine that a reference group for liver functioning would be composed of men who consume excessive amounts of alcohol. In that case, liver functioning indicators that under ordinary circumstances would count as diseased would appear within the normal range. Thus, to a significant degree, the BST depends on getting the "appropriate" reference classes right. Presupposing a sufficient amount of uniformity in the species, Boorse (1977, p. 562) maintains that the appropriate reference class is "a natural class of organisms of uniform functional design; specifically, an age group of a sex of a species." Thus X is in good health as long as every subsystem performs in a statistically typical manner for X's reference class, as defined by the parameters age and sex. According to this picture, if the parts and processes that constitute the author of this book function in a statistically typical manner for male, Caucasian, 39-year-old humans, then he qualifies as healthy.

Although there is clearly much to be said in favor of Boorse's precise analyses, they have also been the subject of a considerable amount of criticism. Authors have criticized the BST for falsely equating medical and statistical normality (Bolton 2008), for simultaneously rejecting and assuming etiological and selectionist accounts of function (Murphy 2006; Ananth 2008), for ultimately providing a value-laden analysis (Fulford 1989, 2001; DeVito 2000; Kingma 2007, 2010; Ereshefsky 2009), for running into massive problems with regard to the choice of reference class (Cooper 2005; Schwartz 2007; Varga 2011a), and for providing a definition that cannot account for counter-examples from the relevant medical literature (DeVito 2000; Nordenfelt 2001). In lengthy responses to his critics, Boorse (1997, 2014) maintains that these criticisms can be overcome, and the BST still provides the best explanation of medical disease judgments. In this context, rather than listing all of the different concerns voiced by other authors, the focus in this chapter is on contributing to the discussion by taking into account new material by Boorse and by putting forward new arguments that seem to challenge the BST. The aim is to present a different kind of objection—one that is connected to the issue of *epistemic authority*, with implications for conceptualizing an adequate way of dealing with the question of health and disease.

2. **Reference class and the question of epistemic authority**

To introduce the issue of epistemic authority, we might start by considering a pivotal aspect of the BST. The critical significance of the choice of reference class for the BST is beyond any reasonable doubt. As disease is only warranted if there is a deviation from *appropriate* reference classes, everything depends on an appropriate justification of the choice of suitable reference classes. The reference class has a crucial role in determining the boundary between disease and health. Thus if a definition of disorder is to be objective, Boorse must demonstrate that the distinguishing of appropriate from inappropriate reference classes builds on strictly empirical facts. To provide a solid justification, Boorse argues that the correct reference class is simply "a natural class of organisms of uniform functional design" (Boorse 1977, p. 562). Two points of clarification are needed here. First, the term "functional design" might suggest that Boorse is attempting to justify his reference classes by recourse to evolutionary biology. However, he explicitly rejects such a strategy of justification (Boorse 1976). Second, the term "natural" does not refer to "whatever occurs in nature," as both appropriate and inappropriate classes occur in nature. Moreover, it cannot mean "innate," because one of the reference classes that Boorse identifies, namely age, is obviously acquired. For example, if the author of this book describes himself as Caucasian, blue-eyed, and moderately tall, Boorse's account has to show that empirical facts determine that only "Caucasian" would count as a determining factor when choosing the appropriate reference class.

In addition, the term "natural" is not to be understood as statistical normality, because, as Kingma (2007) has noted, some age groups have an extremely limited number of members, while various diseases are very common. An additional, even more serious problem with understanding the term "natural" in terms of statistical "normality" is that it would amount to the same thing as saying that the BST is true. In other words, it would make the BST true by definition. Given that Boorse (1976, 1977, 2014) explicitly rejects the notion that the BST depends on evolutionary theory, the last option would be to understand "a natural class of organisms of uniform functional design" (Boorse 1977, p. 562) as natural kinds. However, we must also reject this option. As we discussed in Chapter 6, biological classes such as species can only qualify as natural kinds on the basis of a significantly watered down definition of natural kinds. At this point, although the BST account depends on justifying the appropriate reference classes, Boorse admits that his account "*presupposes* enough uniformity in the species to generate a statistically typical species design" (Boorse 1977, p. 562, italics added). However, he does not provide any evidence as to why we should accept such a far-reaching presupposition.

Building on an idea explored by Hare (1986), we shall continue with an example that challenges the BST, and to which Boorse (1997) has an interesting line of response. Although forms of baldness, particularly premature baldness and *androgenic alopecia* (male- or female-pattern hair loss), are usually recognized as diseases, they can also be used as cases which demonstrate that the person's response to a condition is a part of the concept of health. There are two important details that we should add here. First, in such cases, baldness is not due to the malfunctioning of some other part of the body (e.g. the thyroid). If that was the case, Boorse could rightly claim that baldness is merely a sign of another part of the body being diseased. Second, the example is particularly relevant because baldness is regarded as a disease in the literature (Randall 2010; Lee and Lee 2012), but it does not interfere with survival and/or reproductive success.

Hare (1986) imagines that a genetic engineer designs a product that can prevent hair growth locally and puts it on the market as an effective leg-hair remover for use by women. Is the induced loss of hair in women who use this product a disease? Hare suspects that the relevant professionals would be reluctant to regard the skin of the consumers as non-healthy. But why is it that hair loss from baldness is regarded as a disease, but hair loss caused by the genetically engineered product is not? Hare's answer is that in both cases there is no effect on survival and reproduction or on natural function in the ordinary sense of that expression. Rather, the important difference relates to the affected person's evaluative reactions. However, in that case we might expect that a definition of disease needs to include an evaluative dimension, which, in contradiction to Boorse's theory, would ultimately mean that values are part of the concept of health.[2]

In the case of the genetically engineered product, Boorse admits to not being sure what a pathologist would say about the leg-hair loss. He thinks that if androgenic alopecia affected most men to a statistically significant degree, it would not be a disease, but if the baldness was excessive or premature with respect to the reference class, then we could speak of a dysfunction and hence

[2] Boorse's response to this challenge (Boorse 1997) merits scrutiny, as it reveals something interesting and surprising. He maintains that the BST is able to handle this question, emphasizing the difference between body/leg hair and face/scalp hair. While the former is a vestigial organ, the latter must have a function. It is at this point that Boorse seems to be arguing from evolutionary theory—he interprets the fact that, in the process of evolution, body hair almost disappeared while it remained on the head as demonstrating some proof that hair has a function, probably a protective one. Now we need not be concerned whether he is right about the function of hair from an evolutionary perspective, but drawing on evolutionary theory is problematic, as Boorse (1975) rejects evolutionary (etiological) concepts of function. Although understanding statistically normal functioning in a species as a marker of evolutionary design might be defensible, it is difficult to see how this can be done within the framework of the BST without encountering contradictions.

a disease. However, this answer remains ambiguous. To demonstrate this, we may emphasize that there are significant racial differences in the prevalence and types of androgenic alopecia (Paik et al. 2001; Randall 2010; Lee and Lee 2012). For example, non-Caucasians such as Asians often exhibit significantly less balding than Caucasians. In that case, the reference class for an organism needs to be narrower and to add race to species, gender, and age. However, determining normal function depending on the additional factor, race brings with it major complications with regard to individuals of mixed race, the boundaries of races, etc. Although Boorse admits that "medicine may need to add race" (Boorse 2014, p. 702), he also states that he remains "ambivalent about it." However, such a position is ultimately untenable given the crucial role of reference classes for the BST.

The discussion of reference classes and the recent work of Boorse (2014) in response to criticism unearths other important aspects that are relevant to the goals of this chapter. One line of criticism related to the issue of reference class (DeVito 2000; Cooper 2005; Kingma 2007) has been that the BST cannot answer the question "Is homosexuality a disease?" in a value-free way. The BST is forced to bite the bullet and accept that homosexuality might be a disease (Cooper 2005, p. 17), which Boorse (1997, pp. 11–12) defends by saying that identifying something as a disease does not mean that it ought to be cured by psychiatrists or psychologists. Kingma asks us to imagine two competing concepts for health, the BST and the XST, where the only difference is that the XST includes an additional reference class—sexual orientation:

> Thus on the XST homosexuality is a normal, therefore healthy, function in the reference class of homosexual people. On the BST however, homosexuality interferes with statistically typical reproductive function in the reference class of all men, and is therefore a disease. The question 'is homosexuality a disease?' then reduces to the question 'is the BST or the XST the right account of health?' or, 'is sexual orientation an appropriate reference class or not?' Since, as I have argued, there are no facts that determine which reference classes are appropriate, there is no empirical fact that determines whether homosexuality is an appropriate reference class. Therefore there is no reference class that tells us whether the BST or the XST is correct.
>
> (Kingma 2007, p. 132)

Boorse (2014) responds that his analysis does not choose one of these competing concepts for any (evaluative) reasons. Rather, he is aiming to select the analysis that best fits medical usage (Boorse 1977, p. 551; Boorse 2014). Thus the point is that whereas competing (or candidate) concepts only exist due to the "imagination of philosophers," the medical-theoretical concept of disease that Boorse aims to analyze already exists and influences much of medical practice. In fact, the competing concepts such as the XST actually fail to be health concepts in the first place.

This line of response reveals some interesting aspects of the BST. It reveals the extensive degree to which Boorse considers that the theoretical concept of health should be modeled on the way "biologists" use the term. The underlying assumption is that the expert concepts of disease and health are epistemologically superior to those used by lay people, or simply the "folk." However, such a goal is only interesting if one simultaneously accepts that the way "biologists" use the term does more than merely reflect the practices and conventions of biology. Rather, the underlying assumption must be that the biologists' use of the term is epistemologically insightful, reveals facts about the world, and "carves nature at its joints." In other words, the assumption must be that the concept of disease put forward by certain experts is "natural." Recalling Boorse's original motivation, the BST's aim of showing how experts apply the terms "health" and "disease" is only intelligible if Boorse also believes that pathologists use the term *in the right way*, tracking something objective and carving nature in the right places. This means that the BST attributes a particular *epistemic authority* to the relevant experts. In the following account, the focus is on exploring the implications of this claim and the ramifications for the BST.

3. **Conceptual analysis and epistemic authority: who is the right expert?**

Most of us live in a world that is characterized by an increasing amount of specialization, in which we habitually defer to scientific, expert knowledge in order to orient ourselves or to deal with countless everyday issues. Successful navigation of life in complex modern societies demands that we make a number of judgments and decisions that we cannot ground in reasons and evidence that we ourselves have examined. The special epistemic authority of science stems from the knowledge it holds about aspects of the physical world (Brown 2009). Let us start by identifying who the BST accepts as having expert authority on this field.

Boorse (2014) states that for the BST, as a naturalist theory that defines health as normal physiological functional ability, biology alone is able to tell us what functions are, and ultimately what disease and health are. Distinguishing between health and disease is an "objective matter, to be read off the biological facts of nature, without need of value judgments" (Boorse 1997, p. 4). Biology is thus the paradigm of scientific medicine, and the claim is that goal and function ascriptions by biologists are the key to understanding what disease is. Although it is not always entirely clear what is meant by "biology," it is helpful to note that Boorse introduces an important and sensible distinction between "medical practice" and "medical theory," claiming that while the first term is value-laden, the second is scientific, objective, and value-free (Fulford 2001). Yet who is the *right* biologist with the relevant epistemic authority? This question is important, as Boorse is well aware that different subfields of biology might ascribe different functions, amounting to a plurality of goals of organisms. Plurality and indeterminacy in this context mean that some higher-level goals of organisms may be fixed by the research and classificatory interest of different branches of biology. However, if there is such plurality, then the inevitable conclusion is that biology operates with dissimilar ascriptions of function (particularly with regard to higher-order ones), which would pose an insurmountable problem for the BST. Boorse is well aware of this difficulty. While indeterminacy would be difficult to match with the naturalist aims of the BST, Boorse clarifies that it is exclusively the subspecialization of *physiology* that is relevant to health. Thus, at the end, while Boorse also talks about the usage of the terms "in physiology texts" (Boorse 1977, p. 556), "medicine," and "theoretical medicine" (which might be different from biology), in his more recent work (Boorse 1997, pp. 45–50; Boorse 2014, p. 711) he clearly states that he is interested in the *pathologist's concept of disease*. The accompanying claim with regard to attributing epistemic authority is that from the perspective of the pathologist, medical normality and statistical normality coincide (Boorse 1997, p. 17).

There are at least two problems with the choice concerning epistemic authority. First, the question arises as to why we should assume the epistemic authority of the pathologist and not of the biologist, the clinical doctor, or others. We are not provided with arguments in support of the underlying assumption that it is the pathologist who operates with the concept of disease that "carves nature at its joints." However, in that case it remains entirely unclear how the BST would arbitrate in the event of a disagreement. What if it turned out that even though biologists and pathologists operate with almost identical concepts, there is one condition X that biologists consider to be a disease and pathologists do not? Boorse would most probably choose to rely on the authority of pathologists, but such a choice would be in need of additional substantiation.

Further complicating this issue, Boorse does not seem to want to grant epistemic authority to *all* pathologists, but only to a certain group. For instance, he rejects the work of authors of books on psychopathology, critically noting that they often wrongly assume that psychiatric disorder has less to do with biological dysfunction and more to do with social values (Boorse 2014).

Instead, to fix the extension of the concept of disease, it seems that Boorse relies on the *Standard Nomenclature of Diseases and Operations*, produced by the American Medical Association. However, although epistemic authority is attributed to a limited group of pathologists, some of this authority is also taken back again. This is discernible when Boorse (1997) notes that some cases described in the *Nomenclature* (such as the macacus ear, but also some structural disorders and universal diseases such as the congenital absence of the appendix, dental caries, atherosclerosis, senile decline in function, etc.) should not be regarded as "diseases" because they do not disturb normal function. This move is rather odd, since a descriptive definition aims to provide information about the way in which the relevant pathologists use the term, not how the term *ought* to be used. With such a move Boorse aims to alter the actual use of the term by pathologists—a move that clashes with the method of conceptual analysis, unless the change is very minor and something that all pathologists would readily accept. However, Boorse does not give any indication that this would be the case. Without further evidence, it seems likely that the definition achieved relies on conceptual work in which Boorse both cherry-picks the group of experts on whom he relies for his analysis and only accepts their epistemic authority as far as it matches the BST.

Although our present focus is on the discussion of certain methodological suppositions of the BST, it should be mentioned that even within the narrow group of pathologists, we find the term "disease" used in ways that would not warrant the label from the point of view of the BST. Pathology books do not usually spend time actually defining what disease means, which is another factor that contributes to the diversity of views. Lennart Nordenfelt (2001) has listed a number of such cases, and it seems that with the growing number of diseases listed, this problem will only become more obvious. For example, the second edition of *Contemporary Oral and Maxillofacial Pathology* "presents a substantial expansion in the number of diseases" (Sapp et al. 2004, p. 2), and many of the conditions listed do not qualify as diseases according to the BST. For example, in the case of *microdontia* (the presence of one or more teeth that are smaller than normal) it would be hard to claim that normal functioning is impaired or that there is no statistically typical contribution to the general aims of survival and reproduction. The same is true for a variety of conditions, such as *supernumerary teeth* (teeth in excess of the normal number), *double lip* (redundant mucosal tissue on the inner aspect of the upper lip), or *taurodontism* (meaning "bull-like tooth," where there is a molar or premolar with an elongated crown and apically placed furcation of the roots), which usually require no treatment. It is devastating for the chances of a successful conceptual analysis that some pathologists define pathology and its understanding of disease in such a way that the organism as a whole with all its range of functions is included (Ananth 2008, pp. 140–141). Similarly, many take seriously the literal translation of pathology as the study (*logos*) of suffering (*pathos*). For instance, in a book entitled *Plant Disease*, the authors recognize that the precise contours of the term "plant pathology" probably depend on the interests of the scientist involved (Horsfall and Cowling 1977, p. 3). They subsequently provide a definition that might seem surprising from Boorse's point of view:

> The term pathology, like numerous others in science, stems from the Greek pathos (suffering) and logos (to study). Plant pathology, then, is the study of the suffering plant. A distinguished botanist has expressed surprise to us that plants really suffer.
>
> (Horsfall and Cowling 1977, p. 3)

Thus at least some of the relevant authors want to hold on to the idea that suffering is a part of the concept of disease. Such cases demonstrate the problems involved with the kind of conceptual analysis on which Boorse relies. Any account that puts forward a set of criteria for the concept of disease is vulnerable to counter-examples pointing to a condition that is considered to be a disease without meeting all of the criteria. Such counter-examples require at least the rethinking and adjustment of the BST.

4. Science and epistemic authority

In Section 3 of this chapter, the discussion of an even more basic question concerning epistemic authority on issues of health and disease was omitted. Therefore we should now dig deeper and examine the more general claim about the epistemic authority of experts (such as pathologists) with regard to the concept of disease. The point that the pathologists might not be the right authority to whom to appeal can be made in different ways. One possibility would be to follow William E. Stempsey and argue that pathologists are not the right experts because they are not interested in the study of the concept of disease (and hence experts in conceptual analysis), but rather in the study of the morphological characteristics of disease that usually correlate with a patient's experience (Stempsey 2000). Instead, Stempsey is inclined to think that medical practitioners might be the right group to ask. In the following account, a different path will be attempted. The question is posed as to whether we are warranted in assuming the epistemic authority of pathologists and thinking that the concept of disease used in pathology "carves nature at its joints."

We have developed a trust in the authority of expert scientists that is not easily broken, even if we discover that some important scientific accounts and predictions were in fact wrong. A good example is the extent to which we orient ourselves by relying on forecasts made by meteorologists, even if we simultaneously complain about the mistakes that they incessantly make. Of course there are good reasons for accepting the epistemic authority of the sciences. Science is not about a set of observable facts that laypeople can verify for themselves—if we lack the relevant training, it is unlikely that we will be able to understand the expert's reasons, or indeed to understand why exactly they constitute good reasons. In many cases in the physical sciences, even if a layperson could deal with the relevant equipment, and even if they could successfully make an observation that contradicted scientific statement Z, they would not be able to evaluate the significance of the evidence and understand how it contradicts Z (Polanyi 1962).

However, although in many or indeed most cases we habitually and justifiably rely on experts and attribute epistemic authority to them, we cannot simply assume that such authority is warranted in each and every case. Might it not be that "folk" knowledge has authority on some subjects, or the epistemic authority of expert knowledge is at least disputable in some areas? Translated to the context of the present inquiry, the question is this: why should we assume that the concept of disease used in pathology (not the "folk" concept) is the one that "carves nature at its joints"? Before we start to explore this question, we should note that in recent years the availability of various new media has opened up alternative ways of acquiring information, a development that has led to what we could call the "medicalization" of lay knowledge. Due to such advances, the everyday understanding of the "folk" now includes a good deal of medical knowledge, and the relationship between lay and medical systems of knowledge is increasingly dynamic. Naturally, even if the distances between expert and lay concepts are now decreasing, there are still important differences. What we need to explore is whether these differences are such that we are warranted in assuming that the concept of disease held by certain experts is "natural."

5. Attributing epistemic authority: who is the right expert?

It is helpful to start with cases in which we commonly agree that epistemic authority is rightly attributed to experts. When deciding whether one should take a rain jacket when heading out of the house in the morning, one trusts the judgment of the meteorologist, even though there may at the moment be a perfectly clear sky with absolutely no indication of any rain clouds. Importantly, one accepts the judgment of the meteorologist without needing to know about the kind of evidence and form of reasoning that meteorologists use in order to reach their predictive conclusions (Pierson 1994). Clearly, in such a case, one accepts the epistemic authority of the relevant scientists and modifies one's behavior accordingly. Although there are countless examples of such uncomplicated acceptance in everyday life, it is important to recognize that there is a substantial difference in the way that we attribute epistemic authority to experts. The point is that our attribution of epistemic authority to experts crucially depends on whether we consider the issue at hand to have value-laden aspects or implications. Whereas with regard to issues that are generally considered to be objectively approachable we are inclined to acknowledge the epistemic authority of experts, the situation is very different with regard to value-laden issues.

Let us examine a case in which the attribution of epistemic authority to experts is not so clear-cut. Consider, for instance, the question of how to define the beginning of a human life. This question is to a large extent about a transformation. When does the transformation occur in which two entities that are parts of two human beings become one unique live human being? When is it that the parts of two human beings cease to exist and change into a new, single, whole human being? Although this might initially appear to be a genuinely scientific question, things quickly become complicated when we try to identify the right group of scientists who hold the relevant epistemic authority. Who should answer such a question, about which embryologists, obstetricians, gynecologists, and neurologists might all claim epistemic authority? This is important, as these different groups of experts might reach different conclusions. For instance, it is commonly accepted that, from a neurological perspective, death is ordinarily defined as the termination of recognizable brain activity. Therefore it would make sense for neurologists to argue in favor of defining the start of life as the start of recognizable brain activity, which first appears approximately 25 weeks after conception. From the point of view of genetics, the life of a new human being begins at conception, with the emergence of a new, distinct genome. From the point of view of embryology, life starts when the zygote reaches a certain stage of development, about 2 weeks after fertilization. Such examples indicate that the question of epistemic authority also arises between different experts. In that case, it is difficult to see how a theory such as the BST could have the right criteria for selecting between the possibilities.

In addition, in the case of the BST, the question about the epistemic authority of the pathologist is even more problematic. On second glance, it is not entirely certain whether the BST really attributes complete epistemic authority to the pathologist. In fact the epistemic authority might turn out to be shared by the pathologist and the statistician. To understand this, recall that according to the BST, statistical questions play a central role, as dysfunction only occurs if a function falls *significantly* below the mean. But what counts as significantly low in this context, and what criteria are used to determine it? The BST distinguishes between low-normal function and dysfunction, and holds that the line between health and disease "can only be conventionally chosen, as in any application of statistical normality to a continuous distribution" (Boorse 1977, p. 559). In a later paper, Boorse argues not only that "the concept of a pathological state has vague boundaries," but also that the limit of normal functional ability, and thus "the line between normal and pathological—is arbitrary" (Boorse 1987, p. 371). While noting that experts in statistics regularly utilize a 95% central range, Boorse admits that this choice relies on (statistical) conventions more than on facts in the world (see Schwartz 2007). For my purposes, it is sufficient here to emphasize that the epistemic authority about disease is shared by the pathologist and the statistician, which raises further questions.[3] If it is correct that "the classification of human states as healthy or diseased is an objective matter, to be read off the biological facts of nature without need for value judgments" (Boorse 1997), then the claim that the concept of disease used in pathology "carves nature at its joints" is paired with the claim that a certain conventional methodological choice in statistics also "carves nature at its joints."

6. **Attributing epistemic authority: experts and the "folk"**

While this science-internal question is difficult to answer for the BST, there is an even more fundamental question that is easiest to understand if we assume that our experts agree. To grasp this, let us for a moment return to the "beginning of life" example, and assume that there *is* agreement between embryologists, obstetricians, gynecologists, and neurologists about the beginning of life. Given this agreement, someone could suggest that we simply attribute epistemic authority to the group of agreeing experts and make our decisions dependent on the boundary between non-life and life that they define. Nevertheless, it is my contention that there would be considerable hesitation about accepting this suggestion, leading to the question of whether we (that is, the non-scientists, such as bioethicists, theologians, politicians, etc.) should accept the epistemic authority of the relevant experts in such a case.

[3] However, I should note that the statistical choice of range that ultimately determines the boundary between health and disease is a matter of conventional choice, which makes it a rather poor fit with the naturalistic tenets of the BST.

This question arises because when we ask "When does life begin?", two meanings overlap, so descriptive and normative (or moral) senses are *enmeshed*. At first it seems that the question "When does life begin?" merely aims to identify a relevant and decisive boundary in the biological process of development. However, the question about this particular boundary (that marks the beginning of human life) has only become significant because of its role in a non-descriptive debate. The different positions in contemporary debates on stem-cell research, different methods of abortion, and human embryo research rely on particular ideas about the beginning of human life. The point is that due to such developments, the question "When does life begin?" is inherently entangled with the question of from what moment a human being should be treated as a *person*—as a legitimate bearer of certain rights and dignities. Here we begin to see the limits of a purely scientific and descriptive agenda. For instance, even if there was unanimous agreement between embryologists, obstetricians, gynecologists, and neurologists that, by virtue of its bearing a certain genetic code, human life begins in the zygote at time X, this would not settle the question of whether the zygote at time X is a *person* with legal and moral rights. Science can point out a crucial break in the biological process of development, but it cannot tell us whether this break is *morally relevant*. That is, no legal or moral rights simply derive from facts about the beginning of a human life. To put this in general terms, science has epistemic authority to tell us how the world is, but no moral authority to tell us how it should be.[4]

The aim of this brief detour was to show that the attribution of epistemic authority depends on whether the question is concerned with a value-neutral subject, or one in which value-laden questions are interpenetrated with value-neutral ones. While we might argue that science has a justified epistemic authority in settling the questions about how the world is, this authority is only warranted as long as the question is descriptive and in no way entangled with a normative one. Keeping this point in mind, we may now return to the question of epistemic authority about disease. Recall that Boorse's important starting assumptions were that biology alone is able to tell us what health and disease are, and we should accept the epistemic authority of pathologists with regard to the concept of disease. However, the point is that this

[4] Brown (2009, p. 23) distinguishes between epistemic authority as "the capacity to convince others of how the world is," and moral authority as "the capacity to convince others how the world should be." This distinction is helpful, but the talk of "capacity" is somewhat misleading, as there are people or groups of people who do have the capacity to convince others, although their authority is illegitimate.

starting assumption is only justified if we assume right from the outset that the answer to the question of health and disease is value-neutral. The claim that pathologists have epistemic authority is only meaningful if we suppose that health and disease are value-neutral and objectively definable. However, if this is true, then the BST might be accused of leaping into circularity by presupposing what it attempts to prove. This criticism might prove difficult to counter: if a BST supporter wants to claim that no such assumption is needed, then the BST is pushed into committing the fallacy of *ad verecundiam*. That is, without the assumption that the answer to the question of health and disease is value-neutral, the BST would be erroneously appealing to unqualified authority.

One possible objection that a supporter of the BST might voice is that the comparison between the question about the beginning of life and the question about disease is unfair. They are, so the BST supporter might argue, two very different types of question, where the latter is not one in which descriptive and normative issues are entangled. However, at least in most cases, this objection would be incorrect. Usually, perceiving that a human being is affected by a disease is intertwined with the perception that she both needs and (admittedly to a lesser degree) is morally entitled to medical attention. It should be emphasized that the claim here is not that there are no exceptions to this generalization. Clearly, there will be cases in which there is disease, suffering, and functional impairment, but in which we do not consider that the person automatically needs or is morally entitled to medical attention.

7. The BST and EHCH

In order to discriminate between function and dysfunction, Boorse appeals to "normality" as a standard. Now the "normal" cannot be demarcated in terms of functioning according to its design, because providing criteria for determining what something's design is would invite the charge of essentialism and of ignoring constant adaptation under selection pressures. Well aware of this issue, Boorse focuses on function as a standard causal contribution to the goals *actually* pursued by the organism, which he claims can be ascertained empirically, by studying the (statistically) normal behavior of the organism. However, William Bechtel argues that such a move is flawed, "for normal is being used to define functioning according to design, which was to explicate the notion of normal" (Bechtel 1985, p. 143). Thus the charge is that of circular reasoning. In particular, the main technical terms "function" and "normal (behavior)" that do much of the work are explained by each other. The point is that as Boorse cannot take species design to ground anything, he has to establish that X is a function by determining whether X is a normal behavior.

In his non-evolutionary framework, the criterion for determining the design or function of something is that it has to make "a standard causal contribution to a goal actually pursued by the organism" (Boorse 1975, p. 57). These goals can be identified empirically (statistically) by studying the statistically normal behavior of the organism. However, it then seems that the BST has moved in a circle, since statistic normality is being employed to define functioning according to design, which is then used to elucidate the notion of normal. The problem of circularity arises when function is determined by normal behavior, while normal behavior is simultaneously determined by function. In order for the account to be plausible, it is necessary for the two concepts to be explicated independently.

In his 1997 paper, Boorse denies that his account is circular and tries to explain how such criticism rests on confusion about medical and statistical normality:

> What I proposed was to explicate medical normality as statistical normality of function. ... Medical normality ... is functioning according to design. But species design is, in fact, simply those functions statistically typical in species members. Given a focus on functions, medical normality and statistical (nonsub)normality are the same thing. But one must add the function concept to the statistical-normality concept to get medical normality, so the two kinds of normality differ.
>
> (Boorse 1997, p. 17)

But is Boorse's defense successful, and does he manage to evade the charge of circularity? In support of the BST, Mahesh Ananth argues that the fact that the definition contains the ultimate aims of "survival and reproduction" resolves the problem of circularity:

> Normal is defined in terms of statistically typical activities, but normal is now explained in terms of how such activities ensure survival and reproduction. More carefully, since Boorse is a part-functionalist, normal is explained by the goals and activities of specific parts within the body. Nevertheless, Boorse has provided independent support for his notion of "normal" that is neither circular nor question begging.
>
> (Ananth 2008, p. 130)

Nevertheless, it seems that this line of defense needs further support. It is not clear whether this solution merely pushes the problem further. The point is that even if the normal is explained by the goals of specific parts within the body, that explanation cannot stand alone. Those goals still stand in need of explanation, which can only be provided by referring to the goals of the *organism*. In other words, even if we take "normal" to refer to activities of parts of organisms, this only makes sense in the light of a notion of the "normal" on the level of organism. However, if that is true, then the charge of circularity still stands, as there seems to be no independent support for the notion of "normal."

After presenting a detailed analysis of Boorse's work, Ananth (2008, pp. 171–172) argues that Boorse's naturalistic concept of health and disease is partly unpersuasive, mainly due to his inconsistent views about biology, and particularly about natural selection and environmental factors. Instead of rejecting Boorse's account, Ananth presents a modified version of his concept of health—the evolutionary-homeostasis concept of health (EHCH). Homeostatic mechanisms exist on several levels in organisms, detect internal and external change (such as air temperature), and help to maintain a fairly constant state. For instance, sensory elements of the skin detect cold air and elicit a response that offsets the change, sometimes leading to shivering, in which the muscle contraction produces body heat that counterbalances the cold. Interestingly, Ananth claims that the modified account is supposedly shielded against the difficulties that Boorse's work encounters:

> An organism—within a certain species, gender, age group, and environment—is in a state of health if and only if its relevant parts and overall behavioral activities have and retain evolved functional propensities to secure dual-homeostasis, which in turn confers a survival enhancing functional propensity on the organism as a whole.
>
> (Ananth 2008, p. 196)

In contrast to the BST, the EHCH combines function and homeostasis into an evolutionary concept of health, maintaining that an organism within a specific reference class is healthy when its internal parts are functioning according to their evolved abilities that assist both internal homeostasis and organism homeostasis.

On the positive side, the EHCH is able to acknowledge the role of the environment when making health judgments, and, with its reliance on natural selection and an evolutionary concept of function, it provides a way of distinguishing functions from mere side effects. However, compared with the BST, there are two relatively subtle changes that we should note. First, the EHCH focuses on defining health, while leaving disease underdefined. After all, from the definition it is not clear that *every* interference with homeostatic processes that confer a survival-enhancing functional propensity on the organism qualifies as a disease. This aspect leaves important questions open, which Boorse aimed to answer. Second, it is also the case that, compared with the BST, the EHCH changes the concept of health (and disease) from an absolute to a *relative* one. This means that, according to the EHCH, health and disease are states that admit of degree. That is, different internal and external factors that disrupt various parts of the homeostatic system may only reduce various propensities slightly, rendering an organism only "slightly unhealthy" or "extremely unhealthy" (Ananth 2008, p. 196).

When considering these two aspects, it is unclear to what extent we can regard the EHCH as being a modification of Boorse's account, or something that exists in its own right. Ananth shifts away from conceptual analysis, adopts an evolutionary account of function, and adds the environment to the reference classes, which means that he radically alters aspects that are fundamental to the BST. Overall, then, it seems that Ananth is proposing an account that is quite fundamentally different from that of Boorse and displays instead some similarities with Wakefield's evolutionary account—a topic that will be dealt with later in this chapter. However, we should briefly point out some challenges in Ananth's proposal. While the focus is on explaining the selection of dual homeostasis (cellular-level and organismic) as a relevant measure, the choice of a particular (propensity) interpretation of function, and the choice of the unit of selection fall short on exhaustive argumentation.[5]

It makes perfect sense to argue that homeostasis in an organism makes an important contribution to survival and reproductive success. However, it is hard to see how reference to homeostasis could solve anything. Recall that homeostasis is not a state of internal constancy, but a dynamic process in which an organism maintains important variables *within a range of values.* Consider, for example, the human body's ability to observe and uphold internal states such as temperature at fairly constant levels. We generate body heat to maintain our body temperature at a fairly constant level, about 37°C. However, far from being constant, body temperature varies, being lower at night (during sleep), higher during the daylight hours, and increasingly high with demanding physical activity. Given such temperature fluctuations, the question is how we establish the "normal" range of values. In order to know in what range the temperature *should* fluctuate, we would have to know what the normal range is. However, this information cannot be obtained by looking at evolutionary processes, but probably needs to be established by statistical data. In that case, though, the EHCH—in order to live up to Boorse's

[5] Consider, for instance, the central claim that the individual is the unit of selection. This issue is complex and controversial. Dawkins and others have maintained that the gene must be the unit of selection, while others have argued in favor of group-level selection. Kirmeyer notes that it might even be that our very idea of individual units of selection is culturally biased: "we tend to think of adaptation in terms of individuals rather than groups because of the individualistic bias of Euro-American societies, and we are less likely to recognize and give central place to functions whose main purpose may be intragroup harmony rather than individual fitness" (Kirmeyer 1994, p. 19).

commitment to naturalism—cannot merely rely on evolution, and is then likely to run into the same challenges that Boorse's account faces.

Another difficulty with understanding health in terms of homeostasis is linked to the question of whether we can reliably establish that a primary goal of an organism is to work toward maintaining homeostasis. To get some idea of the complications inherent in such a view, it is helpful to remember that in the case of human beings, homeostasis clearly involves both physiological and psychological dimensions. Yet on the EHCH it remains entirely unclear how we should grasp homeostatic processes in psychological systems. It can hardly mean that in a healthy psychological system, be it our belief system or our emotional life, there could be no frictions, instabilities, or contradictions. Certainly, when dissonances between our fundamental beliefs become very substantial, we might say that we are experiencing a deep ambiguity about our goals in life and possibly a personal crisis that might for a period even diminish our reproductive abilities. Nevertheless, undergoing such a personal crisis would hardly amount to having a disease.

To recapitulate, this chapter has focused on a naturalist view that does not operate with the notion of natural kinds, but holds instead that diseases involve a deviation from the proper physiological or psychological functioning of parts of the organism. Diseases are simply failures of *natural function*, while the malfunctioning can be distinguished from proper functioning by a scientific, value-neutral investigation. This position has a number of variants, and we have so far investigated the BST, which combines biological function and statistical normality, and the EHCH, which understands health in terms of homeostasis. In fact, since the EHCH relies on evolutionary explanations, it provides a useful bridge to the next account we shall consider, which was originally developed by Jerome Wakefield.

8. Wakefield and the HD account

During the last two decades, Wakefield has made a significant contribution to the debates about mental disorder and the theoretical foundations of psychiatry by putting forward a naturalist account of mental disorder as "harmful dysfunction" (HD). Just like Boorse, Wakefield claims that his account applies to physical as well as mental disorders (Wakefield 1992, 1999a, 1999b, 2007, 2010).[6] In addition, Wakefield's motivation (again much like that of Boorse) is closely related to discussions about the scientific nature of medicine and

[6] Wakefield refers to disease as dysfunction. In order to maintain a certain continuity of concepts, I shall continue to use the term "disease."

psychiatry. As Wakefield notes, "a central goal of an analysis of 'mental disorder' is to clarify and reveal the degree of legitimacy in psychiatry's claims to be a truly medical discipline rather than, as anti-psychiatrists and others have claimed, a social control institution masquerading as a medical discipline" (Wakefield 2007, p. 150). For Wakefield, this is crucial because:

> The claim of psychiatry to be a medical discipline depends on there being genuine mental disorders in the same sense of "disorder" that is used in physical medicine. Any proposal to define "mental disorder" in a way unique to psychiatry that does not fall under the broader medical concept of disorder would fail to address this issue. Part of the challenge in resolving this issue is that the medical concept of disorder is itself subject to ongoing dispute. The HD analysis is aimed at addressing this challenge.
>
> (Wakefield 2007, p. 150)

Wakefield argues that a naturalistic account is called for as current diagnostic criteria include many conditions that do not qualify as genuine mental disorders (Wakefield 1999b; see also Horwitz and Wakefield 2007; Wakefield 2010). While using the idea of natural function as informed by evolutionary theory, HD is a "hybrid" theory that combines a factual term (dysfunction) with a value-laden term (harm), attempting to bridge the gap between naturalist and constructivist positions. Thus, in contrast to Boorse, Wakefield accepts a value-laden component in addition to the factual component. In fact, Wakefield (2010) criticizes Boorse for failing to address the value-laden component. Also in contrast to Boorse, Wakefield embraces an evolutionary account of natural functions—that is, the psychological subsystems that constitute a human being were naturally selected to perform certain functions, and such natural functions are objectively discoverable. Wakefield has influentially argued that a condition should be considered to be a disease if and only if that condition "causes some harm or deprivation of benefit to the person as judged by the standards of the person's culture" (Wakefield 1992, p. 385). For instance, assuming that it is correct that dyslexia involves a dysfunction in the corpus callosum resulting in the inability to learn, this condition is harmful only in literate societies where reading is a valued ability (Wakefield 2007, 2010). Accordingly, in preliterate societies, this dysfunction does not qualify as a disorder.

With this move Wakefield creates a "hybrid" definition that tries to bridge the gap between the previously incompatible positions—that is, the social-constructivist position that understood mental disorder as a value-laden social construct and the position that defined mental disorders as natural entities to be understood in biological terms (Jablensky 2007; Varga 2011a):

> I have proposed a hybrid account, the "harmful dysfunction" (HD) analysis of the concept of mental disorder. According to the HD analysis, a disorder is a harmful

> dysfunction, where "harmful" is a value term, referring to conditions judged negative by sociocultural standards, and "dysfunction" is a scientific factual term.
>
> (Wakefield 2007, p. 149)

> A condition is a disorder if and only if (a) the condition causes some harm or deprivation of benefit to the person as judged by the standards of the person's culture (the value criterion), and (b) the condition results from the inability of some internal mechanism to perform its natural function, wherein a natural function is an effect that is part of the evolutionary explanation of the existence and structure of the mechanism (the explanatory criterion).
>
> (Wakefield 1992, p. 384)

We find two distinct but interrelated claims here. First, Wakefield maintains that it is the factual malfunctioning of an internal mechanism that causes dysfunction, which is something that can be established objectively. Second, Wakefield claims that the social definition of "harm" depends on the cultural context. He acknowledges that there is no precise or crisp boundary between disorder and non-disorder, and disorder has areas of fuzziness and vagueness (Wakefield 2010, p. 278). However, while it might be impossible to draw a clear boundary between disorder and non-disorder, he wants to argue that there is a meaningful distinction between clear cases of disorder and non-disorder. For instance, the fact that there is no precise boundary between being a child and being an adult does not mean that there are no clear cases of being a child and of being an adult. As he points out, "boundary setting sometimes in part involves values, and is very sensitive to current social views and knowledge" (Wakefield 2010, p. 278). Different age limits for voting, driving, and drinking show that the boundaries between childhood and adulthood are set differently in different areas, reflecting value-laden conventional choices.

While Wakefield proposes a hybrid construction, he nevertheless remains objectivist about natural function. This is possible as he holds both that the psychological subsystems that constitute a human being were naturally selected to perform certain functions and that natural functions are objectively discoverable. Against such a background, he proposes that dysfunctions should be defined as failures of internal mechanisms to perform functions for which they were naturally selected. He restates his point, adding that "in modern science, 'dysfunction' is ultimately anchored in evolutionary biology and refers to failure of an internal mechanism to perform one of its naturally selected functions" (Wakefield 2007, p. 149). Thus while he accepts that for a condition to be a disorder it is necessary that the dysfunction is harmful, he claims that there has to be an evolutionary dysfunction in order for a condition to qualify as a disease. To reiterate, whether the dysfunction causes significant harm to the person determines whether or not that dysfunction can be classified as a disorder (Wakefield 2010, p. 284).

9. Conceptual analysis and the HD

Wakefield's account is "hybrid" in the sense that he incorporates both value and scientific criteria, which seems like an attractive alternative, particularly insofar as it has been able to demonstrate problems with both constructivist and naturalist views. In a similar way to the BST, Wakefield's HD relies on conceptual analysis. However, in contrast to Boorse, Wakefield is driven by a different idea about the epistemic authority about disease. Instead of being persuaded that we are warranted in assuming that the concept of disease used in pathology "carves nature at its joints," Wakefield seems to think that there is an overarching concept of disease that we can appeal to:

> I approach this problem via a conceptual analysis that asks: what do we mean when we say that a problematic mental condition, such as adolescent antisocial behavior, a child's defiant behavior toward a parent, intense sadness, intense worry, intense shyness, failure to learn to read, or heavy use of illicit drugs, is not merely a form of normal, albeit undesirable and painful, human functioning, but indicative of psychiatric disorder? The credibility and even the coherence of psychiatry as a medical discipline depends on there being a persuasive answer to this question. The answer requires an account of the concept of disorder that generally guides such judgments.
>
> (Wakefield 2007, p. 149)

While Wakefeld here provides the first argument for the necessity of a conceptual analysis, he is well aware that more needs to be said to justify this methodological choice. Indeed, to support his conceptual analysis, Wakefield puts forward interesting arguments that proceed in several steps. There are three arguments at stake, which aim to render it plausible that there is a factual component in our concept of disorder.

(1) *Common conceptual ground.* Wakefield argues that experts and "the folk" regularly discriminate between negative conditions in terms of disorders and non-disorders. As he maintains, "the concept of 'disorder' has been around in physical medicine and applied to some mental conditions for millennia and is broadly understood by lay people and professionals" (Wakefield 2010, p. 287). For instance, intense sadness in connection with grief is in most cases perceived as normal, whereas equally deep sadness is seen as disordered if it is not initiated by loss. Wakefield's point is that a "purely value-based account of 'disorder' does not explain such distinctions among negative conditions" (Wakefield 2010, p. 287).

(2) *Modification of values.* Wakefield points out that in the light of cross-cultural evidence we sometimes modify our views of disorder even if this goes against our own values. To support this point, Wakefield cites the example of polygamy, arguing that although US culture does not value polygamy, partly on the basis of cross-cultural data, Americans do not think that it involves a failure of natural functioning and, hence, do not regard it as a disorder.

(3) *The possibility of being mistaken.* Wakefield takes seriously the widely held idea that diagnosis is misemployed in case it is applied in order to achieve a discrediting political labeling (e.g. drapetomania, Soviet dissidents): "Finally, the possibility that even an entire culture may be mistaken about disorder … suggests that the concept has at least some factual or objective component that is more than simply a value judgment" (Wakefield 2010, p. 286).

For Wakefield, steps (1) to (3) establish that there is more to the concept of mental disorder than just social values, and that the concept entails a factual component (dysfunction). It is against such a background that conceptual analysis is justified, and the HD aims to elucidate and explain the nature of the factual component of dysfunction. Nevertheless, there are some difficulties associated with this argument for conceptual analysis.

(1) In contrast to the BST, epistemic authority in HD is ascribed to both laypeople and experts. An important assumption, which Wakefield presents as an observation, is that the concept of "disorder" is sufficiently stable and used in similar ways by professionals and the "folk" (Wakefield 1992, p. 374; Wakefield 2010). Boorse would clearly disagree with this, and perhaps reasonably so. Recall the examples of *microdontia, supernumerary teeth*, and *taurodontism* from our earlier discussion. Although they are listed as diseases (dysfunctions) and disorders in the professional literature, it is very unlikely that the layperson would regard such conditions as pathological. Therefore if Wakefield, in contrast to Boorse, attributes equal amount of epistemic authority to the laypeople and the professionals, the whole analysis is unlikely to produce solid results. It is far from clear whether the term "carves nature at its joints" or whether professionals and the "folk" operate with the same concept. In fact if the concept of disorder entails dysfunction, and if dysfunction is to be understood in evolutionary terms, then it is difficult to see how laypeople could be attributed epistemic authority here. However, Wakefield could in principle address this concern by, just like Boorse, restricting the HD to the professionals. The claim would be that the defining of mental disorder should be approached via

a conceptual analysis of the term used by experts, which will give us the concept's meaning and extension. As we have seen with the BST, the whole undertaking is only interesting if we simultaneously assume that the way we use the term does not merely reflect the expert's practices and conventions, but is "natural"—that is, epistemologically insightful, "carving nature at its joints." At this point, we leap into the whole host of problems about epistemic authority that we have analyzed in the BST.

(2) Wakefield wants to convince us of the existence of an objective component, by saying that while American culture does not value polygamy, it does not consider it to be a disorder, *because of the lack of failure of natural functioning*. First, it seems rather unlikely that the "folk" in particular would operate with concepts that track underlying fine-grained phenomena known from evolutionary biology. Second, even if this were the case, we might argue that the fact that there is a correlation does not warrant the inference to a causal relationship.

(3) Wakefield wants to claim that *since our intuitions tell us* that an entire culture may be mistaken about disorder, we should assume the existence of a factual or objective component in the notion of disorder, which is dysfunction. But the fact that an entire culture might be mistaken about calling condition X a disorder does not mean that the corrective judgment that X is not a disorder is grounded on or made possible by an underlying objective component. As it stands, the HD does not exclude the possibility that such judgments are entirely value determined.

Overall, Wakefield wants to justify conceptual analysis by demonstrating that the concept of mental disorder involves both values and a factual component (dysfunction). It is against such a background that the HD aims to elucidate and explain the nature of the factual component of dysfunction. However, the three points that Wakefield puts forward in support of the methodological choice fail to demonstrate that the concept of mental disorder actually involves an objective component (dysfunction).

10. **HD and evolution**

The success of the proposal to define mental disorder via a conceptual analysis of the term used by experts hinges on—among other factors—whether there is significant agreement among the experts. Here one might argue that the relevant experts are those who deal with the analysis of diseases in terms of knowledge from evolutionary theory.

During the last few decades, evolutionary theory has been increasingly seen as a valuable framework for explaining both individual behaviors and social structures (Nesse 1984).[7] While few dispute that the human mind has been shaped by evolution (Cosmides and Tooby 1987, 2000), it is not surprising that evolutionary theory has begun to inform psychiatry's attempts to understand and explain psychopathology, resulting in the field of "evolutionary psychiatry" (MacLean 1985). Possibly helped by a growing dissatisfaction with the reductionist views inherent in many biological approaches to psychiatry, recent years have witnessed increased general interest in the application of evolutionary theory to issues in psychopathology (Nesse and Williams 1995; McGuire and Troisi 1998; Stevens and Price 2000). As Nettle (2004) has noted, there has been a genuine "adaptive turn" in psychology and psychiatry, and evolutionary explanations are being proposed to explain an increasing number of aspects of psychopathologies. Evolutionarily informed researchers have been surprised to discover that numerous mental disorders seem to have a genetic basis, while they occur at prevalence rates that are too high to be explained by mutations. Seen from an evolutionary viewpoint, high prevalence rates reveal that the genetic bases of these mental disorders have been promoted by natural selection. Another appealing aspect of the approach is that evolutionary psychiatry is at least potentially able to identify not only proximate but also ultimate causes.[8]

---

[7] The work of Hamilton (1964) and Wilson (1975) has managed to address the unanswered problems that haunted the original Darwinian account, leading to development of the study of behaviors informed by evolutionary theory into an independent discipline. Further propelling this development was the idea of a "modular mind," originally developed by Jerry Fodor (1983). According to this theory, the human mind is composed of numerous separate but interconnected "modules," which are assigned to different information-processing tasks, such as grammar induction, face recognition, etc. (Tooby and Cosmides, 1995; Gerrans 2002).

Mental modules are genetically specified adaptations (Cosmides and Tooby 2000; Fodor 2000) to solve the problems that faced our ancestors (Tooby and Cosmides 1995, p. xiii; Murphy and Stich 2000). They are thus adaptations and domain-specific computational devices with specific purposes.

[8] Whereas *proximate* causes merely explain a process or a structure in an individual organism, *ultimate* (evolutionary) causes provide a bigger picture, as they explain a process or a structure in all members of a species. For instance, the question might be "What causes depression?" A proximate cause could be given by maintaining that specific imbalances in brain chemistry or particular combinations of environmental precipitants result in a depressive episode. Conversely, an ultimate cause could be given with an explanation of the evolutionary function of depression, and hence the way in which this ability has improved survival or reproductive possibilities in the process of natural selection. Thus, although psychiatry has mainly focused on proximate explanations, some of the most appealing aspects in the application of evolutionary principles to psychiatric phenomena are richer explanations, and the possibility of a "bigger picture"

With regard to applications of evolutionary theory to psychopathology, three types of explanation can be distinguished (Murphy 2005; Varga 2011b). A *breakdown explanation* understands mental disorder as the malfunction of some component of the mind or brain in fulfilling its evolutionary function. A *mismatch explanation* understands mental disorder as connected to mechanisms that were once adaptive but are no longer so because of changes in the environment. Thus the pathology lies not in some subsystem of an individual, but in the mismatch between the ancestral environment and our current environment. The more controversial *persistence explanation* holds that some putative disorders qualify as adaptive even in the present environment.

In Sections 10.1 and 10.2, the mismatch and persistence accounts in psychiatry are outlined. The discussion is limited to depression, both because there has been a considerable amount of work on the subject and because the condition has been prevalent throughout history. Whereas the *breakdown explanation* would support the HD, the so-called *mismatch and persistence* explanation would oppose it. Both mismatch and persistence explanations start out from two common assumptions. First, the fact that depression has been prevalent throughout history is seen to be appropriate to investigations of its evolutionary origins. Second, both explanations build on the idea that the mechanisms or devices that are activated in depression evolved to manage hostile situations in which flight was impossible. From here, the two accounts part ways. The point of exploring these accounts is that if either the mismatch explanation or the persistence explanation of depression is true, then the HD is wrong.

10.1. The persistence explanation

According to the persistence explanation, it is argued by researchers such as Price et al. (1994), Hagen (1999), and Watson and Andrews (2002) that alleged psychopathologies such as depression represent adaptive behavioral strategies and function adaptively in the present environment, as they did in the ancestral environment. The fact that distinctive features of depression have been shown to exist almost worldwide (Kohrt et al., 2005; Hadley

that provides a platform for integrating the diverse levels. That said, it might be more precise to use the term "quasi-proximate explanation." Maintaining that an imbalance at brain level causes something at a mental level only qualifies as an explanation if, like some biologically oriented psychiatrists, one embraces an epiphenomenalist outlook. However, from the point of view of physicalism, which has become the consensus view in philosophy, identifying a proximate cause involves identifying a physical reason for brain-level imbalance.

and Patil 2008; Patil and Hadley 2008), and that there is a higher prevalence of depression in Western societies (Patel 2001; Horwitz and Wakefield 2007), is considered to support the persistence view. Importantly, in opposition to Wakefield, the authors consider depression to involve impairment, but maintain that *impairment can be caused by appropriately functioning defense mechanisms*. In order to secure the best allocation of resources to different systems that deal with adaptive challenges, particular stressors trigger evolved stress response mechanisms. Negative emotions constitute good examples of the activation of stress response mechanisms, which then coordinate bodily and cognitive resources to manage the task (LeDoux 1996; Cosmides and Tooby 2000). Such mechanisms can also generate impairments when responding to a particular stressor. Fever might be perceived as an impairment in multiple domains, reducing metabolism, sexual activity, and social activity, for example, although it is an adaptation that evolved to increase fitness by a specific immune system response (Hasday et al. 2000). In much the same way, depression impairs a wide range of life aspects—it is aversive and disruptive, and in many senses it interrupts normal function. Therefore, at first sight, it is difficult not to regard it as a maladaptation. However, one might argue that a brief look at a wide array of our functional capacities, such as experiencing fatigue, nausea, or pain, reveals that it is precisely the aversive and disruptive character of such capacities that is the key to their adaptive capacity—it is their disruptive character that helps us to avoid potentially dangerous and fitness-decreasing situations. Following the same path of thought, Darwin (1859/2003, p. 431) himself considered depression to be an adaptive function.

However, an adequate answer about the status of depression can only be given when considering the situations in which its various characteristics offer fitness advantages. Stevens and Price (2000) maintain that certain forms of depression are conceivable as constructive human responses to situations in which a desired social goal is unachievable. This view gains some additional credence from the fact that depression is common in people who are pursuing unattainable goals and who fail to yield, for example, in the domain of status competition (Davis 1970; Nesse 2000). In addition, depression can become more severe and chronic when individuals remain committed to poor pay-off goals and tasks that they cannot fulfill (McGuire and Troisi 1987; Leahy 2000). Proponents of the persistence view of depression have proposed that the distress and the down-regulation of positive affect systems that characterize depression may push the depressed individual to re-evaluate and then abandon impossible undertakings that have become overly habitual. In this case, depression would be an adaptive response to social circumstances, enhancing our ability to navigate in the social context.[9] Thus depressive pessimism, down-regulation of positive affect, diminished responsiveness, and lack of motivation may be seen as conserving resources, as they foster disengagement from unachievable goals, the pursuit of which would eventually exhaust and harm the individual.

The *analytical rumination hypothesis*, which was proposed by Andrews and Thompson (2009), points in the same direction. It is widely acknowledged that depression causes specific impairments, such as maladaptive cognitions (Beck and Alford 2009) and "depressive rumination" (recyclic negative thinking which is resistant to distraction), which are considered to be important in the development, maintenance, and relapse or recurrence of depression (Treynor et al. 2003), and difficult to suppress (Nolen-Hoeksema 1991; Wenzlaff and Luxton 2003). In contrast, Andrews and Thompson (2009) aim to explain the cognitive impairments associated with depression by hypothesizing that depression is an evolved stress response mechanism and that depressive rumination has a beneficial cognitive effect. Their hypothesis holds that natural selection has promoted specific behaviors and cognitive patterns that force individuals to withdraw when facing complex social problems and to abandon certain formerly pleasurable and even fitness-increasing activities (Andrews and Thompson 2009, p. 623). The withdrawal from activities and commitments to depressive rumination enables the depressed individual to engage in a profound analysis of the triggering problems. The adaptive aspect of depressive rumination is that it assists problem solving before the individual re-engages in social activities and commitments. Crucially, the authors claim that depressive rumination provides adequate cognitive means of solving difficult analytical problems—sufficient to compensate for the substantial costs (Andrews and Thompson 2009, p. 643).

Supporting this view, adopting an adaptationist stance on postpartum depression, Hagen (1999) has maintained that depressed mothers receive more care from both their partner and their social network. In their *social navigation hypothesis*, Watson and Andrews (2002) extend this idea to depression in general, and argue that depressive responses have the function

[9] D.A. Hamburg, an early exponent of this view, has summarized the possible functions of depression, maintaining that in a situation where the individual estimates that the probability of achieving a goal is very low, "the depressive responses can be viewed as adaptive" because "feelings of sadness and discouragement may be a useful stimulus to consider ways of changing (the) situation" (Hamburg 1974, p. 240). For instance, against the background of the mismatch thesis and the work of Nesse (1999) we could speculate that there is a link between growing globalization (and hence growing peer groups) and the increase in the incidence of depression over the last few decades.

of achieving a revitalizing of social relationships. Not only do disinterest in normal fitness-related activities, anhedonia, and psychomotor perturbation impose costs on the depressed individual, but also social partners are aware of the costs imposed on them when a partner is depressed (Segrin and Dillard 1992). Understanding the benefits of avoiding escalating costs, partners in the depressive individual's social network are forced to make "investments" that they would hesitate to make under normal circumstances. In addition to specific partners, depression also motivates the entire social network and functions as something like an extortive mechanism that aims to overcome network members' reluctance to help (Hagen 1999). The fact that there is overwhelming empirical evidence that individuals who are in conflict with significant peers are more likely to become depressed seems to at least partly support the persistence position. For instance, while interpersonal conflict is commonly associated with depression (Hammen 1992), it is striking that in unhappily married people the risk of major depression is about 40 times higher than in happily married ones (Weissman 1987). Overall, even if depression might cause abandonment and sometimes lead to social deterioration, the main idea underlying the social navigation hypothesis is that depression has evolved to serve a social motivation function.

10.2. The mismatch explanation of depression

The basic assumption made by proponents of the mismatch explanation of depression is that numerous pertinent characteristics of the human mind evolved in hunter-gatherer societies that existed around the Pleistocene period (Glantz and Pearce 1989; Cosmides and Tooby 1999). Stevens and Price (2000) emphasize that the human mind broadly consists of hierarchically organized systems of very different evolutionary ages, including "reptilian," "paleo-mammalian" (limbic system), and "neo-mammalian" (cerebral neocortex) systems. The core of their proposal is that whereas our ancestors adapted to the hunting and gathering environment, which predisposed them to behave in ways that were adaptive in that environment, those evolved patterns now promote psychopathological conditions (Baptista et al. 2008). Psychopathology arises in response to a *mismatch* between behavioral, cognitive, and affective predispositions and the current environment with its completely different social settings. As Glantz and Pearce (1989, p. 112) state, "when culture strays too far from biology, it also moves away from sanity." Price et al. (1994), Nesse and Williams (1995), and Gilbert (2006) argue that depression should be understood as an evolved, adaptive response to specific problems that arose in the small, status-oriented social group of our ancestors. The mismatch explanation of depression builds on a set of interlocking arguments that have been put forward by several proponents. However, two main strands of argument can be distinguished that understand depression as adaptive responses for (1) the abandonment of unrealistic goals and (2) the acceptance of social defeat.

(a) It has been suggested that forms of depression assist the restoration of exhausted resources by pushing the individual to withdraw (Schmale 1973). Characteristic and well-known symptoms of depression, such as psychomotor retardation, are considered to be good examples in this context. Nesse (2000) and Nesse and Williams (1995) propose that depression helps to maximize pay-offs by aiding the adjustment of resource allocation to activities. The characteristic sense of lack of capability to fulfill tasks, pessimism, behavioral inactivity, and the well-documented exaggerated interpretation of the difficulty of tasks, prevents the depressive individual from allocating resources to demanding activities with a low probability of success (Sloman et al. 2003). Similarly, Stevens and Price (2000) argue that certain forms of depression are considered to be constructive human responses to situations in which a desired social goal seems impossible to achieve. Recall that it has long been established that depression is common in people who are pursuing unattainable goals and who fail to yield, for example, in the domain of status competition (Davis 1970; Nesse 2000). Thus, in such cases, the distress and the down-regulation of positive affect systems that characterize depression may push the depressed individual to re-evaluate and abandon impossible undertakings. In this sense, depression could be seen as a limiting defense mechanism that could help the individual to disengage from impossible undertakings that have become such a matter of habit that under normal circumstances it would be unfeasible for the person to abandon them. Importantly, for the mismatch theorists the evolved capacity that has functioned as a defense mechanism for enabling disengagement from impossible undertakings now causes conflicts that lead to mental disorders.

(b) The *social rank theory* of depression (Gilbert 1992, 2000) links involuntary subordination to depression and builds on research on the regulators of mood in dominant and subordinate animals in the context of social conflict (Price 1972; Price and Sloman 1987). A central claim is that depression-like states occur in animals and humans who have been defeated and lost rank. More specifically, depression is an adaptive response to the loss of status in such small social groups, which helps the individual to accept their lowered rank once they have lost status (Price et al. 1994; Stevens and Price 2000). Once an individual has been outcompeted, it is of advantage to them to self-evaluate, ruminate upon their weaknesses, and alter their previous behaviors. The idea is that depressed mood helps the individual to accept status loss and motivates them to alter their previous behaviors in order to ameliorate their reproductive chances.[10]

Overall, although such an adaptive response might have been a fruitful strategy resulting in social success in ancient societies organized around small groups, in contemporary life with more sizeable group units, this affect-lowering response to change in status is clearly a *mismatch* (Nesse and Williams 1995). This is not just because the inherited mechanism is no longer adaptive, and now fails to accomplish the goal it was selected to achieve due to a radically changed social setting, but because, in our contemporary social context, it results in inappropriate activation of an affect-lowering response, which is not only an ineffective reaction, but is also inhibiting and decreases fitness.

10.3. Mismatch, persistence, and exaptations

The mismatch and persistence models specifically apply evolutionary theory to depression, provide useful explanations of single aspects of depression, and might develop into promising research platforms. There are objections to both theories,[11] but in the context of our goals here they need not concern

[10] In order to support their argument, some accounts make use of the links between serotonin, social rank, and depression. It has been established that in a sizeable subpopulation of depressive individuals, serotonin levels are abnormally low. In addition, the level of serotonin seems to be correlated with negative self-assessment and pessimism. Moreover, Meyer et al. (2003) have shown that increasing the serotonin levels in healthy individuals reduces such dysfunctional attitudes. Furthermore, when animals change their position in a power hierarchy, their behavioral changes are accompanied by changes in serotonin levels (Kravitz 2000; Drummond et al. 2002). The recourse to research on serotonin is supposed to additionally underpin the central thesis of the social rank theory of depression, namely that depression is both a mechanism that is triggered when an individual is outcompeted and a means of helping them to accept their lower status and of motivating them to change their current behavior to improve their reproductive chances. Status-degraded monkeys display lowered levels of serotonin, and it seems that the stress of the new lower social rank produces a down-regulation of serotonin levels (Grant et al. 1998; McGuire and Troisi 1998; Shively 1999).

[11] I have voiced several concerns about both the mismatch and the persistence accounts (Varga 2011b). For instance, the mismatch theory does not address the individual and social factors. The proponents of the mismatch theory of depression would need to show that those individuals on the international job market who are taking part in global competition would be more vulnerable to depression. Yet it is well known that socio-economic deprivation is linked to a high prevalence of mental illness, such as depression (Thornicroft et al. 1992; Acheson,1998), and many studies have shown that higher rates of depression are associated with lower socio-economic status (Bebbington

us. The point is rather that if either of them turn out to be true, then the HD is false. Now surely the persistence and mismatch explanations could both turn out to be false, and in fact they both exhibit several flaws (Varga 2011b). However, we should recall that the reason for invoking these increasingly popular explanations was to get an idea of how experts think about dysfunctions and disorders in relation to evolutionary theory. On the one hand, the mismatch explanation of depression challenges the HD, because it shows that the depressive responses can be seen as the result of systems performing the functions for which they originally evolved, but in a mismatched context. Thus it would show that there could be a disorder without a dysfunction—the experts in question clearly think that depression is a disorder, but, instead of speaking about a dysfunction, they focus on the mismatch between the evolved response pattern and the current environment. On the other hand, the persistence explanation of depression challenges the HD but in a slightly more complex way. According to the persistence explanation, depression both functions adaptively in the present environment (as it did in the ancestral one) *and* can be identified as a disorder.[12]

In closing this chapter, we may wish to add another challenge to the HD from an evolutionary point of view. Just like the persistence and mismatch explanations, the HD claims that important systems (mental and physical) were most probably designed by evolution to perform a specific function. However, this claim needs to be significantly modified, as a number of systems cannot be viewed as selected, fitness-increased adaptations, but rather

et al. 1981; Kessler et al. 1994; Stansfeld et al. 1998), and with area deprivation (Eachus et al. 1996), unemployment (Meltzer et al. 1995), and employment grade (Stansfeld and Marmot 1992). Thus, contrary to the point of the mismatch theory of depression, it seems that underprivileged and unemployed individuals who typically do not take part in global competition in the international job market are more vulnerable to depression. This individual aspect is much better integrated in the persistence account, where both concrete individual factors and complex social problems come into play. However, this theory fails to demonstrate that depressive rumination promotes productive analysis. Nevertheless, data on depressive rumination suggest that rumination actually maintains and even exacerbates depression (Nolen-Hoeksema 1991)—it impairs problem-solving capacities, hinders instrumental behavior, and undermines social support. In general, people who engage in rumination are more prone to developing depressive disorders and to experiencing prolonged periods of depression (Lyubomirsky and Nolen-Hoeksema 1993; Just and Alloy 1997; Nolan et al. 1998; Kuehner and Weber 1999; Lyubomirsky et al. 1999; Nolen-Hoeksema 2000; Donaldson and Lam 2004; Nolen-Hoeksema et al. 2005).

[12] To be precise, the authors tend to use the term "impairment." However, no reasons are given for thinking that "impairment" does not equal "disorder."

they might be "exaptations," which are not rare phenomena. In fact Dennett (1996) argued that since only a few functions remain constant, it makes sense to regard many adaptations as exaptations. Dennett finds it hard to clearly distinguish between exaptation and adaptation, arguing that if one goes back far enough one will see that every adaptation has developed from a predecessor structure with another or no use (Dennett 1996, p. 281). More support for such a view has been provided by recent scientific research. A very recent study on adaptations in metabolic systems published in *Nature* (Barve and Wagner 2013) concludes that these many metabolic traits have non-adaptive origins, which challenges our ability to distinguish adaptive from non-adaptive traits.

Bearing this in mind, let us consider relatively clear-cut cases of "exaptations." First, there are secondary adaptations, such as the feather system of birds. The feather system originally evolved to enable heat regulation in birds, and in a secondary process it became an instrument for flight. Such secondary exaptations have enhanced fitness at the point of their emergence, but might have subsequently taken on fitness-increasing functions that are different from their original functions. Given the definition of *dysfunction* as failure to fulfill the original function, the HD cannot deal with such secondary adaptations. The broken wing of a bird would not be regarded as a dysfunction, as it might still fulfill its original function as a heat regulator.[13]

Whereas the case of bird feathers is one in which fitness was originally enhanced, there are also *adaptively neutral exaptations*—that is, non-selected features that are merely by-products of adaptations that have not enhanced fitness at the point of their emergence. Gould (1991) has argued that large brain size originally developed as an adaptation for some functions in humans' ancestral past, and the sheer complexity of it produced many by-products. Thus the human brain "throws up spandrels by the thousands for each conceivable adaptation in its initial evolutionary restructuring" (Gould 1991, p. 58; see also Lilienfeld and Marino 1995; Dennett 1996, p. 279). Good examples of such adaptively neutral exaptations that are unlikely to be of direct relevance to increased fitness are, according to Gould's account, psychological capacities such as religion, reading, writing, fine arts, the norms of commerce, arithmetic ability, music, and motor skills. More precisely, it has since been argued that these exaptations might be indirect, domain-general consequences of natural selection, such as general intelligence (Falk 1992; Tooby

[13] Certainly, if one modified the account so that it only referred to current design, then it could accommodate secondary adaptations. However, such a move would raise a host of other concerns—for instance, about the right timescale for establishing what should count as "current design."

and Cosmides 1992). The accommodation of such exaptations is a problematic issue for the HD. Consider, for example, people with *congenital amusia*, which is an established learning disability for music, a deficit that appears to be highly specific to the musical domain (Ayotte et al. 2002). Affected individuals are unable to discriminate the pitch of two successive tones, to recognize familiar melodies, or to remember a tune. Now, according to the HD, amusia would not count as a disorder, as the impaired function is not the outcome of evolution.[14]

Overall, it seems that dysfunction in evolutionary terms is simply neither necessary nor sufficient for disorder. Without modifications, the HD cannot accommodate *adaptively neutral exaptations* and *mismatches* (mechanisms that were once adaptive, but are no longer adequate due to environmental changes). The upshot of this discussion is that, in general, it is not the case that a disease unavoidably involves evolutionary dysfunction. If one is to hold on to an evolutionarily informed account of dysfunction and mental disorder, one must identify the characteristic selection pressures of the time period when a certain function is considered to be adaptive. As we have seen, the same condition might fulfill a function at a time with particular selection pressures, and at a later point in time it might be a mismatched dysfunction.

11. **Conclusion**

This rather lengthy chapter has dealt with *natural function naturalism*—that is, a naturalist approach to defining disease. In order to objectively identify a particular condition as a disease or dysfunction, proponents of this approach draw on the notion of *natural function*, embracing the idea that no value-dependent evaluations are needed to settle whether something is dysfunctional. This chapter has critically engaged with two main forms of natural function naturalism, which understand the "naturalness" of natural functions in different ways. Interestingly, the motivation of both the BST and the HD was to make the ethically and politically laden discussion of health and disease more scientific by proposing an objective, value-free definition of health and disease. Another similarity between the BST and the HD is that they both to varying degrees rely on conceptual analysis. Much of the criticism discussed in this chapter concerns methodological issues relating to conceptual analysis and epistemic authority. However, a considerable amount

[14] Wakefield could respond that amusia is not itself a disorder, but a harmful effect of some hitherto undiscovered underlying dysfunction in the brain. In that case, Wakefield would be correct, given that he can also show that the undiscovered underlying dysfunction has been selected for that task.

of the discussion concerned the argument that the HD's subscribing to evolutionary theory results in major difficulties.

Finally, we might ask what really follows from the failure to provide a wholly naturalist definition of disease and mental disorder. We have to remember that the motivation for a naturalist definition and the idea (both BST and HD) of natural dysfunction as the proper domain of psychiatry emerged in a specific historical context when psychiatry was facing fierce criticism. Importantly, the basic assumption of both anti-psychiatry and natural function naturalism is a clear separation of natural (evolved and innate) and socially cultivated psychological functioning. However, as psychiatry no longer faces such harsh criticism (although this has not disappeared altogether), it might be time to revise this doubtful underlying dichotomy. New developments at the nexus of genetics and psychology, such as the growing emphasis on gene–environment interactions, indicate that psychological phenotypes are not merely evolved functions, nor are they created by environmental circumstances (including social ones) (Bolton 2008, pp. 272–276). Rather, they are the product of complex patterns of interaction between these. If this is the case, and current science is undermining the clear division between the natural (evolved) and the socio-cultural, then such a basic dichotomy presupposed by both sides of the anti-psychiatry debate as well as by the naturalist solutions to the debate must be revised.

Chapter 8

Having it both ways

Over the course of Chapters 6 and 7, the dynamic nature of the concept of mental disorder was highlighted. It seemed to resist any strict naturalistic attempt at definition, particularly in terms of necessary and sufficient conditions. One conclusion of the last two chapters could be that the leading naturalist approaches that attempt to define disease or disorder as a natural kind, a biostatistical fact, or evolutionary dysfunction all exhibit significant flaws and fail to provide an adequate definition. Against such a background, what should be our conclusion? Should we call into question the whole attempt to provide an objective (value-free) definition of health and disease? Some of the figures involved in the debate seem to think so. Invoking Wittgenstein, some argue that it is in principle impossible to provide necessary and sufficient conditions for membership of the category disease, and even more so for mental disorder. In his late work, Wittgenstein maintained that no necessary and sufficient conditions can be provided for certain concepts, such as "game." Rather, akin to members of a family, games are held together by a set of similarities, in the same way that while all members of a family will not share the same feature, any two members will be similar in at least one way. Scott Lilienfeld and Lori Marino have suggested that as mental disorder is characterized by the fact that it is in principle impossible to provide necessary and sufficient conditions for category membership, the criterion for a condition to qualify as a mental disorder should depend on grades of similarity to prototypical cases (Lilienfeld and Marino 1995). Thus it might be that "mental disorder" should be seen as a Wittgensteinian "family resemblance" concept (Mackinejad and Sharifi 2006). According to this view, it is not a set of necessary and sufficient properties, but rather global similarity to a prototype that determines membership. In the debate, many figures, such as Fulford (1999, p. 419), view the reference to prototypes as ducking difficult issues by opting out. It seems that many authors are caught in a logic which dictates that either a concept is objective (non-value-laden) or it is merely an inadequate hodgepodge. However, there is a group of influential researchers who reject some of these assumptions and provide fruitful analyses of the concept of mental disorder.

First of all, we should note that thus far we have accepted the commonly held view that posits a dichotomy between value-laden and value-neutral, scientific accounts. However, prominent figures who have shaped the debate for decades, such as Bill Fulford (Fulford 1989, 1991, 2005; Fulford et al. 2006), Tim Thornton (Thornton 2007), and George Graham (Graham 2010, 2013), reject such a simple dichotomy and the connected Szaszian claim that bodily illness is physiological and value-free, whereas mental disorder is normative. Instead they opt for what we may refer to as a "having it both ways" account. They accept that health and disorder entail values (Fulford 1989, 1999; Graham 2010, pp. 12, 92–95) and, hence, that the concept of mental disorder is value-laden, while simultaneously arguing that this is also the case for the concept of somatic disorder. As Graham (2010, p. 93) argues, we attribute somatic disease against the background of norms and standards of properly functioning parts of the body, and so "the notions of bodily health and physical well-being are evaluative or normative through and through." In general, the authors tend to appreciate the difference between the normativity involved in the standards that govern the attribution of bodily disease, such as hypertension or infection, and the normativity involved in the standards that govern the attribution of mental disorder. The latter is recognized as directly reflecting fundamentally contestable value judgments that are often moral and political in character. In other words, whereas in a diagnosis of a "bodily disorder" the values expressed by the value term "disease" or "disorder" are relatively widely agreed upon, they are much more divergent in the case of "mental disorders" (Fulford 1989; Fulford et al. 2006). Both physical and mental disorders are value-laden, but conditions that constitute physical diseases are often taken to be descriptive. Drawing on the work of R. M. Hare, Fulford notes that the value judgments implicit in value terms are sometimes made on the basis of descriptive criteria. To use Hare's example, the value judgment expressed by the statement "This is a good strawberry" is based on the descriptive criteria of the strawberry being "sweet, grub-free, etc." In such relatively straightforward cases in which there is a widely shared set of descriptive criteria for a value judgment (most people prefer sweet and grub-free strawberries), the descriptive criteria can govern and overshadow the use of the value term (Fulford et al. 2006, pp. 120–122; Fulford 1989). Therefore, in such unproblematic cases, value terms appear as descriptive terms. Conversely, value terms that express problematic, non-shared, contested values appear explicitly value-laden. Fulford (1989) uses this idea to analyze medical language and to argue that mental disorder is overtly value-laden, because psychiatry deals with the complex experiences, deep-seated desires, motives, and values that make us into the individuals whom we are (Thornton 2011).

The second aspect is linked to the view of the relationship between science and psychiatry. Far from being a sign of scientific deficiency, the value-ladenness of mental disorder is seen as a sign of the complexity of the values involved. Thus the view is that *we can have it both ways*—the concept of mental disorder is value-laden, but this does not mean that there can be no scientific account of mental disorder. In addition, it is claimed that the debate should not be between "values-in" and "values-out" accounts, but between reductionism and anti-reductionism. Thus the "having it both ways" view acknowledges that the concept of mental disorder is value-laden, while it simultaneously maintains that there are objective truths about mental disorder attributions. Starting from such shared ground, Graham (2010, 2013) and Thornton (2007) develop their positions in different ways.

1. Graham and the original position

Graham rejects the reduction of mental to neural impairment and argues that mental disorder, unlike neurological disorder, cannot be fully comprehended in "mechanistic" terms. Graham's realism involves maintaining that the language of somatic disease provided by brain science is inadequate to account for mental disorders, since these are characterized by the interactions between "brute, a-rational forces" and rational factors. Alzheimer's disease and Down's syndrome are neurological disorders, because a reference to intentionality and rationality is not part of "the best explanation" of their "origin, source or developmental propensity" (Graham 2010, p. 128). Therefore, in contrast to those who believe that the use of mental terms should be and/or will be replaced by non-mentalistic (neural, chemical, or other) descriptions, Graham (2010, pp. 7, 71, 129) argues that an adequate explanation of mental disorder must include reference both to neural mechanisms and to impaired rationality and reason-responsiveness.[1]

[1] This line of defense can be clarified by introducing a distinction between empirical and metaphysical skepticism. *Metaphysical skepticism* is the view that mental terms are *necessarily* part of an adequate explanation of mental disorders. *Empirical skepticism*, which has been embraced by Emil Kraepelin, Eugen Bleuler, and Wilhelm Griesinger, maintains that eventually mental disorders will be explained as distinct brain diseases. Their view became increasingly popular at the beginning of the twentieth century, as technological advances made it possible to prove that some mental disorders were caused by physical factors (such as the case of *general paresis*). While it may at times seem as if Graham wants to counter metaphysical skepticism, the arguments put forward only target empirical skepticism. Graham does not show that mental disorders are entities of a certain kind that are *necessarily* best understood in terms of reference to rationality and intentionality, but only that mental terms are *contingently* part of an adequate description of mental disorders. Suppose that, one day, strong evidence is discovered in favor of the view (as proposed recently) that inflammation plays a major causal role in the pathophysiology of depression. In that case, following Graham's account, we would have to redefine depression as a biological–neurological disorder that can be fully specified and understood in mechanistic terms.

Graham (2010, p. 21) rejects the idea that there could be necessary and sufficient conditions to define mental disorder, and he denies that mental disorder is a natural kind (Graham 2010, p. 58). However, he wants to salvage naturalism and disagrees with the view that vague and debatable boundaries make mental disorder a "catch-all concept" (Graham 2010, p. 22). First, he claims that mental disorders are "classificatory decision-independent" and that "there are facts of the matter as to whether someone is depressed, agoraphobic or deluded" (Graham 2010, p. 59). Nevertheless, Graham is committed to salvaging naturalism, and he argues that mental disorders have discoverable and objective standards and norms: "to qualify as a disorder a condition or disturbance must meet certain standards or norms. Success or failure in meeting such standards or norms also is discoverable" (Graham 2010, p. 10). This also means that Graham rejects positions in which mental disorders figure as socially constructed or merely reflect cultural conventions (Graham 2010, p. 108). Affirming "the existence of objective truths about mental disorder attributions and diagnoses" (Graham 2010, pp. 154, 9), Graham maintains that "there are facts of the matter as to whether someone is depressed" (Graham 2010, p. 59). Second, the naturalistic tenets are also tangible when Graham argues that mental disorder detects a clinically significant disability or impairment in rationality, not mere distress, performance lapse, error, or anything that is undesirable within a particular cultural horizon. Rather, mental disorders are "undesirable period—unwanted in any or virtually any context or cultural environment … no matter when or where we are" (Graham 2010, p. 113).

But how can one be a naturalist about the concept of mental disorder while admitting that the concept has such vague boundaries? Graham's response to this question is that a solid characterization of some entity can be extracted from *exemplary* applications. Taking this seriously, he argues in favor of a *prototypical account* of mental disorders, while holding on to naturalism—although mental disorders may have fuzzy boundaries, they have discoverable and objective standards and norms:

> Fortunately, there is another way in which to characterize mental disorder. … This is to recognize that the concept of a mental disorder has uncontroversial or prototypical instances of application or exemplars. An uncontroversial instance or exemplar is a case that *competent and informed observers or qualified judges agree* (or at least currently or widely agree) is a mental disorder.
>
> (Graham 2010, p. 26, added emphasis)

Thus Graham emphasizes the value of a prototype account but needs to delimit the range of potential prototype candidates. Drawing on anthropology, he first establishes a list of candidates for exemplary disorders (those that are not manifestly culture-bound, such as the Chinese railroad psychosis), a list that is additionally limited by taking into account international surveys and reports of the complaints that clinicians mostly deal with (Graham 2010, pp. 38–39). Although Graham admits that there is no perfect match between the lists, he goes on to suggest five heuristic general types of disorder, namely depression (including major depression and depression with mania), anxiety disorders (including phobias and some types of paranoia), disorders of incoherence (including delusional disorders), disorders of reactivity or impulse (including addiction or substance abuse), and some forms of mania and obsession (Graham 2010, p. 40).

This view is rich in details, but for our purposes here it is best to confine the discussion to an aspect that is fundamental to the whole account. According to Graham's account, mental disorder involves impairment that affects the reason-responsive operation of one or more *basic psychological capacities* (brought about by a combination of mental activity and neural mechanisms), resulting in harmful consequences for the individual. A condition is significant or serious enough to qualify as a mental disorder if there is an impairment occurring in a basic psychological capacity, the term "basic" being used to refer to "something without which it is difficult, and indeed in most cases, impossible to lead *a decent or personally satisfying life*" (Graham 2010, pp. 131–132, emphasis added). It is apparent that the notions of a "basic psychological capacity" and "a decent or personally satisfying life" are at the core of the proposal, and providing support for these key concepts will be decisive for the overall credibility of the account.

Graham obtains a list of *basic psychological capacities* by using Rawls' famous thought experiment. He argues that basic mental capacities are like "primary goods" that everyone would choose without having knowledge about their social status, talents, and abilities, and their the idea of "the good life." Rawls assumes that individuals in the "original position" would nonetheless strive to advance some interests and exhibit a preference for more rather than fewer primary goods. Graham's list of what we could call "primary psychological goods" includes the ability to locate oneself bodily/spatially and historically/temporally, the ability to comprehend self and world, and the ability to communicate, to engage emotionally, to assume self-responsibility, and to make decisions (Graham 2010, pp. 147–149). With the list of "primary psychological goods" in place, Graham presents his prototypical definition of mental disorder:

> The concept of a mental disorder, prototypically understood and regimentally clarified, is the concept of a (i) (rationality-disability thesis) disability, incapacity or

> impairment in the rational or reason-responsive operation or exercise of one or more fundamental mental faculties or basic psychological capacities of a person, that (ii) (harm thesis) causes harmful or potentially harmful symptoms/consequences for the person (and perhaps also for others). The disability also possesses a special sort of source, genesis or set of propensity conditions. It is (iii) (mixed-source thesis) brought about by a balance or mix of intentionalistic activity, on the one hand, and brute a-rational neural causes or mechanisms, on the other, and (iv) (some preservation of rationality thesis) the combination or intersection of such activities infuses a mental disorder with a truncated 'logic' or compromised rationale of its own, i.e., when a capacity is impaired or disabled in a mental disorder it is compromised in its reason-responsive operation but not destroyed. (The incapacitation or impairment—which, remember, is subject to contextual parameters—is not an obliteration of reason or reason-responsiveness.)
>
> (Graham 2010, p. 156)

Graham's approach is subtle, and the scope of the claims is very reasonable. In addition, he is well aware that the list of capacities and the notion of the "decent life" are vague. Rather than claiming that the impairment or partial disabling of one of the basic psychological capacities directly leads to disorder, he merely claims that it "raises the risks or likelihood of harm or losses of freedom" necessary for a decent life (Graham 2010, p. 150; Graham 2013, p. 160). Further limiting possible objections, Graham also distinguishes a "decent life" from a "flourishing life," arguing that only impairments that put at risk the possibility of living a "decent life" count as determining factors with regard to mental disorders. Nevertheless, there is also a more firm and universal claim in that the list of capacities is understood as "general capacities or competencies that we and other persons are bound to value and need" (Graham 2013, p. 157).[2]

1.1. The problem of being either too definite or too vague

A considerable number of books and articles have been devoted at least partially to Rawls' central ideas, and many of them contain critical comments. At this point, only those issues that are directly relevant to our discussion will be considered. Recall that Rawls (1971) invites us to imagine the original position under "the veil of ignorance" where the parties lack all relevant knowledge about their goals, personal characteristics, historical and political

[2] In the second and revised edition of the book, Graham (2013) adds some changes to the content of the relevant chapter. For instance, he relies more on Frankfurt's (2004) ideas of universal needs (Graham 2013, p. 150) and omits the talk of hyper-sociological method (Graham 2010, p. 145). However, from the perspective of this discussion, the changes are not decisive.

circumstances, social class, natural talents, status acquired through birth or achievement. The idea is that, because they lack this information, the parties of the original position are compelled to imagine themselves being disadvantaged by social, natural, historical, economical, or other relevant circumstances. These individuals lack the kind of knowledge that may typically incite people to seek advantages on morally irrelevant grounds. Rawls assumes that individuals in such a position would nevertheless attempt to act in a way that would advance their interests and exhibit a preference for more primary goods. In such a case, individuals would advance their interests by ensuring the equal distribution of *primary goods*—that is, goods that are necessary conditions for the realization of *any* idea of a good life, in the sense that their distribution does not promote any particular idea of a good life. It is against such a background, Rawls argues, that in a liberal society a state may intervene to ensure the distribution of primary goods—that is, resources that improve the chances of attaining the kind of life that individuals might choose. Primary goods are "things that every rational man is presumed to want. These goods normally have a use whatever a person's rational plan of life" (Rawls 1971, p. 62). Such primary goods are neutral and independent with respect to any particular conception of a good life and provide preconditions for autonomy, such as the capacity to choose and engage in life plans free from coercion. Rawls does not consider the list of primary goods that he offers to be completely fixed, but only provisional. In fact, in *Justice as Fairness* (Rawls 1985), he expands the list and includes basic healthcare and leisure time.

Graham's choice of Rawls' work might at first seem peculiar, as Rawls' goals are quite far removed from an account of health or mental disorder. However, in support of Graham, we might point out that Rawls distinguishes between *social primary goods* (rights, liberties, opportunities, income, and wealth) and *natural primary goods* (health, vigor, intelligence, and imagination), which are both seen as neutral resources that are required if one is to make autonomous choices about any kind of goods. Thus, in the Rawlsian vocabulary, the basic psychological capacities are not merely primary goods, but natural primary goods.[3]

1.2. The original position as thought experiment

The thought experiment method, which involves studying imaginary examples, can be a very useful philosophical tool that stretches the concept under

[3] The talk of "natural" should not mislead one into thinking that such goods are innate. Basic education enhances general emotional and cognitive traits in children and provides them with social skills that are needed for any life plan they may choose.

scrutiny and may reveal aspects that would otherwise remain hidden, pertaining both to the scope and the extent of the concept. As will be argued in the following sections, one drawback of this method is that it may lead to unreliable results because it is sometimes very difficult to control the parameters by which one's imagination is set to work. In the following account, three general concerns about the reliability of this method are described, followed by a discussion of some specific problems associated with the concrete thought experiment. Nothing of what follows implies a wholesale rejection of thought experiments, which can clearly be valuable and powerful tools. Nevertheless, just as with empirical experiments, the consistency of the premises, the clarity of background conditions, and the thoroughness with which the conclusions are derived will determine the reliability of the results of the thought experiment.

It is widely held that successful philosophical thought experiments are those that elicit "strong beliefs" in the vast majority of those exposed to them (Parfit 1984). Nevertheless, if the results of recent experimental philosophy are credible, then it would appear that consensus on the evoked idea necessitates something like a common cultural background. For instance, it seems that East Asian intuitions about various well-known philosophical thought experiments are significantly different from those that philosophical literature assumes to be universal (Weinberg et al. 2001). Intuitions are influenced not only by cultural background, but also by other unrelated factors, such as educational background (Swain et al. 2008). If consensus on the evoked intuition depends on a common cultural and educational background, this begins to indicate that the proper analysis of a concept should not merely rely on intuitions, since they reflect no universal norms.[4] Also, however, while it is crucial to the reliability of the outcome to provide support for the methodological choices, no independent argument is given in favor of relying on *folk* psychological intuitions. It is often the case that strong folk intuitions about the mind cannot be rendered compatible with scientific-psychological findings (Dennett 1984), which is one of the reasons why philosophers such as Kathleen Wilkes oppose them. As Wilkes (1988) notes, one of the most serious problems with thought experiments is that they are underdetermined, which means that the background conditions of the experiment and possible tests of validity are not provided. It is extremely difficult to be certain that the crucial apparatus of the experiment—the imagination—is used in the correct way. The risk is that thought experiments could lead us astray because

[4] In addition, the method can be questioned on evolutionary grounds (Brown and Fehige 2014).

imagination, representations, and representational schemas can be extremely difficult to control. As will be shown, that concern is justified here. The results of the experiment might be misleading, because we cannot regard ourselves as required by the experiment.

1.3. Liberalism and the problem of neutrality

Graham's approach is susceptible to criticisms reminiscent of those launched against Rawls. In *Liberalism and the Limits of Justice*, Michael Sandel (1982) famously argued that the thought experiment hinges on accepting an overly stripped notion of the person, divorced from all goals, inclinations, commitments, and capacities. As Rainer Forst (2002) rightly notes, Sandel's critique can be understood in the context of the critique by Taylor (1979) of the reliance of liberal deontological theories on a concept of liberty that operates with a thin, "atomistic," and non-situated concept of the self. Opposing such a view, Taylor emphasizes the historically, culturally, and communally "situated" nature of identity—an idea which is employed in Sandel's critique of Rawls. Rather than being "thin," selves are constituted by their values, goals, and commitments, which only become intelligible to them by their being participatively immersed in the social life of communities. Understood normatively, there is no self prior to its ends; rather, we are self-interpreting beings who reflectively participate in the constitution of our identities. Without such "situatedness" it is highly questionable whether such a "thin" self can be the object of self-reflection. It is not possible for Rawls to provide a quick solution to this problem, because universalist moral accounts can in general only be reached by "detached" understanding of individuals (Taylor 1991a; see also Williams 1981).

A more important issue that is worth emphasizing here is that this "thin" notion of the self is far from being neutral. Instead, Rawls has to embrace a certain "philosophical anthropology" and make certain assumptions that enable the description of the self in the original position (Sandel 1982, p. 50; Taylor 1979). In other words, Rawls' notion of the self is not neutral, but rather certain values enter its description—values that reflect the standards of political liberalism. First, Rawls already assumes that rational individuals are prudent and care for their future good when they formulate a conception of their good upon reflection on values, ambitions, commitments, goals, etc. that they can order into a "rational plan of life" (Rawls 1971, §45). In addition, we are called upon to accept a neutral description of the human self as a "subject of possession" with mutual disinterest (Sandel 1982, p. 48), as an antecedently individuated entity, with a sense of identity that is not constitutively tied to a social world. In addition to the description of an "atomist" and "self-possessing" subject, there is also a portion of voluntarism at stake in Rawls' description of the self in the original position, as the important determinations of personal identity are chosen qualitatively in the same way that we choose external goods and objects. However, such voluntarism is ultimately untenable, as many key normative aspects essential for an identity are discovered in communal life rather than being chosen in solitude. Thus the thought experiment is set up in a way that might bias the answer, disfavoring members of non-individualistic cultures, in which acting informed by a collective orientation (prioritizing the good of the community, embracing the culture of their ancestors, etc.) might weigh heavier than individualistic concerns. At the same time, it encourages the pursuit of the good from an individualistic perspective (see also Taylor 1994). We might say that the original thought experiment represents a particular "philosophical anthropology," which might be widely accepted in certain areas of the Western world, but that certainly conveys a false picture about allegedly universal human interests. In short, the problem is that this method of universalizability or objectivity yields a determinate set of human goods that either clash with standards embedded in the traditions of particular societies or become far too vague and abstract to provide useful standards.

The question is now how Graham's account of mental disorder is affected by the fact that the thought experiment might yield descriptively questionable and normatively loaded results. In a similar manner, the "basic psychological capacities" that Graham puts forward are both too vague and too narrow. On the one hand, capacities for comprehension of self and the world, communication, and decision making are too vague and are unable to specify the type of comprehensive, communicative, and decision-making capacities that individuals need in order to lead a good life. For instance, it is not clear whether, and at what point, intense feelings of care or love that alter comprehension of self and the world and decision making should count as impairment. On the other hand, less vague descriptions and further specifications of the relevant psychological capacities would most probably make these too narrow, thus excluding particular ideas of the good life. It is extremely difficult to eliminate the possibility that rational individuals may be hindered in pursuing their vision of a good life by possessing a particular primary good. Consider, for instance, the ability to have emotional commitments to others, which Graham includes in his list. A warrior and a devoted monk might both hold that in order to achieve a "personally satisfying life" it would be better for them not to have emotional commitments to other people.

In summary, it seems virtually impossible to identify universal psychological capacities that are needed to realize any type of good life, without the choice of those capacities itself being led by a particular idea of the good life.[5] In defense of Graham's view, one could emphasize that we should not forget that the goal is not to provide necessary and sufficient conditions, but rather to offer a prototype account of mental disorder. Certainly this fact together with the modest scale of Graham's overall goals makes the problem less acute, but it does not disappear. Even a prototype account suffers from the individualistic bias that it inherits from Rawls, potentially leading to biased answers that might disfavor some individuals, particularly those with a non-individualistic orientation. The original thought experiment relies on a certain conception of self and the social sphere which is commonly accepted in the Western world, but that clashes with standards embedded in the traditions of other societies.

In addition, it might be that such a Rawls-based account promotes values that are contested even within the ideological framework of contemporary Western culture. For instance, Graham (2013, p. 156) notes that speaker and listener competences are important for communicative abilities, which are again important for a "decent" life. Nevertheless, not even something as seemingly "natural" as normal auditory perception can be unconditionally identified as a primary natural good. During the past two decades we have witnessed the emergence of novel medical solutions to the problem of hearing loss. The new cochlear implants compensate for damaged auditory nerves and thereby restore normal auditory perception. Nonetheless, these implants have been met with resistance. Advocates of the deaf-culture movement argue that deaf people are not disabled, but merely constitute a visually oriented subculture or linguistic community (Tucker 1994, 1998). Because they do not regard deafness as a handicap, but rather as something constitutive for an identity of a community and a crucial component of what they view as a good life, advocates of the deaf-culture movement are extremely skeptical about cochlear implants. Similarly, some people think of blindness in terms of difference instead of disability, while maintaining that sighted people attach too much importance to seeing and too little to information brought to us by the other senses and language (Glover 2006).

[5] While Rawls maintains that procedurally structured fair construction of principles of justice and rightness in liberal democracies must be prior to and unbiased by specific and comprehensive conceptions of a good life, he also recognizes that in order to establish these principles we must rely on some thin notion of goodness (Rawls 1971, p. 396). However, his claim is that such a thin notion is morally neutral and suitable for all rational individuals whatever their ethical orientation.

2. **Relaxed naturalism**

Just like Graham, Thornton (2002, 2007) opposes a certain type of reductive naturalism in psychiatry. Yet, being a proponent of a "having it both ways" view, Thornton pairs his rejection of hard-nosed naturalism with an acceptance of what he calls "relaxed naturalism" (Thornton 2007, p. 235), which is taken from the work of John McDowell. This view is multifaceted, and "reduction" is countered in several ways—for instance, by arguing that psychiatric practice relies on skilled clinical judgment that cannot be grasped in terms of algorithmic processes. For present purposes we shall only be concerned with the manner in which naturalism is salvaged parallel to the recognition of the value-ladenness of the concepts of mental disorder.

Philosophers such as Crispin Wright have been concerned with the question of how to give a correct characterization of true statements within discourse. Highlighting faultless disagreement as a criterion for differentiating between subjective and objective aspects of discourse, Wright proposes a test that he calls "cognitive command":

> It is a priori that differences of opinion formulated within the discourse, unless excusable as a result of vagueness in a disputed statement, or in the standards of acceptability, or variation in personal evidence thresholds, so to speak, will involve something which may properly be regarded as a cognitive shortcoming.
>
> (Wright 1992, p. 144)

Typical utterances in scientific or mathematical discourse will pass the test of cognitive command, whereas "subjective" disagreements in discourses about taste, values, humor, etc. will fail, as such "subjective" disagreements are faultless. Using humor to illustrate this point, it seems intuitively appealing to say that two or more individuals can disagree about whether a joke is funny, without either of them making a mistake. Such faultless disagreements only occur in "subjective" discourses, whereas a difference in opinion in scientific or mathematical discourse implies at least one mistake. It should be added here that while this position is hostile to moral realism, secondary qualities such as color will also pass the test. So what about disagreement about the boundaries of "mental disorder"? In the light of Wright's suggestion, such judgments about mental disorder would fail to pass the test of cognitive command, as they are not describing facts but expressing certain values. The failure to pass the test leads to the conclusion that judgments about the boundaries of mental disorder cannot be objective (or valid)—a view that Szaszian "categorical criticism" would readily accept, claiming that mental disorder is defined in terms of value (social, ethical, etc.), and hence is fundamentally evaluative. Thus a disagreement about the boundaries of mental disorder need not imply that any mistake has been made.

Thornton's aim is to challenge this view by arguing that it is not necessarily the case that the presence of values in a judgment will lead to the failure of the test (Thornton 2002, pp. 232–233; Thornton 2007, p. 176). Although it is intuitively plausible, Thornton urges us not to accept the view that the failure of cognitive command necessarily precludes objectivity and validity. The central move that allows Thornton to "have it both ways" involves opposing a Humean, projectionist account of value, according to which values are intrinsically subjective and projected on to an otherwise neutral world. The view that no *ought* can be derived from an *is*, and thus the semantic idea that value judgments are not reducible to non-value judgments, is in this view complemented by the idea that values are not found in nature but *projected* on to it. In the words of McDowell (1998, p. 175), such a view amounts to an understanding of reality as:

> exhausted by the natural world, in the sense of the world as the natural sciences are capable of revealing to us. Part of the truth in the idea that science disenchants nature is that science is committed to a dehumanized stance for investigation; that is taken to be a matter of conforming to a metaphysical insight into the character of reality as such.
>
> (McDowell 1998, p. 175)

According to the projectionist view, features of reality that science cannot capture are "mere" projections that arise from human interaction with nature.

Following McDowell, Thornton resists the projectionist view and maintains that values are a part of the world, while arguing that the "disenchanted" image of nature has resulted in an incorrect framing of conceptual issues in many areas. It is not just that we take it for granted that a disagreement over values cannot be comprehended in terms of someone making a mistake. In addition, as Thornton also points out, this flawed view has misled many into thinking that validity is the property of classifications that map on to distinctions in the world from a perspective that is independent of human interests. According to such a view, "[a] classificatory judgment is valid if it can be characterized using the resources only of a dehumanized natural scientific standpoint fully independent of human interests" (Thornton 2007, p. 178). Both McDowell and Thornton doubt that such a perspective is achievable, or that it would result in an accurate picture of the world. However, more importantly, the "disenchanted" view has also led to the dubious conviction that if diagnosis involves value-laden concepts, then, given the subjective and "projected" nature of values, the scientific validity of psychiatric categories is undermined. Thornton's point is that if validity is concerned with getting to the structure of the world, and if values can be said to be a part of the structure of the world, then it is no longer clear that we have to accept that a classificatory judgment involving evaluative elements *must* be invalid.

Thornton thus explores a different path to defend the scientific status of psychiatry and the validity of psychiatric diagnosis. Compared with Boorse and Wakefield, Thornton moves the debate in a distinctive direction.[6] Sidestepping a host of minor and major issues that the BST and HD need to address, Thornton can focus on substantiating one major point, which if successful could change the debate about the scientific status of psychiatry. That is, placing values in the natural world, demonstrating that the world contains value-laden structural components could not only change the debate but also, it would appear, effectively block the "categorical criticism." However, Thornton's position, and ultimately his defense of the scientific status of value-laden psychiatric classification, depend on McDowell's "relaxed naturalism" being correct. Whether or not such a move is warranted will be explored in the rest of this chapter.

2.1. McDowell and relaxed naturalism

Over the last few decades, McDowell has contributed to meta-ethical debates with important views on moral reasons and moral objectivity. Reflecting on the question of reduction of value properties to natural properties, he develops a certain take on cognitivism (the idea that *moral* statements articulate beliefs apt for truth and falsity) that has come to be known as *secondary property realism*. His account is best viewed together with his later work in *Mind and World* (McDowell 1996), in which he replaces a reductively naturalistic account with a "relaxed" naturalistic view, for which it is important that the unique capabilities of our minds are cultural achievements linked to our "second nature." To understand McDowell's position, it is useful to consider the view that he critically engages with when developing "relaxed" naturalism. This is the popular view, espoused by Mackie, for example, which insists on a parallel between values and secondary qualities and concludes that values cannot pass the test for objectivity:

> There are no objective values. ... The claim that values are not objective, are not part of the fabric of the world, is meant to include not only moral goodness, which might be most naturally equated with moral value, but also other things that could be more loosely called moral values or disvalues—rightness and wrongness, duty, obligation.

[6] It is worth noting that Boorse (2014) also embraces a realist position about value. However, in that case a similar line of argument would also be available for Boorse.

> An action's being rotten and contemptible, and so on. It also includes non-moral values, notably aesthetic ones, beauty and various kinds of artistic merit.
>
> (Mackie 1977, p. 15)

Mackie denies that values are a part of the world in the sense that they can be *discovered* in the world, providing answers to certain kinds of concerns. Mackie's observation that, phenomenologically, whenever we evaluate things in the world it seems to us that we respond to aspects of the world is to a large extent shared by McDowell. However, whereas Mackie would claim that this phenomenology deceives us, McDowell wants to take it seriously. Rejecting Mackie's "error theory" that moral language only appears to refer to something in the world, McDowell argues that it wrongly equates value properties to primary qualities which have an objective, mind-independent existence, being "simply there, independently of human sensibility" McDowell (1985, p. 167). Such a step is flawed because it excludes secondary qualities, which are only conceivable in connection to non-objective "human sensibility." In addition, McDowell thinks that there is a mistaken concept of value at stake, in which value appears to be valuable from no perspective at all. Instead he suggests that we conceive of values in terms of their being linked to human sensibility. Adopting a broadly Aristotelian view, McDowell thinks that such sensibility must be educated—a process that "attunes" the individual to the values in the world.

A critical engagement with Bernard Williams' idea of the "absolute conception of reality" (that is, reality as "what there is anyway," independent of the human point of view) helps McDowell to develop the analogy between values and secondary qualities. According to Williams, we may speak of progress in science in case particular conceptions of the world are gradually replaced toward the absolute conception. Ideally, the absolute conception includes all correct representations, permitting a proper knowledge of an entity, since it would incorporate the contrast between world and representation. McDowell objects to this line of thought, maintaining that there is:

> a general difficulty about the idea that we can firmly detach subjective properties from objects in the world, eschewing all need for the idea of an object's really possessing such a property, while retaining the thought that such properties 'figure in our experience,' so that we can regard them as projected on to the world from there.
>
> (McDowell 1998, p. 124)

However, such a general objection needs more support, as the undeniable progress of science seems to support the opposite view. Williams takes the progress of science to support his view and particularly the progress science has made in distinguishing features believed to be a part of the world from features related to our perspective on the world. For instance, one area in which science has managed to describe the world apart from our situated, sensory experiences is with secondary qualities such as colors. Colors are now grasped more precisely as primary qualities, and understood in terms of wavelength. Our scientific account of color is now objective, as it no longer relies on sensory experience and secondary qualities that are not part of the world. At first glance, the parallel sounds quite convincing. The premise is acknowledging that we adequately make sense of color experience by referring to what really are colorless features of the world. Having accepted this premise, in a second step we can draw a parallel between colors and values, anticipating that we might explicate value experience by referring to what really are value-free qualities of the world. Thus, so the argument goes, values and colors reflect the way our minds represent the world, rather than reflecting genuine parts of the fabric of the world (Wynn 2004).

McDowell (1981, 1998) objects to this line of thought and defends moral cognitivism by comparing the everyday experience of values and secondary qualities. For example, "red" is something that would look red to an observer. This case has close parallels to a value term such as "funny," which is to be an occasion for laughter at least for people with a certain sense of humor. As Milgram (1999, p. 253) notes, "because the shape of a secondary quality follows the shape of the relevant pattern of reactions, a joke can be funny in virtue of being a well-turned member of such a genre." Importantly, there are certain limits to the parallel with secondary qualities. McDowell also maintains that values cannot be understood in purely quantitative terms. To prove this point, he uses the example of something being funny, maintaining that it cannot be explained or specified independently of those reactions that human beings usually display when in funny situations. Thus, in contrast to the case of colors, where we have a way of grouping them together without reference to subjective experience, in the case of things and events that we label as funny, the only way we have of grouping them together is by referring to their tendency to evoke the response of laughing or being amused. In other words, whereas "green" can be identified by reference to something that can be picked out in terms of wavelength (which is a color-neutral term), "funny" can only be identified by reference to responses of being amused. Values are specific in the sense that they are only intelligible for creatures with a particular sensibility. McDowell admits that not all forms of human sensibility have access to values in the world, in the sense that they become motivationally efficacious. Just as Aristotle maintained, this requires education and virtuous character.

It is against such a background that McDowell wants to claim that some values are not the result of human projection of qualities on to a value-free world. Just as sensory qualities are subjective, but at the same time also parts of the world, values genuinely make up parts of the world and are open to be identified by evaluative experience. In other words, the fact that some quality is conceptually dependent on experience does not warrant thinking that it cannot be a part of the world. This is a crucial point that Thornton applies with regard to the validity of psychiatric judgment. In contrast to the common view held by Hempel and many others, Thornton concludes that "there can be no swift argument from the dependence of a property on human interests to its not being valid … the presence of values would not imply the lack of validity" (Thornton 2007, p. 179).

It is against such a background that Thornton claims to be able to "have it both ways," by opposing a certain type of reductive naturalism, accepting what he calls "relaxed naturalism," and salvaging the scientific validity of psychiatric judgment while acknowledging the value-ladenness of the concept of mental disorder. If we replace such an "absolute conception" of objectivity with a "relaxed" one, it is possible to maintain that value can be objective, something we can find out about by finding out about the world. This means that in cases where there are differences of opinion in judgments about the boundaries of mental disorder, it is possible that at least one of the disputants is making a mistake. If there is no inference from the presence of values to the lack of objectivity, then the value-laden nature of psychiatric assessments does not render them invalid.

2.2. **Values and secondary qualities**

For present purposes, we may agree with McDowell's position that the world contains features and properties to which we have access via the possession of certain (conceptual, sensible) abilities. We may agree that some qualities cannot be explained without reference to a subjective perspective, which raises questions about the potential of the "view from nowhere" approach. We may also agree with McDowell's rejection of error theory, and adopt his view that values are a part of the world, accessible to certain morally sensitive individuals. Presumably it is safe to assume that, due to different educational backgrounds, social and cultural backgrounds, gender, etc., individuals exhibit different levels of sensitivity. Just as the education of one's color vision will result in one perceiving the world with a richer palette of colors, and just as educating one's sense of humor will give access to a richer palette of witticisms, educating one's moral vision will result in one perceiving the world with a fuller palette of values. Nevertheless, the position defended here is that while claiming that values are a part of the world might convince some that psychiatry is to be taken seriously as a scientific discipline, it seems to do little to help to solve the problem that originally motivated the discussion. To demonstrate this, we need to look more closely at the parallel between values and secondary qualities on which the argument hinges.

2.2.1. The instability of values

Much of the force of McDowell's argument depends on the analogy between secondary qualities and values. Both McDowell and others such as Mackie (1977) and Wynn (2004) assume that we are warranted in treating secondary properties such as color and values in the same manner. Thus any reasonable demonstration that secondary qualities and values are significantly different in a variety of aspects would weaken the position and reduce the plausibility of its application for psychiatric matters.

A good place to start is by reflecting on the differences in the ways that we explain our actions. In the case of color experience, we can give a perfectly adequate explanation of why we responded in a particular manner, by simply indicating how we were (causally) affected. Whereas in the case of secondary qualities there is no need for further explanation, this is not the case with values. Consider, for instance, a particular response to a situation that requires moral action. Here an adequate explanation of why we responded in a particular manner requires more than our indicating how we were causally affected. We must explain our reasons for our response to the situation, which must be flexible, and exhibit a readiness to change the response if good reasons are presented. While this begins to indicate that value terms are less stable than secondary properties, highlighting another way in which value terms and secondary properties such as "green" differ from each other can strengthen this point. Compared with values, secondary properties do not "fade." Whereas a green object still looks green the twentieth time we look at it, the "funniness" of a joke is significantly reduced even the second time we hear it, and the "compellingness" of a moral situation in most cases has less of a grip on us by the ninth or tenth time we encounter it. Thus, compared with secondary properties, values are unstable, and their presence is in a sense unpredictable. We might agree with Aristotle that the morally educated person is able to *see* moral values, but we have to add that the instability of our grasp of values is still at stake. In addition, whether or not we will be able to *see* such values also depends on something as fleeting as momentary mood states. For instance, a recent study published in the journal *Cognition* by Pastötter et al. (2013) explores how people deal with the hypothetical "trolley problem," demonstrating that people's mood strongly influences their perception of and response to the scenario. However, in that case it turns out that value terms and secondary properties differ from each other in a crucial way—it would be implausible to claim that seeing the property "green" is mood dependent in the same way. That said, it is of course correct that the mere instability of values (in the world) does not mean that one cannot "get them right," or that a disagreement about them does not involve a mistake.

Adding to the instability of values, in contrast to our experience of secondary qualities, our responses to values admit of interest dependence. We might agree with McDowell that the world presents itself to us with aspects of value-ladenness, but what exactly does this mean? In many cases it is not that we directly perceive or somehow encounter the values in a situation (Tollefsen 2000). Whereas we directly encounter objects as red or green, our evaluative experiences of situations as affording certain actions merely indicate the possible attainment of certain values. For instance, we might see the possibility of attaining the values of integrity or friendship in a situation, but the actual realization of the relevant value will depend on our active responses to that situation. In these cases, values do guide our actions, but at that point they only potentially exist. This is possible because, as Heidegger and Taylor have noted, we already always care about the world; we can see facts of the world as directive because of our interests and concerns that define our conception of the good. The agent who does not "care" about integrity or friendship will probably fail to see facts of the world in that situation as directive and will fail to be guided by the values of integrity or friendship. In order to *see* the situation as affording the possibility of realizing the values of integrity or friendship, and for them to be able to guide our responses, one already has to be indebted to those values. In other words, the world only presents us with the possibility of those values if we are indebted to a certain normative ideal of how the world should be. Thus, unlike the perception of secondary qualities such as color, the perception of (potential) values is generally interest dependent.

2.2.2. The plurality of values

Another difference is that, in contrast to the case of secondary qualities such as colors, the values that we "see" in the world are dissimilar, contrasting, and divergent. While it is unquestionable that color vision is extremely stable cross-culturally, the situation is very different with regard to humor, pride, shame, etc. That is, people from different cultural backgrounds have strikingly different sensibilities with regard to the latter. In other words, in contrast to such things as colors, what qualifies as witty, shameful, or good is exceptionally contestable. McDowell (1985, p. 144) is well aware of this asymmetry, but he does not consider it a threat to his argument. However, we might reach a different conclusion if we take into account several ways in which a plurality can be understood.

In a sense, the picture that Taylor paints is to a large extent compatible with McDowell's "relaxed naturalism." Just like McDowell, Taylor criticizes philosophy and psychology in the twentieth century for imitating the outlook of the natural sciences and for adopting *naturalist* meta-theory (Taylor 1982, 1989) that dictates the studying of human life in objective, value-neutral, culture-independent terms. In addition, Taylor recognizes that regarding the world *objectively* in the strict naturalist sense comes at the price of disregarding the human life-world, the rich appearance of objects, and the world as enshrined in experiences of value and meaning.[7] Invoking Williams' absolute conception, Taylor criticizes a certain branch of naturalism for aiming to explain human beings as other entities in nature, and for embracing a conception of objectivity that in all cases tries to eschew what he calls "subject-related properties" (Taylor 1982, p. 140)—thus "properties which things bear only insofar as they are objects of experience of subjects."

> Our value terms purport to give us insight into what it is to live in the universe as a human being, and this is a quite different matter from that which physical science claims to reveal and explain. This reality is, of course, dependent on us, in the sense that a condition for its existence is our existence. But once granted that we exist, it is no more a subjective projection than what physics deals with
>
> (Taylor 1989, p. 69)

The point is that if we want to explain phenomena tied to individuals and their lives, then the terms in which they live their lives cannot be removed from the explanandum (Taylor 1989, p. 68). Interestingly, Taylor also draws a parallel with secondary qualities, arguing that the logic of values such as courage or generosity is such "that they have to be construed as picking out projectible properties, just as 'red' or 'square' do, an essential feature of which is precisely their value." While the existence of such properties essentially depends on the existence of human beings with a certain form of life and patterns of caring, "these properties are no less real features of the world which does contain humans than any 'neutral' properties are" (Taylor 1989, p. 68).

Overall, then, much like McDowell, Taylor (1982, 1989, 1991a) rejects the absolute conception and focuses on exploring a path between naturalism and neo-Humean projectivism, arguing that some values (courage, dignity, etc.) are not projections, but really exist, albeit bound to our experience of the world. Like McDowell, Taylor argues that it is only possible to understand values as "real" once naturalism has been rejected. As Taylor argues, some values seem "objective" to us, largely because they are being "privileged over

[7] Taylor also adds that, with the emergence of this idea of objectivity, a new idea of *subjectivity* emerges, which understands the subject as independent of the external order of a collective horizon (Taylor 1989, 1991a). Such an individual understands herself as an atom, a distinct center of experience, and seeks self-comprehension in solitude, away from social constellations.

others because in our civilization they come less into dispute" (Taylor 1982, pp. 139–140).

However, there are some crucial differences. For present purposes it will suffice to highlight two of these. The first crucial difference is that Taylor emphasizes the plurality and incommensurability of values. There are at least two ways in which we can maintain the existence of a plurality of value features and properties in the world to which the morally educated person has access. First, we may note that there is an *inter-cultural plurality of values*. If somebody has been schooled within a different cultural context, embedded in a different normative horizon, we might assume that the values she "discovers" in the world will be somewhat different. Second, we may also claim that there is an *intra-cultural plurality of values*. Even within the same cultural outlook, the same moral community, human sensibility can be developed in many ways—whereas the virtuous might perceive X as the requirement of the situation that manifests value Y, the mean but sensible might perceive Z as the requirement of the situation that manifests value Y. There is plenty of evidence that, even under ideal conditions, there is rather little convergence of values, even if we compare culturally and linguistically similar populations, such as US Americans living in the northern and southern parts of the USA (Nisbett and Cohen 1996; Doris and Stich 2013).

Supporting this view, philosophers such as Taylor have argued that there is a plurality of values even at the most basic level. First, this plurality of values emerges, as Taylor maintains, because a community of valuers is constitutive of the existence of values. Second, as "all moral reasoning is carried out within a community" (Taylor 1982, p. 131), values are internal to and dependent on socio-cultural formations and practices. However, these two claims indicate that we should doubt the existence of one value subsuming all others. Taylor (1982, 1991a) has persuasively argued against the formalist and utilitarian idea that the domain of moral values can be reduced to a single consistent domain. Rather than any "reduction" and "homogenization" (Taylor 1982, p. 132) of the domain of moral values, we should acknowledge that values such as solidarity, personal excellence, personal integrity, honesty, the Christian "agape," and rationality are at times conflicting. These are all moral values that many recognize as valid, but they are based on very different philosophical anthropologies, leading to incompatible ideas about the good life. In fact the whole idea of drawing "objective" boundaries for the moral domain is impossible—that issue is itself a question that is inherently bound to the way in which we interpret ourselves.

In addition, Taylor's middle path ties values not simply to our sensibilities, but to processes of self-interpretation (Taylor 1989, p. 342)—some values are simply inseparable from our self-interpretation. This brings out another important aspect that should make us doubt the validity of the parallel with secondary qualities. In contrast to the case of colors, in the case of values their presence (in the world) might change through critical reflection and interpretation. For instance, the presence and grip of some values might simply disappear if we found that there was a perfectly justifiable argument that spoke convincingly against our understanding of them. This is not the case with colors. Chapter 9 will shed more light on this alternative, but we must first direct our attention to the extent to which "relaxed naturalism" can advance the debate.

2.3. **Does "relaxed naturalism" help?**

We might agree that we have access to value features and properties via the possession of certain (conceptual, sensible) abilities, that objectivity has to be established from a practice-internal perspective (no "view from nowhere"), and that secondary properties are no less real than those described by sciences. In the last sections of this chapter we have acknowledged that the morally educated individual might be able to *see* moral values, but we have highlighted the fact that there are important differences between secondary properties and values, as the latter are essentially unstable and not universal. With this in mind, we may now proceed to explore what is really gained by adopting McDowell's "relaxed naturalism." From the point of view of the discussions in this book, how would adopting "relaxed naturalism" help? Certainly adopting McDowell's view might help to make it more plausible that we need a different understanding of objectivity, and that psychiatric (scientific) classification can be both valid and value-laden, which might help us to reach agreement about the scientific status of psychiatry.

This might indeed be a reasonable achievement, but we need to investigate how adopting McDowell's relaxed naturalism might assist in advancing the debate with naturalists such as Boorse. Let us for a moment assume that the naturalist adopts a "relaxed" view. In fact, Boorse has recently hinted at such a position. He indicates that he rejects relativist meta-ethics (Boorse 2012, p. 7) and maintains that the BST is successful even if it is agreed that health is not value-free because science itself is value-laden. As he notes, "If health and disease are only as value-laden as astrophysics and inorganic chemistry, I am content" (Boorse 1997, p. 56). The underlying point is that even though there might be value aspects to science, they are negligible and not significant enough to undermine its scientific status. Now Boorse might have been too hasty here, and might be contradicting some of his earlier claims, but let us assume for now that—with some modifications—he would be able to accept that values are a part of the world. In a second step, he could then simply insist that the BST gets those values right. This scenario is of course speculative, but it is nevertheless helpful in indicating how it would affect the debate.

If a relaxed naturalist BST grants that values are a part of the world and subsequently claims to track the right values, then it seems that relaxed naturalism does not notably advance the debate about the boundary of mental disorder. In fact, it might simply lead to a stalemate. Given the vast range of at least partly conflicting and even incommensurable values, this would just mean that different strands of relaxed naturalism could claim with an increased sense of authority that their judgment is grounded "in the nature of things." In other words, we might accept both that values are involved in drawing the boundaries between health and disorder, and that the relevant values are a part of the world, but the question that arises upon such acceptance does not seem significantly easier to answer, or more manageable. From the diversity of values that exist, which ones should we take to guide our decisions about the concept of mental disorder? It would seem that this question can only be answered if the relaxed naturalist simultaneously denies the plurality of values.

What begins to emerge from this discussion is that the question about the ontological status and location of values might not be the real problem here. That question is ultimately neutral with regard to the plurality of values, which seems to be the root problem. Providing an answer to the metaphysical question of whether or to what extent values can be a part of the world does not help to answer the question about how to pick out the *right* values that should guide our decision concerning the concept of mental disorder. Relaxed naturalism would only advance the debate if one could simultaneously deny the plurality and incommensurability of values and posit that arguments about values are in fact rationally resolvable. Otherwise, in view of the instability of value perception and the plurality of values, the defense for drawing firm boundaries between disorder and health might turn out to be an insurmountable problem.[8]

[8] In McDowell's view there are both projected and non-projected values. Which of these should guide our decisions? An additional concern is linked to the question of epistemic authority. If we, like McDowell, assume that perception of the relevant values is available only to those who have been adequately acculturated, then we might have to attribute epistemic authority about mental disorder to those who have been properly acculturated. Deciding who those individuals might be would involve reflecting on the kind of upbringing and acculturation that is likely to enable an individual to track the relevant values in the world.

3. Conclusion

After arguing that the concept of mental disorder might resist strict naturalistic definitions, be these in terms of natural kind, a biostatistical fact, or evolutionary dysfunction, this chapter discussed views that reject the idea that bodily illness is value-free whereas mental illness is normative. Such views hold that both mental and "somatic" disorders inescapably involve values, while recognizing those involved in mental disorder as reflecting fundamentally contestable value judgments, complex experiences, desires, and motives that are constitutive of our identities. While these are genuine achievements, the focus was on their thoughts on the relationship between science and psychiatric inquiry and a solution referred to as "having it both ways." While Graham (2010, 2013) and Thornton (2007) develop this idea in distinct ways, the shared starting point is that the fact of mental disorder being value-laden does not preclude the existence of objective truths about mental disorder attributions.

Graham maintains that although mental disorders involve values, they have objective standards and pick out clinically significant impairments, not mere distress or anything that counts as undesirable only within a certain cultural horizon. Graham is universalist in the sense that a condition qualifies as a mental disorder if there is an impairment in a basic fundamental psychological competence needed for any kind of a "decent or personally satisfying life." These capacities are like "primary goods" that each person would choose under the veil of ignorance. However, Graham's approach is susceptible to arguments reminiscent of those launched against Rawls' liberalism. First, the "thin" notion of the self, separate from all goals, inclinations, and capacities, is confused, as selves are constituted by the values and commitments that they have acquired as a result of being immersed in communal life. Second, the supposedly "thin" notion is too "thick," being permeated by certain individualistic values that reflect the standards of a certain political liberalism. Thus the thought experiment is set up in a way that might bias the answer, not only potentially disfavoring members of collectively orientated cultures, but also promoting values that are contested even within the ideological framework of contemporary Western culture. The method yields human goods that either clash with standards embedded in the traditions of particular societies, or become far too vague and abstract to provide useful standards.

Thornton (2007) attempts a different approach to "having it both ways," largely inspired by McDowell's secondary property realism. McDowell rejects what he sees as a flawed account of objectivity as "what there is anyway" independent of the human point of view, and he replaces it with a "relaxed" account, according to which values can be objective. According to this view, some values are not projections on to a value-free world, but are genuinely "in the world" and open to evaluative experience. The fact that they conceptually depend on experience and human sensibility does not preclude their being part of the world. Drawing on McDowell, Thornton's point, which has interesting consequences for psychiatry, is that the dependence of a property on human interests does not warrant the denial of its being valid. Thus Thornton argues that accepting "relaxed naturalism" allows us to "have it both ways"—securing the scientific validity of psychiatric judgment while acknowledging the value-ladenness of the concept of mental disorder. Although many of McDowell's points are convincing, when used in the context of the debates in the philosophy of psychiatry, at least in this current form, their usefulness is limited. Certainly McDowell's view might help to convince others to adopt a more relaxed notion of objectivity, which might lead to an increased recognition of the scientific status of psychiatry, but there are many question left unresolved. For instance, whereas the asymmetry between colors and values might not pose a problem for McDowell, it proves problematic in our context because, in contrast to the situation with colors, people from different cultural backgrounds have dramatically different sensibilities, which indicates that there will be a plurality of values. In other words, the problems that psychiatry faces and the question of agreement about a concept of mental disorder are relatively independent of the question about the metaphysical status of the relevant values. Overall, it seems that unless one is prepared to deny the plurality and incommensurability of values, and accept that arguments about relevant values are in fact rationally resolvable, the benefits to be gained from adopting "relaxed naturalism" are not decisive.

In conclusion, both of the accounts that have been analyzed in this chapter are sophisticated and attempt to hold on to some form of naturalism while accepting the value-ladenness involved in mental disorder. They also reveal some new possibilities and limitations when reflecting on a concept of mental disorder once the value component is acknowledged. In Chapter 9 it will be argued that it is not entirely surprising that both the naturalist account and the "having it both ways" account face difficulties in providing a more precise definition of mental disorder. The point will be made that the key to understanding these difficulties lies in the nature of a group of concepts to which "mental disorder" belongs.

Chapter 9

Self-interpretation, rationality, and mental disorder

So far, the main focus of Part II of this book has been to analyze the debate and to provide new arguments that, although favoring accounts that argue in favor of value-ladenness, actually attempt to navigate between the available positions. In this chapter, the aim is to go further and to provide something like an *explanation* of the elusiveness of the concept of mental disorder. In other words, drawing from hermeneutical sources, the argument will be that the concept of mental disorder belongs to a particular class of concepts that will be referred to as *identity-tied concepts*. Such concepts are elusive because they are dynamic, and they are dynamic because they supervene on our self-interpretation.

How are we to understand the concept of "mental disorder"? After what we have seen in Chapters 6, 7, and 8, it is safe to exclude the possibility that it is anything like a classical concept such as "bachelor," with a definitional structure composed of simpler constituent concepts ("unmarried" and "man") that articulate the necessary and sufficient conditions for falling within it. In the case of classical concepts, paradigmatic conceptual analysis is usually successful in providing a definition, in part by testing against counter-examples created in thought experiments. However, if we are not dealing with such a classical concept here, what type of structure does it have? One possibility is that the concept "mental disorder" has probabilistic rather than definitional structure, which means that something falls within it if it satisfies an appropriate number of criteria encoded by its constituents. Thus it might be best to think of "mental disorder" in terms of a prototype connecting the entities that fall within it by "family resemblance" as Wittgenstein has described it. In the case of prototype concepts, the process of categorization unfolds as a comparison of constituents that are shared by the concepts under comparison. In the case of mental disorders, it might be that schizophrenia is considered to be more typical than attention deficit hyperactivity disorder (ADHD), in case it is judged that the concept schizophrenia shares more of its constituents with mental disorder.

Seeing the concept of mental disorder in terms of a prototype theory could partly explain why attempts to produce an adequate definition are unsuccessful. However, there are also important limitations with regard to understanding concepts as prototypes, which may lead us to think that prototype theory is not able to fully account for the elusiveness of the concept. Many think that understanding concepts as propotypes has crucial limitations. For instance, in some cases, the issue of compositionality arises with concepts of prototype structure. Some of these concepts might exhibit emergent properties that cannot be reduced to (the prototypes of) its constituents. A useful example here is "pet fish," which encodes properties such as "exotically colored," which do not stem from the structure for either "pet" or "fish" (Margolis and Lawrence 2011).

One of the ideas that will be defended in this chapter is that at least some of the elusiveness of the concept of mental disorder (but also disease) and its resistance to a definition can be explained by its being value-laden. However, stating that the concept of "mental disorder" is value-laden does not in fact tell us much about the precise way in which it is value-laden. Thus it would be premature to conclude that the debate comes to an end when it is established beyond reasonable doubt that the concept of mental disorder is value-laden. In fact, as we have seen in the second part of Chapter 8, some fundamental questions arise upon such acceptance. The present chapter seeks to provide answers to some of these questions.

1. Rationality and mental disorder

Before we start to unfold the argument, it is important to make a point about the relationship between rationality and mental disorder. Graham's (2010) reflections on the nature of mental disorder provide rich sources that might help explain the closely tied relationship between rationality and mental disorder. Graham starts out by noting that elements of rationality actively constitute characteristically mental activities such as believing, thinking, desiring, hoping, deciding, and so on. In a second step, he demonstrates that the distinction between mental disorders and neurological disorders such as Alzheimer's disease can only be understood by recourse to the concept of rationality. Quite simply, certain behaviors can only be considered as symptoms of a mental disorder if they satisfy a minimal standard of coherence or "logic" while at the same time reflecting impaired or truncated rationality. In short, mental disorder "gums up" rationality.

For additional evidence about the closely tied relationship between rationality and mental disorder, we may turn to Foucault's thoughts in *Madness and*

Civilization (Foucault 2005). One of the most important aims in this early work of his is to write the archaeology of the "silence"—that is, the historical process in which madness is silenced and constituted as the "other" of rationality. While pointing out that the Greek word *logos* had no opposite, Foucault demonstrated how oppositions between "rational" and "mad" (mentally ill) are put to work to enforce social and epistemological norms in classical and modern discourses. In this process, mental disorder is recognized as the "other," or the negative of rationality, while the ascendance of rationality as a central concept for Western self-understanding is paired with silencing "the voice of madness," and excluding the mentally ill from society by placing them in institutions of confinement. Despite Foucault's sometimes rushed generalizations, the general point is an interesting and valid one—from the Enlightenment period we began to conceptualize madness as the "other" of reason, no longer as strange, but as *mentally ill* and hence to be treated by physicians. The previously "undifferentiated experience" of madness became systematized and classified in terms of mental disorder, no longer thought of as a moral or spiritual problem but as an essentially medical one.

This point about the relationship between rationality and mental disorder can be rendered more precise by some further reflection on concepts that lie in a binary, but inherently incompatible, relationship to each other. Clearly, in this context, incompatibility amounts to irreconcilability between the two members of the rational/insane pair of opposites. Whereas we usually refer to such a relationship as "opposite," in this case the more restricted and precise term "antonym" is warranted. Antonyms may take on several forms, but at this point it is useful to focus on *relational antonyms,* which are considered to be a subcategory of complementary antonyms. This is because an antonym forms part of a pair, in which one opposite only makes sense in the context of the relationship between the two members of the pair. Classic examples include doctor/patient, teacher/pupil, and organic/inorganic. Against this background, the point is that "rational" and "insane" are relational antonyms, admitting of degree without any loss of correspondence in terms of semantic structure. The point that the relationship between *rationality and mental disorder* can be thought of as relational antonyms is meant to enforce the claim that their meanings are tied together in a special way. For now, suffice it to say that this link means that any major conceptual change in one part of the pair is accompanied by a change in its opposite.

Overall, the idea that *rationality and mental disorder* are inherently tied together can be at least partly substantiated by the fact that from the classical age onward, the rational/insane distinction has become a crucial distinction. This can be rendered more precise by pointing out that the irreconcilability between the two members of the rational/insane pair of opposites warrants the label *relational antonyms.*

2. Self-interpreting animals

One of the most noteworthy achievements of philosophical thought in the last centuries is the increased awareness about the nature of normativity and its internal relationship to thought and action. The contrast class to this normativity has been the form of intelligibility that characterizes nature's causally determined events. Whereas natural phenomena and the objects of natural science are intelligible as events subjected to the norms of causal forces, human thoughts and actions are subject to an entirely different class of norms, or rather reasons, which can render them right or wrong, true or false, etc. (Smith 2004). Influential philosophers such as Kant argued that, rather than stemming from the forces of a "natural" or "supernatural" order, the roots of normativity are to be located in human existence and subjectivity (Korsgaard 1996). In particular, the tradition of philosophical hermeneutics emphasized that the source of normativity is to be found in the existential structure of our being embedded in the world, shaped by the multiplicity of our distinct concerns. These concerns are not given to us, but present themselves in interpretations. This means that our answer to the question of what it is to be a human being will depend on how our capacity to interpret the world and ourselves (our primary concerns) is exerted. One of Heidegger's insights, later taken up by Taylor, is that it is in the process of interpretation that human identities take shape. In other words, it is in the course of a constant process of interpretation that human life achieves its distinctive narrative unity, formed by "care" and concern for worldly affairs.

Thus interpretation again enters the picture and takes on a crucial role. Who we are—the question of our identities as human beings—is to a significant extent determined by how we interpret ourselves, that is, how we interpret the goals, commitments, and concerns that we care about. While Part I of this book was concerned with the interpretation of texts and utterances, here interpretation is primarily understood in an ontological fashion, so that the human capacity for interpretation is given ontological significance. The point relevant to our present goals is this—our natures are not simply given to us, but rather our existence as human beings is such that who we are is (at least to a large degree) constituted by the manner in which we interpret ourselves. This set of ideas are most clearly and lucidly expressed in Taylor's work, particularly in his captivating claim that human beings are "self-interpreting animals" (Taylor 1985b, p. 45). Just like Heidegger and Gadamer, Taylor

(1985a, 1991a, 1989) also ascribes a crucial significance to language, conceptualizing it as the medium through which we interpret and thereby also shape ourselves.

This view accompanies a rejection of a view of the self as reducible to neurophysiological states and processes that are in principle available to scientific research, or as an individuated psychological entity that exists prior to its own self-interpretations. Self-interpretation is an ongoing process that cannot be finalized or somehow concluded, and the largely interminable nature of this process of self-interpretation opens up the possibility of re-interpretations attempting to achieve an ever deeper understanding (Taylor 1985a). Self-interpretation is continuing in the sense that it cannot be terminated at a point where we arrive at a full description immune to further (re)interpretation.[1]

It would be incorrect to think of the process of self-interpretation as something that is achieved in solitude and solely in the realm of thought. Rather it is to a large extent a question of shared practice. Yet how does this process unfold? First, we interpret ourselves and thereby constitute our identities by situating ourselves in a moral landscape—a background of implicit understandings and practices that can never be fully charted by an agent. Self-interpretation proceeds by a process that is fundamentally of a collective and dialogical nature, and these are characteristics that limit the possible ways in which we are free to interpret ourselves. Although we constitute ourselves through self-interpretations, this is only intelligible against a shared background ("web of interlocutions"), which constrains the extent to which who we are is something that can be fully determined by us. Concrete self-interpretations are always drawn from interchanges within a community.

Also, the condition of our ability to constitute our self is our being embedded in a horizon of significance—that is, a collectively shaped background of a particular historical–cultural context. Interpretation (and self-interpretation) are dependent on such frameworks of understanding and collective "vocabularies" that enable us to hold a view (Taylor 1985a, 1985b). Self-interpretation makes little sense in abstraction from the interpretive horizons and practices

[1] We should note that there is a tension in Taylor's account between the idea that we constitute ourselves through certain "strong" evaluative judgments and the idea that some of our self-interpretations might be mistaken. While one might see that it is important for Taylor to hold on to the latter idea in order to avoid relativism, the tension is nevertheless palpable. Given the aims of the present inquiry, we need not be concerned about this tension. However, according to a sensible interpretation, taking seriously that Taylor often suffices with saying that self-interpretations "in part" constitute who we are, the tension can be minimized.

that make it possible in the first place. This view is shared by Habermas (2003), who maintains that in self-interpretation we reflect on what it means to be a human being, not merely as a member of a certain cultural, religious, or national community.[2] In a critique of Taylor, Appiah (2005) argues that he overemphasizes the active role and self-shaping powers of the self, neglecting the Wittgensteinian idea that, at some point, practical reasoning (whether or not it is in the form of interpretation) must come to an end. However, the point is that the self-constitution through self-interpretation that Taylor describes involves both active creation and "discovery," where the agent's self-identity is shaped through the acknowledgment of belonging to a communal horizon and cultural practices.

3. The ontology of values

The next step is to clarify how self-interpretation proceeds. Rather than being something optional that gives our lives an extra dimension, orienting ourselves toward values is a basic condition of interpreting ourselves and becoming moral agents with a sense of self-identity. As creatures living in time, our self-interpretation involves understanding ourselves both by remembering a re-interpretable past and by projecting ourselves into the future and, thus, by creating narrative connections between our past and our future. Importantly, our narratives unfold around our understanding values and around our aims in which we see these values realized. Lastly, we might say that our narratives make sense of our irreducibly first-person experience of the way in which the worlds matters to us.

In other words, who we are and where we situate ourselves in a collective normative context becomes intelligible to us in terms of *qualitative distinctions of worth* (Taylor 1989, 1991a, 1991b, 2007). We situate ourselves in relation to what we view as having or lacking worth. When interpreting ourselves, and when evaluating our wishes and motivations, we do not simply calculate the options without questioning the intrinsic worth of the desire that motivates us (Taylor 1985a, 1989, 1991a).[3] Rather we deploy *the language*

---

2 The self-understanding that this everyday practice of collective self-interpretation provides us with is not a set of axioms that we are free to choose, but rather it is a milieu made up of culturally shared notions, narratives, and historically shaped values that we grow into and further unfold.

3 A subject who only evaluates weakly—that is, who makes decisions such as whether to eat now or later, or take a holiday in the north or the south—might be described as a simple weigher of alternatives. In weak evaluation, "for something to be judged good it is sufficient that it be desired" (Taylor 1985a, p. 18; Taylor 1991).

of evaluative contrasts, assessing what is desirable by a qualitative portrayal of the options—as noble or base, higher or lower, virtuous or vicious, more or less refined, profound or superficial, etc. When making such qualitative distinctions, we not only evaluate our motivations but also express our ambition to be a specific kind of person and hope for our acts to express this. In the type of "strong" evaluation that relies on qualitative distinctions of worth, "there is also a use of 'good' or some other evaluative term for which being desired is not sufficient" (Taylor 1985a, p. 18). Such identity-constitutive orientation toward the good compels us to distinguish between "right or wrong, better or worse, higher or lower, which are not rendered valid by our own desires, inclinations, or choices, but rather stand independent of these and offer standards by which they can be judged" (Taylor 1989, p. 4).

We have said that in order to interpret and constitute ourselves, we must be embedded in a collectively constituted cultural horizon of significance. It is such an embeddedness that provides us with the necessary "vocabularies" that make it possible for us to interpret ourselves. The next important step is to highlight that within any vocabulary there will be some concepts and distinctions that weigh heavier than others. As Rorty (1989) has observed, the languages in which we describe ourselves contain concepts and distinctions that are more essential to our self-interpretations than others.[4] However, from this short description, it might seem that Taylor's account of practical reason fails to distinguish between different types of claims that different values make on us. For instance, much of Habermas' work aims to maintain a distinction between the realm of "ethical" values that make claims on agents in relation to their practical identities, and the realm of certain "moral" values (treating others as ends, respecting basic rights, and minimizing suffering) that apply to every agent irrespective of the goals and aims that they identify with. The latter realm is one of moral obligations that are universally binding, and that in many cases trump "ethical" values that we might endorse. In other words, Habermas (1993) distinguishes between the "ethical" and "moral" use of practical reason—the former is about self-expression and self-constitution, whereas the latter proceeds by the norm of universalizability in which "ethical" conceptions of the good are disregarded in favor of "moral" claims. One important advantage of maintaining this distinction is that it allows us to

[4] "All vocabularies, even those which contain the words which we take most seriously, the ones most essential to our self-descriptions—are human creations, tools for the creation of such other human artifacts as poems, utopian societies, scientific theories, and future generations" (Rorty 1989, p. 53).

hold on to the idea that practical reason is able to arbitrate conflicts between "ethical" visions of the good on moral grounds (Smith 2004).

Rather than ignoring such an important distinction and explaining away the force of certain moral demands, Taylor offers a different explanation for what Habermas (and Kantians) understand as the priority of the moral. Instead of distinguishing between moral and ethical realms and uses of practical reason, treating others as ends, respecting basic rights, and minimizing suffering are regarded as "higher-order" (or "second-order") values that make possible judgments about other goods. Without abstracting the "right" from the "good," Taylor's distinction functions just like the one that Habermas uses to distinguish between moral and ethical realms. In different ways, both claim to enable an arbitration of conflicts between "ethical" visions of the good.[5] Second-order values (and the qualitative distinctions based on them) define first-order values, and provide a basis for discriminating between them and for deliberating about their importance for our lives. Taylor (1989, p. 65) calls such moral sources "hypergoods," "i.e., goods which not only are incomparably more important than others but provide the standpoint from which these must be weighed, judged, decided about":

> Hypergoods are generally a source of conflict. ... Hypergoods are understood by those who espouse them as a step to a higher moral consciousness. To take perhaps the most salient example of modern culture, many accept as their highest good (or perhaps we should say at this stage, principle of right) a notion of universal justice and/or benevolence, in which all human beings are to be treated equally with respect, regardless of race, class, sex, culture, religion.
>
> (Taylor 1989, p. 64)

With this distinction between first- and second-order values, we can now return to the issue that certain values and distinctions of worth weigh heavier than others in our self-interpretation. Taylor's point is that second-order values are constitutive of the normative grip that first-order values might have on us. They define the first-order values that we identify with.

Against this background, the aim is now to substantiate two claims. First, it will be demonstrated that possibly to an even larger extent than the distinctions "virtuous," "profound," or "noble," "rational" is a qualitative distinction

[5] We should note that this account reduces the complexity of Taylor's account of values. Taylor also distinguishes between "life goods" (ordinary aims that we pursue and which give our lives direction), and "constitutive goods" that are the sources of life goods, such as "features of the universe, or God, or human beings ... which command our moral awe or allegiance, and ... the contemplation of or contact with which empowers us to be good." (Taylor 1991b, p. 243; see also Laitinen 2004).

that has, at least in Western cultural history, continuously been tied to self-interpretation. Second, it will be shown that "rationality" is a first-order value that is limited and formed by second-order values.

4. Rationality is a central concept

There is a long tradition in Western cultural history, dating back to Aristotle, according to which the rationality of human beings, minimally defined as the basic capacity of agents to adopt and reject beliefs on the basis of appropriate reasons, distinguishes them from other creatures. According to this view, there is simply a difference in kind between animal sensations and appetites and the human capability of rational thought, because the latter is capable of transforming other mental capacities (Boyle 2012). Kant famously emphasized that rational human agents have a unique status in the world—not only are they capable of attaining autonomy, but also their will is the source of the moral law. Kant attributes to human beings an intrinsic worth ("dignity") insofar as they are rational agents, capable of self-determination and generating goals and actions guided by reason. In fact, as rational beings embody the moral law, appreciation of the moral law reflects an appreciation of rational agency that expresses the essence of human beings.

At least since Kant's time, rationality expressed in rational agency has been a crucial value that served as a source of admiration. Certainly some of our philosophical thinking about rationality has fundamentally changed over the centuries. For instance, contemporary philosophers seem to be more focused on how human rationality is continuous with the minds of animals, and not so much on finding the one characteristic that marks the difference. The criteria that Aristotle established have been altered in that we now think of rationality as embodied, social, not entirely dispassionate (Lakoff and Johnson 1999), and, we may add, a not entirely unbiased human ideal. However, these relatively "local" changes in philosophical discussions of rationality should not allow us to neglect the fact that the basic meaning of the concept referring to the human capacity to understand, investigate, and manipulate the world has proved extremely stable as a crucial part of our self-understanding.

In support of this thesis, it is also valuable to highlight another line of thought. The point is that the significant extent to which the concept of rationality has been deployed in the self-interpretation of dominant cultures (male, white, propertied) becomes apparent if we consider how the same development excluded women, ethical and racial minorities, and the mentally ill (Heikes 2010). Post-structuralist thinkers have demonstrated how various forms of social marginalization are built into the very definitions of central values such as rationality. Much of Foucault's most stimulating early work focused on showing how seemingly universal values may promote inequality and oppression.[6] In particular, his work is dedicated to showing how the ideal of rationality has shaped the identities of the ruling classes while excluding and controlling women, the lower classes, certain races, and the mentally ill. It is also noteworthy that when the voices of the excluded became louder, their strategy was not to reject the concept of rationality as a part of their self-understanding, but to contest a highly biased concept of rationality.

If it is accurate that the concept of rationality is tied to self-interpretation, then we have reasons to think that it is value-laden. This is because its meaning stems not only from how we see ourselves, but also from how we interpret our goals and relations and the goods we strive to achieve. It is a term of a qualitative contrast, functioning as the basis of admiration and as something that warrants respect (Taylor 1982, p. 142). However, although—at least from the point of view defended here—it is natural to claim that "rationality" is a value-laden concept, we may also draw on other sources to support this claim. For instance, Hilary Putnam acknowledges that the concept of rationality is linked to and reflects ideas of human flourishing:

> If 'rationality' is an ability ... which enables the possessor to determine what questions are relevant questions to ask and what answers it is warranted to accept, then its value is on its sleeve. But it needs no argument that such a conception of rationality is as value loaded as the notion of relevance itself.
>
> (Putnam 1981, p. 202; Timmons 1999, p. 103)

Putnam's point is rather plausible. If rationality permits one to establish the range of meaningful questions and to take a stand on the range of answers that are reasonable, then the conclusion that it is value-laden is warranted. Elsewhere, Putnam also acknowledges the value-laden nature of the concept of rationality, indicating that:

> there are disagreements between cultures (and within one culture) over what is or is not coherent or simple (or "justified" or "plausible," etc.). These controversies are no more settleable than are controversies over the nature of justice. Our views on the nature of coherence and simplicity are historically conditioned just as our views on

[6] Taylor (1989) shows that the Western concept of rationality is linked to a form of theoretical understanding (theoria) which is often used as a supposedly universal measure by which a-theoretical cultures appear less rational. In such cases, the attribution of less rationality does not depend on identifying something like logical contradictions. One crucial difference is that the Western concept of rationality has developed from denoting the capacity to grasp the order of being to being inherently linked to an interest in how things "really are"—that is, outside of the world of social practices.

> the nature of justice or good-ness are. There is no neutral conception of rationality to which one can appeal when the nature of rationality is itself what is at issue.
>
> (Putnam, 1982, pp. 7–8)

In conclusion, certain concepts such as rationality are crucial for processes of self-interpretation, and thus belong to that specific part of our vocabulary within which we think and describe our identities as human beings. Such concepts are quite straightforwardly value-laden in that they are linked to our concept of who we are and the goods that we strive to achieve.

5. Rationality and second-order values

In earlier sections of this chapter we have explicated the distinction between first- and second-order values and maintained that certain values and distinctions of worth weigh heavier than others in our self-interpretation. More specifically, the claim was that second-order values to a significant extent influence first-order values. The aim is now to expand and substantiate this claim by presenting concrete examples that demonstrate how changes in the concept of "rationality" are determined by specific changes in second-order moral values.

5.1. Rationality and the boundaries of the moral community

As Taylor shows, basic, second-order goods (treating others as ends, respecting basic rights, and minimizing suffering) have been a part of our moral vocabulary at least since the Enlightenment. However, specifying what it means to have basic moral respect for others is a matter of considerable controversy. In fact, a sustained look reveals what is best seen as an intriguing inconsistency in Enlightenment thought—the supposedly universal ambition for basic moral respect (but also for liberty and equality) was often limited to a racially demarcated realm of individuals. Some groups were deemed to be outside of the moral sphere by virtue of their racial (and also gender) membership, and the substantially inferior forms of rationality that were supposedly associated with such membership. Although it seems to go against the image of Enlightenment philosophers such as Hume and Kant, the work of both also contains shockingly racially prejudiced passages. In the 1753–1754 edition of Hume's *Essays and Treatises on Several Subjects*, an infamous footnote added to the essay "Of National Characters" states:

> I am apt to suspect the negroes, and in general all the other species of men … to be naturally inferior to the whites. There never was a civilized nation of any other complexion than white, nor even any individual eminent either in action or speculation.

> No ingenious manufactures amongst them, no arts, no sciences. … Such a uniform and constant difference could not happen, in so many countries and ages, if nature had not made an original distinction betwixt these breeds of men. Not to mention our colonies, there are negroe slaves dispersed all over Europe, of which none ever discovered any symptom of ingenuity; tho' low people, without education, will start up amongst us, and distinguish themselves in every profession. In Jamaica, indeed, they talk of one negroe as a man of parts and learning; but 'tis likely he is admired for very slender accomplishments, like a parrot, who speaks a few words plainly.
>
> (Hume, cited in Garrett 2000, pp. 171–172)

It is difficult to explain away such a passage as a momentary digression, as it was published with few minor changes in the 1768, 1770, and 1777 versions (Garrett 2000). In a similar way, in "Observations on the Feelings of the Beautiful and the Sublime," Kant commits the classical fallacy of *ad hominem* when he rejects the content of an utterance of a black person because "this fellow was quite black from head to toe, a clear proof that what he said was stupid" (Mills 1997, 70). Furthermore, Kant explains that the difference between the two races is "as great in regard to mental capacities as in color." Crucially, the difference is not so much in the amount of talent and skill, but the incapability of following the precepts of reason.

Of course, one might note that Kant at the same time also claimed that moral progress at some point will encompass every human being, that he unambiguously held that slavery was unjustifiable, and that Hume has clearly objected to cruel practices in ancient slavery.[7] The aim here is not so much to clarify the forms of racism in Enlightenment thought, as to understand what the inconsistency in limiting basic moral respect to racially demarcated groups reveals. The point that is relevant to the aims of this chapter is linked to the interpretation of second-order values concerning basic moral values that allowed the exclusion of supposedly inferior forms of rationality. The point is not just that the boundaries of the moral community were to a significant extent determined and justified by a concept of rationality. Rather, the more significant point for our present purposes is that the concept of rationality was itself guided by a particular interpretation of second-order values, in such a way that the boundaries of the moral community and the boundaries of the rational community fell together.

The change that we see in thinkers such as Johann Gottfried Herder is first and foremost a change in the understanding of second-order values. Herder was outraged by the way that certain groups were, under the pretext of

[7] Some argue that Kant's moral view still stands, as intellectual inferiority does not warrant denying respect to persons in virtue of being persons.

rationality, excluded from moral concern. In his mature work *Ideas Towards a Philosophy of the History of Humanity*, Herder (1800) argues that a unified human nature bridges the gaps between radical differences, and Book Seven, Chapter One begins with the following sentence: "Notwithstanding the varieties of the human form, there is but one and the same species of man throughout the whole of our earth." With regard to two important aspects, Herder continues Enlightenment thinking. First, he subscribes to the thesis that rational capacities characterize human beings and raise them above the animal kingdom. In fact he speaks of human beings in terms of "high rational destination" (Herder 1800, p. 92). Second, he also believes that the boundaries of the moral community and the boundaries of the rational community fall together. Third, he occasionally attributes to groups more or less capacity for certain accomplishments. For example, his description of Africans in *Ideas* reveals that he does not see them as capable of the same intellectual achievements as Europeans.

However, these continuities with Enlightenment thought appear in a different light once we consider what might be one of Herder's most important achievements. He breaks with Enlightenment thought about rationality and race by reinterpreting basic second-order values in a way that enlarges the moral community and emphasizes human diversity. Yet, we might ask, how is it possible for Herder to widen the boundaries of the moral community, while still holding that the boundaries of moral community and the boundaries of the rational community fall together? The answer is that at the same time as he widens the boundaries of the moral community, he also widens the boundaries of the "rational." In other words, Herder allows a certain *pluralism about rationality,* in which rationality is not merely the faculty that is somehow superimposed on animal nature. Although some groups might exhibit fewer capacities for certain accomplishments, Herder clearly insists that they display *different* forms of rationality that allow them to be citizens in the moral realm. He thus acknowledges the *embedded nature* of rationality, denying that there is a neutral, context-free rationality that can be measured by a yardstick that is external to the culture and the distinct *Lebensform* (form of life) in which it is embedded. As capacities are constitutively formed by their socio-cultural embeddedness, there is no absolute benchmark of effective rationality with which one might measure the different groups with regard to their value (Sikka 2011). The fact that some groups, such as races, might not exhibit the same rational capacities is interpreted as a "natural variation" in the possession of rational skills. In this sense, Herder's pluralism means that not only different goods but also rationality might be realized in different forms across humanity.

The lesson to be drawn here concerns the relationship between first- and second-order values, and more precisely between rationality and basic moral respect. Herder's thinking indicates a reorientation that demonstrates how a change in the boundaries of the moral community ultimately enables a change in the concept of rationality. It is the inclusion of all human life forms within the realm of moral concern that makes it possible for Herder to validate different forms of thinking as rational and as having a value of their own. In this case, a change in the boundaries of the moral community led to a change in the understanding of what rationality is and the forms of thinking and behavior that it includes.

5.2. **Psychiatry, rationality, and the boundaries of the moral community**

The example elaborated in Section 5.1 made clearer something fundamental about the relationship between basic moral respect (as a second-order value) and rationality, demonstrating the manner in which a change in the boundaries of the moral community enables a change in the concept of rationality. In the following account, the aim is to gather further support for this thesis, while at the same time returning to psychiatry.

In the early 1850s, Samuel Cartwright, a physician in the South of the USA, coined the term "drapetomania" for a mental disorder that he believed was absent from the relevant medical literature of his time. He considered "drapetomania" to be a specifically Southern condition that could contribute to a variety of emerging diagnoses, such as kleptomania, pyromania, and nymphomania, all of which were characterized by impulsive behaviors. He believed that black slaves suffering from drapetomania had the defining "symptom" of an irrational desire to run away from the conditions of slavery. In his function as the chairman of a Louisiana State Medical Convention committee, Cartwright's task was to chart the disorder of black slaves of the South. The commission's report, entitled "A Report on the Diseases and Physical Peculiarities of the Negro Race," was presented at the Annual Meeting of the Association in March 1851, and later published in the *New Orleans Medical and Surgical Journal* (Bynum 2000). It contained this new diagnostic category.

Importantly, Cartwright's writings reveal that the diagnostic category of "drapetomania," characterized by a desire to escape from slavery, was only possible on a certain interpretation of second-order values concerning the boundaries of the moral community:

> Our Declaration of Independence, which was drawn up at a time when negroes were scarcely considered as human beings, '*That all men are by nature free and equal*,' and only intended to apply to white men, is often quoted in support of the false dogma

> that all mankind possess the same mental, physiological and anatomical organization, and that the liberty, free institutions, and whatever else would be a blessing to one portion, would, under the same external circumstances, be to all, without regard to any original or internal differences, inherent in the organization. … for here, in a country where two races of men dwell together, both born on the same soil, breathing the same air, and surrounded by the same external agents—liberty, which is elevating the one race of people above all other nations, sinks the other into beastly sloth and torpidity; and the slavery, which the one would prefer death rather than endure, improves the other in body, mind and morals; thus proving the dogma false, and establishing the truth that there is a radical, internal, or physical difference between the two races, so great in kind, as to make what is wholesome and beneficial for the white man, as liberty, republican or free institutions, etc., not only unsuitable to the negro race, but actually poisonous to its happiness.
>
> (Cartwright 1851, p. 715)

Cartwright invokes the Scriptures to show that the black race was intended to occupy a position of submission, and that both their exclusion from the moral community and slavery itself reflect a natural order and "unalterable physiological laws." As well as morally neutral differences such as the color of skin, the color of blood and bile (all darker colors), and the senses of hearing and smell (better than in whites), the decisive difference that excluded black slaves from the moral community was a "defective hematosis, or atmospherization of the blood, conjoined with a deficiency of cerebral matter in the cranium, and an excess of nervous matter distributed to the organs of sensation and assimilation, that is the true cause of that debasement of mind, which has rendered the people of Africa unable to take care of themselves." Such deficiency not only resulted in the features characteristic of black slaves, but also Cartwright lists submissiveness, worshipping authority, tranquility and sensual enjoyment, idleness and lack of proper rationality. According to Cartwright (1851, p. 694) this also explained why black slaves were unfit for the enjoyment of freedom and would "always prefer the same kind of government, which we call slavery." He held that because they were creatures incapable of rational thought, freedom would only bring them misery, which is why the inclination to seek this state was the result of mental disorder:

> The black blood distributed to the brain chains the mind to ignorance, superstition and barbarism, and bolts the door against civilization, moral culture and religious truth. The compulsory power of the white man, by making the slothful negro take active exercise, puts into active play the lungs, through whose agency the vitalized blood is sent to the brain, to give liberty to the mind, and to open the door to intellectual improvement. The very exercise, so beneficial to the negro, is expended in cultivating the burning fields in cotton, sugar, rice and tobacco, which, but for his labor, would, from the heat of the climate, go uncultivated, and their products lost to

> the world. Both parties are benefitted—the negro as well as his master—even more. But there is a third party benefitted—the world at large. The three millions of bales of cotton, made by negro labor, afford a cheap clothing for the civilized world. The laboring classes of all mankind, having less to pay for clothing, have more money to spend in educating their children, and in intellectual, moral and religious progress.
>
> (Cartwright 1851, p. 714)

We see that the exclusion from the moral community allowed people like Cartwright to classify the attempts to escape of black slaves as irrational to the point of being a mental disorder. Otherwise, as we have seen in Herder's work, the extension of the boundaries of the moral community to include black slaves would have compelled Cartwright to acknowledge them as capable of forms of thinking that deserve the label of rationality. However, in that case it would not have been possible to maintain that running away from servitude under horrific circumstances is a deeply irrational behavior caused by an underlying mental disorder. The abolition *zeitgeist*'s extension of the moral community makes possible to understand the "symptoms" of a desire to flee from slavery as reflecting perfectly rational thought.

6. Rationality (and mental disorder) is identity-tied

Before we proceed to the next step of the argument, let us briefly summarize what we have achieved so far. It was argued that who we are is (at least partly) constituted by the manner in which we interpret ourselves. Then, it was established that rationality is a central concept in our self-understanding, that it is value-laden, and that rationality and mental disorder are both for several reasons strongly tied together, and can be thought of as relational antonyms. The point that follows if we draw together these considerations is that rationality and mental disorder, due to their particular role, are "tied to our identities." They are *identity-tied concepts.* This means that, far from being fixed, the concept of rationality depends on how we interpret and understand our identities, which is again spelled out in relation to second-order values.

While this is a crucial point to establish, it has to be rendered more precise in order to understand the most important implications for the context of this inquiry. Given that the strength of dependence can vary, we need to specify what special kind of dependence relationship we are dealing with. For instance, an entity X might depend for its existence upon entity Y in an ontological and not merely causal sense. However, the dependence relationship that is relevant for us in this context is a kind of logical dependence. The proposal here is that the relation between central concepts that we use to describe ourselves and our identity (the result of our self-interpretation) is best described as a *supervenience relation*.[8] That is, the concept of rationality (or mental disorder) X that we use to describe ourselves supervenes on identity Y. This means that there cannot be a change in the meaning of concept X without at the same time changing our identities—there cannot be an X difference without a Y difference. Importantly, further precision is needed here in that supervenience relations can take several forms. In our case, rationality/mental disorder stand in an *asymmetrical supervenience* relation to our identities. The fact that the relationship is asymmetrical means that concept X supervenes on identity Y, but not vice versa. In terms of change, this means that we might change our identities by redefining the way we understand ourselves, without there necessarily being a change in our concepts of rationality and mental disorder. The concept of, say, the value of solidarity might become more important to us than the value of individual uniqueness, resulting in a change in the way that we describe ourselves. Such changes will not necessarily affect the concepts of rationality and mental disorder. However, the asymmetrical nature of the supervenience relation means that this is not the case in the other direction. There cannot be any significant change in the concepts of rationality and mental disorder without there being a change at the level of identity.

7. The limits of naturalism

If it is true that the concept of mental disorder is ultimately identity-tied, what are the implications for the attempt to locate an adequate concept of mental disorder? The first impression is surely that being identity-tied, and thereby dependent on how we interpret and understand ourselves, the concept will be extremely fluid and ever changing. Recall Hacking's thesis about classifications that attempt to describe the kinds involved in mental disorder (Hacking 1999). In contrast to the natural sciences, the classifications in social sciences are distinctive and track "human kinds," which are essentially "interactive kinds" that interact with what they classify. In Chapter 6 we saw how Hacking emphasizes that mental disorders might be interactive kinds because the classification enters into interaction with and influences what it classifies. In other words, interactive kinds are subject to a "looping effect" and hence become rather elusive "moving targets."

[8] This relationship is metaphysically contingent. Of course, a *supervenience relation* between entities can be claimed in different strengths. In the present context, saying that "there cannot be an X difference without a Y difference" should not be understood in the sense that it cannot happen consistently with the laws of nature.

It is not difficult to discern that there are some parallels between the idea of "identity-tied concepts" and the idea of looping effects. However, the picture is more complicated in the former case. It is not that experts create a classification that some people appropriate, and, in a second step, those so classified react and create a new scenario that might lead to further changes in the classification. Basically, our case is different because we are not dealing with the process of "making up people," as Hacking (1995, 2007) describes it, but with the process of "making up ourselves." What we should emphasize here is that when we engage in self-interpretation we are "making up ourselves," coming to understand ourselves in a new light, and seek to attain different or just more precisely articulated aims. Although this process has similar effects to those that Hacking describes, for instance certain alterations in the way that we understand our own past, the results are more far-reaching.

Due to these characteristics, and particularly the complex forms of looping, serious limitations arise for any naturalist, objective concept of mental disorder. In addition, limitations also arise concerning the possibility of a scientific discovery that would tell us where to draw the boundaries of mental disorder. Discovery, understood in a strictly naturalistic sense, seems impossible due to the intimate intertwining of the concepts of rationality and mental disorder with a particular way of understanding ourselves. Instead, the solution might be something like a "relaxed naturalism" that incorporates the view proposed here, yet avoids sliding into relativism. Indeed, the point that this section puts forward is that there is an alternative between naturalism and relativism. First, however, it should be indicated that it is indeed possible to operate with a concept of "discovery" that is able to incorporate the points made here. For instance, when we try to make sense of ourselves, the process usually involves not only actively constituting ourselves, but also a dimension of "discovery." We might find ourselves puzzled by discovering that we are indebted to a certain ideal or goal, or surprised by finding that we are no longer wholeheartedly committed to something that used to be crucial to us. This is of course a limited sense of "discovery," as it depends on a *previous* change in the conception of who we believe ourselves to be as human beings.

8. Beyond relativism (and naturalism)

To clarify the position between naturalism and relativism, it is useful to recall the challenge of categorical and dimensional criticism. We need to ask whether the recognition of the elusive nature of a concept of mental disorder will result in an overly expansive concept, which might lead to a medicalization of suffering. Surely, acknowledging that values shape our understanding of what mental disorder is, and simultaneously conceding the plurality of values, we cannot expect anything but continuing disagreement about the boundaries of mental disorder. But does this not mean that nothing can prevent the slide into a detrimental relativism about mental disorder?

In short, the answer is no. The acknowledgement of the nature of self-interpretation and the link to rationality and mental disorder sets particular limitations with regard to what can count as a disorder. However, such limitations can first become intelligible if we pay close attention to the nature of the second-order values that ultimately help determine the concept of mental disorder. It is first then that we can see how the perspective offered here affords us with a stand that is not available to relativists. The problem of the relativist (who sees mental disorder as entirely socially constructed) is that relativism makes it difficult to critically engage with the values involved in the process in which mental disorder is supposedly socially constructed. Because the relativist regularly thinks of (moral) values themselves as little more than reflecting societal power structures, she implicitly discounts the possibility of a critical dialog about justified and non-justified interpretations of the relevant values. However, in that case the relativist has no basis for engaging in moral reasoning.

This is very different from the perspectice proposed here. We may agree with naturalism that it is indeed possible to identify cases of abuse and overextension. Nonetheless, we may simultaneously claim that such identification proceeds in a manner that is in opposition to a naturalist position. The point is that cases of abuse and overextension cannot be identified by a purely theoretical inquiry into culture-independent standards; they cannot be considered independently of a practical point of view that is socially and historically mediated. However, in opposition to the relativist position, this does not mean that there cannot be limitations or normative standards that one could appeal to in order to criticize concepts of mental disorder. Rather, limitations become intelligible when we are properly engaged in the process of interpreting the relevant second-order values that shape the concepts of rationality and mental disorder. Restrictions emerge because these values cannot be interpreted arbitrarily; they have limitations and will resist certain interpretations.

While naturalism must appeal to a flawed idea of a neutral standard, relativism recognizes value-ladenness, but leaves us without normative standards to appeal to in order to criticize concepts of mental disorder and classifications informed by them. The approach proposed here can be seen as lying between these two positions. On the one hand it holds on to the idea that there are legitimate standards that one can appeal to in order to criticize concepts of mental disorder. On the other hand, it acknowledges the value-ladenness of the concept, and that critique can only be *immanent*—that is, the standards that are employed in a criticism must be internal to the practices that one wishes to criticize (see Stahl 2013). A critical engagement cannot build on a preconceived normative standard that is justified independently of any examination of the social practices in question.

However, one may ask how such a critical engagement can ever actually transform anything or induce changes if the normative principles that it employs stem from the self-understanding and practices themselves. Will such a critique not merely reinforce these norms instead of challenging them? In order to see why this is not the case, we need to shed light on certain aspects of this process. By demonstrating that certain ideals and values might have a more diverse meaning than the ones currently acknowledged, and by revealing internal tensions, criticism might help to transform the understanding of values that provide the framework for practices. The inconsistencies *within* self-understandings, and those *between* self-understandings and the practices that they guide, might convince agents that these inconsistencies constitute reason for change. Still, such criticism should not be seen as a mere consistency check of accepted norms. When examining the self-understanding of the members of a practice, one usually unearths hitherto unacknowledged interpretative possibilities. These create implications for a self-understanding that enable one to address and evaluate both the self-understanding and the practice, without having to employ external standards. This is why such criticism not only reproduces and applies the acknowledged norms of a community, but also investigates them in a way that results in new interpretative possibilities that exceed what is currently accepted.

Overall, the view sketched in this section aims to steer clear of both naturalism and relativism, and claims that the discussion of the boundaries of mental disorder should not be separated from discussions about moral values. Instead, a fruitful dialog about mental disorder is best achieved by integrating it with a discussion about self-interpretations and the values that are reflected in them. The point is to generate an awareness that simultaneously tracks changes in the definitions of mental disorders *and* changes in our self-interpretations. This involves not only critically evaluating whether the relevant values are interpreted in ways that are justified, but also ensuring that the dialog unfolds in a domination-free context.

9. **Conclusion**

In the course of Part II of this book, the idea that mental disorder is a classical concept with necessary and sufficient conditions for falling within it was rejected. It was also argued that even thinking of it in terms of having a prototype structure (connecting the relevant entities by "family resemblance") and being value-laden does not fully account for the elusiveness of the concept. Against such a background, this chapter set out to provide some explanation for its elusive and dynamic nature. First, it was emphasized that both rationality and mental disorder are for several reasons strongly tied together and can be thought of as relational antonyms. After this crucial point had been made, it was argued that who we are is (at least partly) constituted by the manner in which we interpret ourselves. Yet such self-interpretation does not take place in a vacuum; rather, it necessitates a cultural background horizon that is constituted by values that guide the ways in which we lead our lives. Although there are second-order values that are so deeply ingrained in who we are that some are inclined to see them as "objective," we have focused on rationality as a central concept in our self-understanding. Drawing together these considerations, one crucial conclusion is that rationality (and mental disorder) are particular concepts that are "tied to our identities." At least to some extent, the concept of rationality depends on how we interpret and understand ourselves, which better explains its elusive, dynamic nature.

The reflections in this chapter closed with the implications of this result with regard to the limits of empirical discovery. To some extent, the view sketched here enables us to explore a way of thinking about mental disorder that steers clear of the pitfalls to which naturalism and relativism fall victim. In closing, it is important to emphasize that the serious limitations of naturalism that were addressed in Part II of this book should not be taken to mean that concepts such as "mental disorder" and "rationality" do not form a "kind" that can be the proper object of scientific inquiry. Rather, the point is that any enterprise that fails to appreciate the role of interpretation and self-interpretation discussed in this book inevitably runs the risk of compromising its results.

Chapter 10

Conclusion

In most Western countries, the publication of the influential DSM-5 has initiated new debates about conceptual philosophical problems in psychiatry, and about psychiatry's status as a medico-scientific discipline. For instance, in May 2013, one of the UK's best-known broadsheets, *The Observer*, published a lengthy article with the telling title "Medicine's big new battleground: does mental illness really exist?" (Doward 2013) giving voice to professionals and laypeople who not only questioned whether forms of shyness, depression after bereavement, and Internet addiction should be classified as mental disorders, but also posed a more fundamental question about the role and scientific status of psychiatric diagnosis. At the same time, Allen Frances, former chair of the DSM-IV Task Force, called the American Psychiatric Association's approval of DSM-5 "a sad day for psychiatry," openly admitting that it was "the saddest moment" of his almost 50-year-long career in psychiatric research, teaching, and practice (Frances 2012). Frances fears not only that the DSM-5 lacks a solid scientific basis, but also that it will lead to massive overdiagnosis and overmedication. Large false-positive populations will be created as common phenomena such as memory lapses that are characteristic of old age (with no risk for dementia) can now be diagnosed as Minor Neurocognitive Disorder. The fact that for most conditions the DSM-5 loosens the diagnosis criteria leads many, like Frances, to fear that the existing diagnostic inflation will turn into a hyperinflation.

This is not the place to roll out the whole debate in detail, but rather it is appropriate to focus on one aspect in this debate that is closely related to the aims of this book. In 2013, the Division of Clinical Psychology (DCP) in the UK issued a Position Statement (Division of Clinical Psychology 2013) concerning the DSM-5 that has some overlap in content with Frances' critique. Importantly, however, the first key conceptual issue that the Position Statement puts forward is concerned with an issue that lies at the heart of this book. Criticizing the DSM-5 for what has been referred to in general terms as a "naturalist position," the first paragraph of the statement states:

> Interpretation presented as objective fact: Psychiatric diagnosis is often presented as an objective statement of fact, but is, in essence, a clinical judgement based on

> observation and interpretation of behaviour and self-report, and thus subject to variation and bias.
>
> (Division of Clinical Psychology 2013, p. 3)

The abstract of the whole statement reads as follows:

> The DCP is of the view that it is timely and appropriate to affirm publicly that the current classification system as outlined in DSM and ICD, in respect of the functional psychiatric diagnoses, has significant conceptual and empirical limitations. Consequently, there is a need for a paradigm shift in relation to the experiences that these diagnoses refer to, towards a conceptual system not based on a 'disease' model.
>
> (Division of Clinical Psychology 2013, p. 1)

What we see here is that the Division of Clinical Psychology in the UK raises issues that correspond to a surprising degree to the aims of this book. The focus is on the neglected role of interpretation in clinical settings and on the naturalistic, "disease model" determining the concept of mental disorder. This book has attempted to contribute to both of these issues by explaining why it is important to focus on interpretation in psychiatric theorizing, empirical research, and clinical practice. One of the main lessons of Part I was precisely that hermeneutical sensibility is needed for an adequate historical understanding of conditions and an adequate, second-person understanding in clinical contexts. Chapter 3 argued that any reliable understanding of texts relevant to psychiatric inquiry must be interpreted with particular care, taking into account quality, representativity, genre, and cultural–historical embeddedness. Chapter 4 made a related point concerning second-person encounters between the patient and the psychiatrist or therapist in clinical settings. As the meaning structures that shape the patient's self-understanding and the specific profile of their mental distress cannot be clearly separated, it is of crucial importance to develop receptivity toward the processes of interpretation that are involved.

Part II of this book has contributed to the second issue raised by the Position Statement of the Division of Clinical Psychology. Thinking of mental disorder in terms of identity-tied concepts helps to resist decontextualizing tendencies, in which the diagnosis downplays the connection between psychological distress and historical and socio-cultural contexts. It might help to identify and also to resist what might be perceived as an ethnocentric Western bias of psychiatric diagnosis.

This investigation will conclude with some reflections on the limitations of the project. Hopefully it has become clear how the amalgamated nature of psychiatry leads to rather unique methodological challenges concerning processes of human understanding. This book has also aimed to establish that ideas and arguments from philosophical hermeneutics should be incorporated more thoroughly in the field of philosophy and psychiatry. By outlining how such ideas could be incorporated, not as a unified position, but rather as a set of methodologically interconnected aspects, this book hopes to have demonstrated the potential benefits of philosophical reflection for current debates in psychiatry. However, it is fair to ask whether the approach outlined in this book has helped to provide a more satisfactory answer to the forms of criticism that have been presented here, and that are clearly resurfacing in contemporary debates in the wake of the publication of the DSM-5. The answer is modest, but nevertheless positive. The contribution has been rather indirect, in that it aimed to clarify some of the assumptions on which contemporary debates are based. Clearly the idea that "mental disorder" belongs to a class of concepts that are identity-tied will not satisfy some, and particularly not the categorical critic. However, if the thesis is correct, it will establish that the categorical criticism is itself based on flawed naturalistic assumptions and an inflated idea of what we can expect from psychiatric diagnosis.

References

Acheson, O. (1998). Independent Inquiry into Inequalities in Health. London: HMSO.

Alford, A., & Beck, A. T. (1997). *The integrative power of cognitive therapy.* New York: Guilford Press.

American Psychiatric Association. (1980). Diagnostic and statistical manual of mental disorders (3rd ed.). Arlington, VA.

American Psychiatric Association. (2000). *Diagnostic and Statistical Manual of Mental Disorders* (4th ed., TR). Washington, DC: American Psychiatric Association.

Amundson, R. (2000). Against Normal Function *Stud. Hist. Phil. Biol. & Biomed. Sci.*, **31** (1): 33–53.

Ananth, M. (2008). *In Defense of an Evolutionary Concept of Health. Nature, Norms, and Human Biology.* London: Ashgate.

Anderson, L. (2001). *Autobiography.* London and New York: Routledge.

Andrews, P. W., & Thompson, A. J. (2009). The bright side of being blue: Depression as an adaptation for analyzing complex problems. *Psychological Review*, **116**, 620–654.

Angel, K. (2003). "Defining Psychiatry: Aubrey Lewis's 1938 Report and the Rockefeller Foundation," in *European Psychiatry on the Eve of War: Aubrey Lewis, the Maudsley Hospital and the Rockefeller Foundation in the 1930s* (Katherine Angel, Edgar Jones, and Michael Neve, Eds.) (London: Wellcome Trust Centre for the History of Medicine at University College London, Medical History Supplement 22), pp. 39–56.

Appiah, K. A. (2003). *Thinking It Through: An Introduction to Contemporary Philosophy,* New York: Oxford University Press.

Appiah, K. A. (2005). *The Ethics of Identity,* Princeton: Princeton University Press.

Aristotle. (1984 edition). *Problematal* in: *The Complete Works of Aristotle* **Vol. 2** (ed. Jonathan Barnes), Princeton University Press.

Armstrong, D. M. (1968). *A Materialist Theory of the Mind.* London: Routledge and Kegan Paul.

Armstrong, D. M. (1981). *The Nature of Mind and Other Essays.* New York:

Arnason, V. (2000). Gadamerian dialogue in the patient-professional interaction. *Medicine, Health Care and Philosophy* **3**(1): 17–23.

Ayotte, J., Peretz, I., Hyde, K. (2002). Congenital amusia. A group study of adults afflicted with a music-specific disorder. *Brain* **125**(2): 238–251.

Babb, L. (1951). *The Elizabethan Malady: A Study of* Melancholia *in English Literature from 1580 to 1642.* Michigan State University Press.

Banner, N. F. & Thornton, T. (2007). The new philosophy of psychiatry: its (recent) past, present and future: a review of the Oxford University Press series *International Perspectives in Philosophy and Psychiatry*, Philosophy, Ethics, and Humanities in Medicine, **2**:9.

Baptista, T., Aldana, E., Angeles, F., & Beaulieu, S. (2008). Evolution theory: An overview of its applications in psychiatry. *Psychopathology*, **41**, 17–27.

Barker, G., & Kitcher, P. (2013). *Philosophy of Science: A New Introduction*, Oxford University Press.

Bartlett, E. (1844). *Essay on the Philosophy of Medical Science*, Philadelphia: Lea and Blanchard.

Barton, W. (1973). Letter from Walter Barton to Sidney Malitz, dated March 20 1973. *Archives of the American Psychiatric Association*. Professional Affairs. Box 2. Folder 74.

Barve, A., & Wagner, A. (2013). A latent capacity for evolutionary innovation through exaptation in metabolic systems, *Nature* **500**, 203–206

Beach, S., & Amir, N. (2003). Is Depression Taxonic, Dimensional, or Both? *Journal of Abnormal Psychology*, **112**, 228–236.

Bebbington, P. E., Hurry, J. & Tennant, C. (1981). Psychotic disorders in selected immigrant groups in Camberwell. Social Psychiatry, **16**, 43–51.

Bechtel, W. (1985). In Defense of a Naturalistic Concept of Health. In *Biomedical Ethics Reviews*. Edited by Humber, JM and Almeder, RF. Clifton: Humana Press, 131–170.

Beck, A. T. (1967). *Depression: Clinical, Experimental and Theoretical Aspects*, New York: Hoeber.

Beck, A. T. (1983). Cognitive therapy of depression: New perspectives. In P. J. Clayton & J. E. Barrett (Eds.), *Treatment of depression: Old controversies and new approaches* (pp. 265–284). New York: Raven Press.

Beck, A. T., & Alford, B. A. (2009). *Depression: Causes and Treatments* (2nd ed). Philadelphia: University of Pennsylvania Press.

Beck, A. T., Rush, A. J., Shaw, B. F., et al. (1979). *Cognitive therapy of depression*. New York: Guilford Press.

Beck, A. T., Steer, R. A., & Brown, G. K. (1996). *Manual for the* Beck *Depression Inventory-II*. San Antonio, TX: Psychological Corporation.

Beck, J. S. 1995. *Cognitive therapy: Basics and beyond*. New York: Guilford.

Becker, G. (1997). *Disrupted Lives: How People Create Meaning in a Chaotic World*. Berkeley, CA: University of California Press.

Beebee, H., & Sabbarton-Leary, N. (2010). Are Psychiatric Kinds Real? *European Journal of Analytic Philosophy* 6 (*1*): 11–27.

Bermúdez, J. L. (2003). *Thinking Without Words*, New York. Oxford University Press.

Berrios, G. E. (1988). "Melancholia and Depression During the 19th Century: A Conceptual History" *British Journal of Psychiatry, 153*, 298–304.

Berrios, G. E. (1996). *The History of Mental Symptoms*. Cambridge, Cambridge University Press.

Berrios, G., & Porter, R. (1998). *The History of Clinical Psychiatry: The Origin and History of Psychiatric Disorders*. New York: New York University Press.

Berrios, G. E., & Beer, D. (1994). The notion of unitary psychosis: a conceptual history. *History of Psychiatry*, **5**: 13–36.

Bird, A. (2007). *Nature's Metaphysics: Laws and Properties*. Oxford: Oxford University.

Bird, A. (2009). "Essences and Natural Kinds" *Routledge Companion to Metaphysics* (eds R. Le Poidevin, P. Simons, A. McGonigal, and R. Cameron) Abingdon: Routledge 497–506.

Bird, A., & Tobin, E. (2008). Natural Kinds. In: *Stanford Encyclopedia of Philosophy*. <http://plato.stanford.edu/entries/natural-kinds>

Blackburn, S. (1999). *Think: A Compelling Introduction to Philosophy*, Oxford: OUP.

Blackmore, R. (1725). *A Treatise of the Spleen and Vapours: or, Hypocondriacal and Hysterical Affections*. London: J. Pemberton.

Blatt, S. J. (2004). *Experiences of depression: Theoretical, clinical, and research perspectives*. Washington, DC: American Psychological Association.

Bola, J. R., Mosher, L. R., & Cohen, D. (2005). Treatment of newly diagnosed psychosis without antipsychotic medications: the Soteria project. In S. Kirk (Ed), *Mental disorders in the Social Environment: critical perspectives*. New York: Columbia University Press. pp. 368–84.

Bolton, D. (2008). *What is mental disorder? An essay in philosophy, science and values*. Oxford: Oxford University Press.

Boorse, C. (1975). On the distinction between disease and illness. *Philosophy and Public Affairs* 5:49–68.

Boorse, C. (1976). What a theory of mental health should be. *Journal of the Theory of Social Behaviour* **6**:61–84.

Boorse, C. (1977). Health as a Theoretical Concept. *Philosophy of Science* 1977, **44**:542–573.

Boorse, C. (1987). "Concepts of health." In Donald VanDeVeer and Tom Regan, ed., *Health Care Ethics: An Introduction*, Philadelphia: Temple University Press, 359–393.

Boorse, C. (1997). A Rebuttal on health. In What is Disease?. Edited by: Humber JF, Almeder RF. Totowa NJ: Humana Press:, *Biomedical Ethics Reviews*, 1–134.

Boorse, C. (2014). "A Second Rebuttal On Health" *Journal of Medicine and Philosophy*, **39**: 683–724.

Boyd, R. (1991). "Realism, Anti-Foundationalism and the Enthusiasm for Natural Kinds," *Philosophical Studies* **61**:127–148.

Boyd, R. (1999). "Homeostasis, Species, and Higher Taxa," in Robert A. Wilson (ed.), *Species: New Interdisciplinary Essays*, Cambridge: MIT Press.

Boyle, M. (2012). Essentially Rational Animals, in *Rethinking Epistemology*, ed. G. Abel and J.Conant (Eds.) *Berlin Studies in Knowledge Research* **Vol. 2**, Berlin/New York.

Bracken, P. J. (1999). "The Importance of Heidegger for Psychiatry." *Philosophy, Psychiatry, & Psychology 6.2: 83–85.*

Bracken, P., & Thomas, P. (2010). From Szasz to Foucault: On the Role of Critical Psychiatry, *Philosophy, Psychiatry, & Psychology* **17** (3): 219–228.

Brewin, C. R. (2006). Understanding cognitive behaviour therapy: A retrieval competition account. *Behaviour Research and Therapy* **44**: 765–784.

Bright, T. (orig. 1586). *Treatise on Melancholy*. New York: Columbia University Press, 1940 edition.

Brown, J. R., & Fehige, Y. (2014). "Thought Experiments", *The Stanford Encyclopedia of Philosophy*, Edward N. Zalta (ed.). <http://plato.stanford.edu/archives/fall2014/entries/thought-experiment/>

Brown, T. L. (2009). *Imperfect Oracle: The Epistemic and Moral Authority of Science*. University Park, PA: Pennsylvania State University Press.

Bucknill, J. C., & Tuke, D.H. (1858). *Manual of psychological medicine: containing the history, nosology, description, statistics, diagnosis, pathology, and treatment of insanity*, J.&A. Churchill, London.

Bunyan, J. (1666/2007). *Grace Abounding to the Chief of Sinners: In a Faithful Account of the Life and Death of John Bunyan*, New York: Cosimo.

Burt, D. B., Zembar, M. J., & Niederehe, G. (1995). Depression and memory impairment: A meta-analysis of the association, its pattern and specificity. *Psychological Bulletin* **117**: 285–305.

Burton, R. (1621/1850). *The Anatomy of Melancholy*. New York: Wiley.

Bury, M. (2001). Illness narratives: fact or fiction? *Sociology of Health and Illness* **23** (3): 263–285.

Butera, G. (2011). Thomas aquinas and cognitive therapy: An exploration of the promise of the thomistic psychology. *Philosophy, Psychiatry, and Psychology* **17**(4), 347–366.

Bynum, B. (2000). Discarded Diagnoses, *The Lancet* **356** (9241) 1615.

Byrne, A. (2011). Knowing that I am thinking. In A. Hatzimoysis (Ed.), *Self-Knowledge* (pp. 105–124). Oxford: OUP.

Caplan, P. (2012). Psychiatric Diagnosis: Too Little Science, Too Many Conflicts of Interest. www.awpsych.org/index.php?option=com_content&view=article&id=101&catid=74&Itemid=126. Psychiatric Diagnosis: Too Little Science, Too Many Conflicts of Interest, [[Homepage of the Association for Women in Psychology, Retrieved 02.2014]]

Carruthers, P. (2009). How we know our own minds: The relationship between mind-reading and metacognition. *Behavioral and Brain Sciences* **32**(2), 121–138.

Carter, K. C. (2003). *The Rise of Causal Concepts of Disease: Case Histories*. Ashgate Publishing Company: Burlington, VT.

Cartwright, S., et al. (1851). "Report on the Diseases and Physical Peculiarities of the Negro Race," *New Orleans Medical and Surgical journal* **7**: 691–715.

Cautin, R. L. (2011). A Century of Psychotherapy, 1860–1960. In J.C. Norcross, G.R. VandenBos, & D.K. Freedheim (Eds.), *History of Psychotherapy, Second Edition* (pp. 3–62). Washington, DC: American Psychological Association.

Charland, L. C. (2006). The cognitive modularity of emotions. *Canadian Journal of Philosophy* **32**, 213–228.

Clark, D. A., Beck, A. T., & Brown, G. (1989). Cognitive mediation in general psychiatric outpatients: A test of the cognitive content-specificity hypothesis. *Journal of Personality and Social Psychology* **56**: 958–964.

Clark, D. A., Beck, A. T., & Stewart, B. (1990). Cognitive specificity and positive-negative affectivity: Complementary or contradictory views on anxiety and depression? *Journal of Abnormal Psychology* **99**: 148–155.

Clark, D. A., Beck, A. T., & Alford, B. A. (1999). *Scientific foundations of cognitive theory and therapy of depression*. New York: Wiley.

Colby, V. (1978). "Browning's "Saul": The Exorcism of Romantic Melancholy" *Victorian Poetry*, **Vol. 16**, No. 1/2, 88–99.

Conway, K. (2007). *Illness and the Limits of Expression*. Ann Arbor, MI: The University of Michigan Press.

Cooper, D. (1967). *Psychiatry and anti-psychiatry*, Tavistock Publications: London.

Cooper, R. (2005). *Classifying Madness* (Dordrecht: Springer).

Cosmides, L., & Tooby, J. (1987). From evolution to behavior: evolutionary psychology as the missing link. In *The latest on the best. Essays on evolution and optimality*, ed. J. Dupre, 277–306. Cambridge, MA: MIT Press.

Cosmides, L., & Tooby, J. (1999). Toward an evolutionary taxonomy of treatable conditions. *Journal of Abnormal Psychology* **108**: 453–464.

Cosmides, L., & Tooby, J. (2000). Consider the source: The evolution of adaptations for decoupling and metarepresentation.' In *Metarepresentations*, ed. D. Sperber. Oxford: Oxford University Press.

Craver, C. F. (2009). "Mechanisms and Natural Kinds," *Philosophical Psychology* **22** (5):575–594.

Cushman, P. (1992). *Constructing the self, constructing America: Studies in the cultural history of psychotherapy.* New York: Addison-Wesley.

Daly, C. (1998). Natural kinds. In *Routledge Encyclopedia of Philosophy, Version 1.0*, London: Routledge.

Daly, R. W. (2007). "Before Depression: The Medieval Vice of Acedia" *Psychiatry* **70** (1), 30–51.

Darwin, C. (1859/2003). *On the Origin of Species*, Joseph Carroll (ed.) Peterborough: Broadview Press.

Davidson, D. (1987). Knowing one's own mind. *Proceedings and Addresses of the American Philosophical Association* **60**(3): 441–458.

Davies, M. (1998). Language, thought, and the language of thought (Aunty's own argument revisited). In P. Carruthers & J. Boucher (Eds.), *Language and thought* (pp. 226–247). Cambridge: Cambridge University Press.

Davis, D. R. 1970. Depression as adaptation to crisis. British Journal of Medical Psychology **43**: 109–116.

De Man, P. (1979). Autobiograpy as De-Facement. *Modern Language Notes*, **94**: 919–930.

Dennett, D. C. (1984). *Elbow Room: The Varieties of Free Will Worth Wanting*, Cambridge: MIT Press.

Dennett, D. C. (1996). *Darwin's dangerous idea*, New York: Simon & Schuster.

Derrida, J. (1980). The Law of Genre. *Critical Inquiry*, **Vol.** 7, No. 1, pp. 55–81.

DeRubeis, R. J., Siegle, G. J., & Hollon, S. D. (2008). Cognitive therapy versus medications for depression: Treatment outcomes and neural mechanisms. Nature Reviews Neuroscience, **9**, 788–796.

DeVito, S. (2000). On the Value-Neutrality of the Concepts of Health and Disease: Unto the Breach Again *Journal of Medicine and Philosophy* **25** (5): 539–567

Dilthey, W. (1989). *Introduction to the Human Sciences, Selected Works* **Vol. 1**, R.A. Makkreel and F. Rodi (eds.), Princeton, NJ: Princeton University Press.

Division of Clinical Psychology. (2013). *Position Statement on the Classification of Behaviour and Experience in Relation to Functional Psychiatric Diagnoses: time for a paradigm shift.* Leicester: The British Psychological Society.

Dobson, K. S., & Dozois, D. J. A. (2010). Historical and philosophical bases of the cognitive- behavioral therapies. In K. S. Dobson (Ed.), *Handbook of cognitive behavioural therapies* (pp. 2–38). NY: Guilford Press.

Donaldson, C., & Lam, D. (2004). Rumination, mood and social problem-solving in major depression. *Psychological Medicine* **34**: 1309–1318.

Doris & Stich. (2013). Empirical Approaches to Meta-Ethics, in. Stich and Mellon (2013) *Traditional and Experimental* Readings.

Doward, J. (2013). Medicine's big new battleground: does mental illness really exist? *The Observer*, 11 May 2013.

Drummond, J. M., Issa, F. A., Song, C. K., Heberholz, J., Yeh, S. R., & Edwards, D. H. (2002). Neural mechanisms of dominance hierarchies in crayfish. In The crustacean nervous system, ed. K. Wiese, 124–135. Berlin: Springer.

Dryden, W., David, D., & Ellis, A. (2010). Rational emotive behavior therapy. In K. S. Dobson (Ed.), *Handbook of cognitive behavioural therapies* (pp. 226–276). NY: Guilford Press.

Dupre, J. (2011). Foreword, Joseph Keim Campbell, Michael O'Rourke, and Matthew H. Slater (eds.), *Carving Nature at Its Joints: Natural Kinds in Metaphysics and Science*, Cambridge: MIT.

Dupree, J. (2000). "Natural Kinds," in W.H.Newton Smith (ed), *A Companion to the Philosophy of Science*, Routledge, 311–319.

Eachus, J., Williams, M., Chan, P., et al. (1996). Deprivation and cause specific morbidity: Evidence from the Somerset and Avon survey of health. *British Medical Journal* **312**: 287–292.

Eakin, J. P. (1992). *Touching the World: Reference in Autobiography*. Princeton New Jersey: Princeton University Press.

Ellis, B. (2001). *Scientific Essentialism*, Cambridge Studies in Philosophy. Cambridge: Cambridge University Press.

Ellis, B. (2005). "Physical Realism," *Ratio* **18**: 371–384.

Engstrom, E. J. (2003). *Clinical Psychiatry in Imperial Germany: A History of Psychiatric Practice*, Ithaca, NY: Cornell University Press.

Epp A. M., Dobson, K. S., & Cottraux, J. (2009). Applications of Individual Cognitive-Behavioral Therapy to Specific Disorders, in *Textbook of Psychotherapeutic Treatments*. Edited by Gabbard GO, Washington DC, American Psychiatric Publishing Inc. 239–247.

Ershefsky, M. (2007). Psychological categories as homologies: lessons from ethology. *Biol Philos* 22:659–674

Ereshefsky, M. (2009). "Defining 'health' and 'disease'." *Studies in History and Philosophy of Biological and Biomedical Sciences* **40**:221–227.

Esquirol. E. (1845). *Mental Maladies: A Treatise on Insanity*. Transl. by E. K. Hunt. Philadelphia: Lea and Blanchard.

Evans, G. (1982). The Varieties of Reference, Oxford: Clarendon Press.

Falk, D. (1992). *Braindance: New Discoveries About Human Origins and Brain Evolution*. New York: Holt.

Fodor, J. (1983). The modularity of mind: An essay in faculty psychology. Cambridge: The MIT Press.

Fodor, J. (2000). *The mind doesn't work that way*. Cambridge MA: MIT Press.

Forst, R. (2002). *Contexts of Justice Political Philosophy beyond Liberalism and Communitarianism*, Berkeley and Los Angeles: University of California Press.

Foucault, M. (1970). *The Order of Things*: An Archaeology of Human Sciences, NY: Pantheon Books (1994 edition).

Foucault, M. (1967). *Madness and civilization: a history of insanity in the age of reason*. London: Routledge (2005 edition).

Foucault, M. (2006). *History of Madness.* Jean Khalfa (ed.), Jonathan Murphy and Jean Khalfa (trans.), New York: Routledge; *(original: Histoire de la folie à l'âge classique - Folie et déraison* Paris: Plon, 1961).

France, C. M., Lysaker, P. H., & Robinson, R. P. (2007). The Chemical Imbalance Explanation for Depression: Origins, Lay Endorsement, and Clinical Implications, *Professional Psychology: Research and Practice* **38**(4): 411–420.

Frances, A. (2010). DSM in philosophyland: Curiouser and curiouser. *Bulletin of the Association for the Advancement of Philosophy and Psychiatry* (AAPP) **17** (2): 3–7.

Frances, A. (2012). DSM-5 in distress:the DSM's impact on mental health practice and research. *Psychology Today,* 2 December.

Frank, A. W. (2000). Illness and autobiographical work: dialogue as narrative destabilisation. *Qualitative Sociology* **23** (1), 135–156.

Frankfurt, H. G. (2004). *The Reasons of Love.* Princeton University Press, Princeton, NJ.

Franklin, C. L., Strong, D. R., & Greene, R. L. (2002). A taxometric analysis of the MMPI-2 depression scales. *Journal of Personality Assessment,* **79,** 110–121.

Freud, S. (1969/1917). "Mourning and Melancholia" *The Standard Edition of the Complete Psychological Works of Sigmund Freud.* The Hogarth Press: London. **Vol. 14**, London: Hogarth Press, 239–260.

Fulford, K. W. M. (1989). *Moral Theory and Medical Practice,* Cambridge, UK: Cambridge University Press.

Fulford, K. W. M. (1991). *Evaluative delusions: Their significance* for philosophy and psychiatry. *British Journal of Psychiatry,* **159,** 108–112.

Fulford, K. W. M (1999). Nine variations and a coda on the theme of an evolutionary definition of dysfunction. *Journal of Abnormal Psychology* 1999, **108**:412–420.

Fulford, K. W. M. (2000). Philosophy Meets Psychiatry in the Twentieth Century—Four Looks Back and a Brief Look Forward. In **Louhiala, P., Stenman, S.** (eds.): Philosophy Meets Medicine. Helsinki: Helsinki University Press; p. 114–131.

Fulford, K. W. M. (2001). 'What is (mental) disease?': an open letter to Christopher Boorse *J Med Ethics* 2001;**27**:*80–85 doi:10.1136/jme.27.2.80.*

Fulford, K. W. M. (2005). Values in psychiatric diagnosis: Developments in policy, training and research. *Psychopathology* **38**: 171–176.

Fulford, K. W. M., Morris, K., Sadler, J.Z., & Stanghellini, G. (2003). Past improbable, future possible: The renaissance in philosophy and psychiatry. In Fulford, K. W. M., Morris, K. J., Sadler, J. Z., & Stanghellini, G. (Eds) *Nature and Narrative: an Introduction to the new Philosophy of Psychiatry.* Oxford University Press, Oxford, 1–41.

Fulford, K. W. M., Thornton, T., & Graham, G. (eds) (2006). *Oxford textbook of philosophy and psychiatry.* Oxford: Oxford University Press.

Gach, J. (2010). Biological Psychiatry in the Nineteenth and Twenieth Century, in Edwin R. Wallace IV and John *Gach* (Eds.). *History of Psychiatry and Medical Psychology: With an Epilogue on Psychiatry* and the Mind–Body Relation. New York: Springer. 381–418.

Gadamer, H.-G. (1972/2006). "The incapacity of conversation," *Continental Philosophy Review.* **39**(4), 351–359.

Gadamer, H.-G. (1976). *Philosophical Hermeneutics*, translated and edited by David E. Linge (Berkeley and Los Angeles: University of California Press, 1976).

Gadamer, H.-G. (1989). *Truth and method.* New York: Continuum.

Gadamer, H.-G. (1996). *The Enigma of Health: The Art of Healing in a Scientific Age*, trans. by John Gaiger and Nicholas Walker, Oxford: Polity Press.

Gadamer, H.-G. (2001). *Gadamer in Conversation*, edited and translated by Richard Palmer (New Haven, Conn.: Yale University Press

Gallagher, S. (2004). Hermeneutics and the cognitive sciences. *Journal of Consciousness Studies* **11**, 162–74.

Garrett, A. (2000). "Hume's Revised Racism Revisited." *Hume Studies* **26** (1): 171–177.

Gerrans, P. (2002). The theory of mind module in evolutionary psychology, *Biology and Philosophy* **17**: 305–321.

Ghaemi, S. N. (2007). *The Concepts of Psychiatry.* Baltimore, MD: Johns Hopkins University Press.

Gilbert, P. (1992). *Depression: The evolution of powerlessness.* London: Lawrence Erlbaum Associates.

Gilbert, P. (2000). Varieties of submissive behavior as forms of social defense: Evolution and psychopathology. In Subordination: Evolution and Mood Disorders, Sloman L, Gilbert P (eds). Lawrence Erlbaum: New York, pp. 3–45.

Gilbert, P. (2006). Emotion and Depression: Issues and Implications. *Psychological Medicine*, **36**:287–297.

Glantz, K., & Pearce, J. (1989). *Exiles from Eden: Psychotherapy from an evolutionary perspective.* New York: Norton.

Glover, J. (2006). *Choosing Children Genes, Disability, and Design*, Oxford: Oxford University.

Goldie, P. (2011). "Grief: a narrative account" *Ratio* **24** (2): 119–137.

Gould, S. J. (1991). Exaptation: A crucial tool for evolutionary psychology. *Journal of Social Issues* **47**:43–65.

Graham, G. (2010). *The Disordered Mind: An Introduction to Philosophy of Mind and Mental Illness.* London and New York: Routledge.

Graham, G. (2013). *The Disordered Mind: An Introduction to Philosophy of Mind and Mental Illness.* London and New York: Routledge. (2nd Edition).

Graham, G., & Stephens, L. (eds.) (1994). *Philosophical Psychopathology*, Cambridge, MA: MIT Press.

Grant, K. A., Shively, C. A., Nader, M. S., Ehrenkaufer, R. L., Line, S. W., Morton, T. E., Gage, H.D., & Mach, R. H. (1998). Effects of socialstatus on striatal dopamine D2 receptor binding characteristics incynomologus monkeys assessed with positron emission tomogrphy. Synapse **29**: 80–83.

Greenberg, P. E., Kessler, R. C., Birnbaum, H. G., et al. (2003). The economic burden of depression in the United States: how did it change between 1990 and 2000? *Journal of Clinical Psychiatry* 64(12), 1465–1475.

Griesinger, W. (1871). *Pathologie und Therapie. psychischen Krankheiten für Aerzte und Studirende* Braunschweig: Verlag von Friedrich Wreden.

Griffiths, P. (1999). "Squaring the Circle: Natural Kinds with Historical Essences." In *Species: New Interdisciplinary Essays*, ed. Robert Wilson, 209–228. Cambridge, Massachusetts: MIT Press.

Gruenberg, A. M., Goldstein, R. D., & Pincus, H. A. (2005). "Classification of Depression: Research and Diagnostic Criteria: DSM-IV and ICD-10" In: *Biology of Depression*. Edited by Julio Licinio and Ma-Li Wong. Weinheim: WILEY-VCH Verlag GmbH & Co, 1–12.

Guze, S. (1992). *Why psychiatry is a branch of medicine*. New York: Oxford University Press.

Guze, S. B. (1989). Biological psychiatry: is there any other kind? *Psychological Medicine* **19**: 315–323.

Habermas, J. (1993). "On the Pragmatic, Ethical, and Moral Employments of Practical Reason," in *Justification and Application: Remarks on Discourse Ethics*, trans. C. Cronin (Cambridge, Mass.: MIT Press, 1993), 1–18.

Habermas, J. (2003). *The Future of Human Nature*, Hella Beister, Max Pensky and William Rehg (trans.). Cambridge: Polity Press.

Hacking, I. (1995). The looping effects of human kinds. In D. Sperber and A. Premark (eds.)*Causal Cognition*. Oxford: Clarendon Press, 351–394.

Hacking, I. (1999). *The Social Construction of What?* Cambridge, Massachusetts: Harvard University Press.

Hacking, I. (2007). Kinds of People: Moving Targets. *Proceedings of the British Academy* **151**: 285–318.

Hadley, C., & Patil, C.L. (2008). Seasonal changes in household food insecurity and symptoms of anxiety and depression. *American Journal of Physical Anthropology* **135**: 225–232.

Hagen, E. H. (1999). The functions of postpartum depression. *Evolution of Human Behaviour* **20**: 325–359.

Hamburg, D. A.(1974). Coping behavior in life threatening circumstances. *Psychother Psychosom* **23**: 13–25.

Hamilton, W. D. (1964). The genetical evolution of social behaviour II. *Journal of Theoretical Biology* 7: 17–32.

Hammen, C. (1992). Life events and depression: The plot thickens. *American Journal of Community Psychology* **20**: 179–193.

Hammen, C. (1997). *Depression*. Hove: Erlbaum.

Hare, R. M. (1986). "Health," *Journal of Medical Ethics* **12**: 174–81.

Hasday, J. D., Fairchild, K. D., & Shanholtz, C. (2000).. The role of fever in the infected host. Microbes and Infection **2**: 1891–1904.

Haslam, J. (1809). *Observations on Madness and Melancholy*. London: J. Callow.

Haslam, N. (2003). The dimensional view of personality disorders: A review of the taxometric evidence. *Clinical Psychology Review* 23: 75–93.

Hawking, S., & Mlodinow, L. (2010). *The Grand Design*, London: Bantam.

Hawkins, A. H. (1993). *Reconstructing Illness: Studies in Pathography*. West Lafayette, IN: Purdue University Press.

Heikes, D. K. (2010). *Rationality and feminist philosophy*, NY: Continuum

Hempel, C. G. (1961). Introduction to problems of taxonomy. In: Zubin J, editor. *Field studies in the mental disorders*. New York: Grune and Stratton, pp. 3–22.

Hempel, C. G. (1966). *Philosophy of Natural Science*. Englewood Cliffs, NJ: Prentice-Hall.

Herbert, J. D., & Forman, E. M. (2011). The Evolution of Cognitive Behavior Therapy: The Rise of Psychological Acceptance and Mindfulness, in *Acceptance and Mindfulness in Cognitive Behavior Therapy: Understanding and Applying the New Therapies* (eds J. D. Herbert and E. M. Forman), John Wiley & Sons, Inc., Hoboken, NJ, USA.

Herder, J. G. (1800). *Ideas towards a Philosophy of the History of Humanity*, trans. T. Churchill, New York: Bergmann Publishers.

Hobbes, T. (2006/1651). *Leviathan*, Dover Publications, Mineola, New York.

Hoffmann, F. (1971). *Fundamenta Medicinae*, trans. L.S. King, London.

Hollon, S. D., & Beck, A. T. (2004). Cognitive and cognitive behavioral therapies. In M. J. Lambert (Ed.), Handbook of psychotherapy and behavior change (5th ed., pp. 447–492). New York: Wiley.

Hornstein, G. (2002). Narratives of madness, as told from within. *Chronicle of Higher Education*, 25 January, 7–10.

Horsfall, J. G., & Cowling, E. B. (1977). *Plant Disease: An Advanced Treatise: How Disease Is Managed*, Academic Press, New York.

Horst, S. (2007). *Beyond Reduction: Philosophy of Mind and Post-Reductionist Philosophy of Science*, Oxford University Press.

Horwitz, A. V., & Wakefield, J. C. (2005). The age of depression. *Public Interest*, **158**, 39–58.

Horwitz, A. V., & Wakefield, J. C. (2007). *The Loss of Sadness: How Psychiatry Transformed Normal Sorrow into Depressive Disorder*. New York: Oxford University Press.

Hull, D. L. (1989). The ontological status of species as evolutionary units. In *Philosophy of biology*, ed. M. Ruse, 146–155. New York: Macmillan.

Humphrey, N., & Dennett, D. C. (1989). "Speaking for our selves: an assessment of multiple personality disorder," *Raritan* **9** (1) 68–98.

Hyden, L.-C. (1997). Illness and narrative. *Sociology of Health and Illness* **19**: 48–69.

Hyman, S. E. (1998). NIMH during the tenure of Director Steven E. Hyman, MD: The now and future of NIMH. American Journal of Psychiatry. 1998;**155**(Suppl):36–40.

Ingram, A. (2011). Deciphering Difference: A Study in Medical Literacy. In: *Melancholy Experience in Literature of the Long Eighteenth Century: Before Depression, 1660-1800*. Palgrave Macmillan, Basingstoke, pp. 170–202.

Insel, T. R., & Quirion, R. (2005). Psychiatry as a clinical neuroscience discipline. JAMA.**294**(17):2221–2224.

Jablensky A. (1999). The nature of psychiatric classification. Issues beyond ICD-10 and DSM-IV. *Australian and New Zealand Journal of Psychiatry* **33**: 137–144.

Jackson, S. W. (1983). "Melancholia and Mechanical Explanation in Eighteenth-Century Medicine" *The Journal of the History of Medicine and Allied Sciences* **38**, **3**, 298–319.

Jablensky, A. (2007). Does psychiatry need an overarching concept of "mental disorder"? World Psychiatry. 2007;**6**(3):157–158.

Jackson, S. W. (1986). *Melancholia and depression: from Hippocratic times to modern times*, Yale University Press, New Haven; London.

Jackson, S. W. (2008). "A History of Melancholia and Depression," in Wallace, Edwin R. & Gach, J. (Ed.) *History of Psychiatry and Medical Psychology. With an Epilogue on Psychiatry and the Mind-Body Relation.* New York: Springer

Jackson, S. W. (1999). *Care of the psyche: A history of psychological healing.* New Haven: Yale University Press.

James, W. (2002/1902). *The Varieties of Religious Experience: A Study in Human Nature*, New York: Routlegde.

Jaspers, K. (1963). *General Psychopathology.* Manchester, Manchester University Press (first published in German in 1913 by Springer, Berlin).

Johnsen, R. (2009). *The Great Health of Melancholy—A Study of the Pathologies of Performativity*, Copenhagen: CBS.

Jones, W. H. S. (1972). *Hippocrates General Introduction* **vol. 1**. London: Heinemann.

Just, N., & Alloy, L. B. (1997). The response styles theory of depression: Tests and an extension of the theory. *Journal of Abnormal Psychology* **106**: 221–229.

Kandel, E. R. (1998). A New Intellectual Framework for Psychiatry, Am J Psychiatry **155**:457–469.

Kendell, R. E. (1975). The concept of disease and its implications for psychiatry. *Br J Psychiatry.*;**127**:305–315.

Kendell, R. E. (1986). What are mental disorders? In: Freedman AM, Brotman R, Silverman I, et al., editors. *Issues in psychiatric classification: science, practice and social policy.* New York: Human Sciences Press; 1986. pp. 23–45.

Kendler, K. S. (2005). Toward a Philosophical Structure for Psychiatry. Am J Psychiatry **162**:433–440.

Kendler, K. S., & Gardner, C. O. (1998). Boundaries of major depression: an evaluation of DSM-IV criteria. *Am J Psychiatry* **155**:172–177.

Kendler, K. S., Zachar, P., & Craver, C. (2011). What kinds of things are psychiatric disorders? *Psychological Medicine* **41**, 1143–1150.

Kessler, R. C., McGonagle, K. A., Zhao, S., et al. (1994). Lifetime and 12-month prevalence of DSM-III-R psychiatric disorders in the United States. *Archives of General Psychiatry* **51**: 8–19.

Keyes, C. L. M., & Ryff, C. D. (2000). Subjective change and mental health: A self-concept theory. *Social Psychology Quarterly*, **63**(3), 264–279.

Kiesler, D. J. (1999). *Beyond the disease model of mental disorders.* Westport, Conn: Praeger.

Kingma, E. (2007). "What is it to be healthy?" *Analysis* **67**:128–133.

Kingma, E. (2010). "Paracetamol, poison, and polio: why Boorse's account of function fails to distinguish health and disease." *British Journal for the Philosophy of Science* **61**:241–64.

Kirmeyer, L. J. (1994). Rejoinder to Professor Wakefield. Debate on 'Is the concept of mental disorder culturally relative? In *Controversial Issues in Mental Health.* Edited by: Kirk SA. Einbinder SD Boston: Allyn and Bacon, 17–20.

Kleinman, A. (1988). *The Illness Narratives: Suffering, Healing and the Human Condition*, New York, NY: Basic Books.

Klerman, G. L., Vaillant, G. E., Spitzer, R. L., & Michels, R. (1984). A debate on DSM-III. *Am J Psychiatry* **141**(4):539–553.

Klibansky, R., Panofsky, E., & Saxl, F. (2001/1964). *Saturn and Melancholy: Studies in the History of Natural Philosophy, Religion, and Art*, New York: Basic Books.

Kohrt, B. A., Kunz, R. D., Baldwin, J. L., Koirala, N. R., Sharma, V. D., & Nepal, M. K. (2005). "Somatization" and "comorbidity": A study of jhum-jhum and depression in rural Nepal. *Ethos* **33**: 125–147.

Korsgaard, C.(1996). *The Sources of Normativity*, Ed. O'Neill. New York: Cambridge University Press.

Kovacs, M., & Beck, A. J. (1978). Maladaptive cognitive structures in depression. *American Journal of Psychiatry*, **135**: 525–533.

Kravitz, E. A. (2000). Serotonin and aggression: Insights gained from alobster model system and speculations on the role of amineneurons in a complex behavior. Journal of Comparative Physiology **186**: 221–238.

Kripke, S. (1980). *Naming and Necessity*. Oxford: Blackwell.

Krupnick, J. L., Sotsky, S. M., Simmens, S., Moyer, J., et al. (1999). The Role of the Therapeutic Alliance in Psychotherapy and Pharmacotherapy Outcome: Findings in the National Institute of Mental Health Treatment of Depression Collaborative Research Program, *Journal of Consulting and Clinical Psychology* **64**:532–539.

Kuehner, C., & Weber, I. (1999). Responses to depression in unipolar depressed patients: An investigation of Nolen-Hoeksema's response styles theory. *Psychological Medicine* **29**: 1323–1333.

Kuhn, T. S. (1970).*The structure of scientific revolutions*. Chicago: University of Chicago Press.

Kutchins, H., & Kirk, S. (1997). *Making Us Crazy*. New York: The Free Press.

Kuyken, W., & Dalgleish, T. (1995). Autobiographical memory and depression. British Journal of Clinical Psychology, **33**, 89–92.

Kuyken, W., Watkins, E., & Beck, A. (2005). CBT for mood disorders. In G. Gabbard, J. Beck, & J. Holmes (Eds.), *Oxford textbook of psychotherapy* (pp. 111–126). Oxford: OUP.

Lacewing, M. (2004). Emotion and cognition: Recent developments and therapeutic practice. *Philosophy, Psychiatry and Psychology* **11**(2), 175–186.

Laitinen, A. (2004). "A Critique of Charles Taylor's Notions of 'Moral Sources' and 'Constitutive Goods'." *Acta Philosophica Fennica* **76**: 73–104.

Lakoff, G., & Johnson, M. (1999). *Philosophy in the flesh: The embodied mind and its challenge to western thought*. New York: Basic Books.

Lambert, M. J., & Ogles, B. M. (2004). The efficacy and effectiveness of psychotherapy. In M. J. Lambert (Ed.), *Handbook of psychotherapy and behavior change*. New York: John Wiley and Sons

Lawlor, C. (2011). Fashionable Melancholy. In: *Melancholy Experience in Literature of the Long Eighteenth Century: Before Depression, 1660-1800*. Palgrave Macmillan, Basingstoke, pp. 25–53.

Lawrence, C. (1994). *Medicine in the Making of Modern Britain, 1700–1920*. London: Routledge.

Leahy, R. L. (2000). Sunk costs and resistance to change. Journal of Cognitive Psychotherapy: An International Quarterly **14**: 355–371.

Leder, D. (1990). Clinical Interpretation: The Hermeneutics of Medicine, *Theoretical Medicine* **11**: 9–24.

LeDoux, J. E. (1996). *The emotional brain.* New York: Simon & Schuster.

Lee, W.-S., & Lee, H.-J. (2012). Characteristics of androgenetic alopecia in Asian. *Ann Dermatol* **24** (3): 243–252.

Leff, J., Sartorius, N., Jablensky, A., Korten, A., & Ernberg, G. (1992). The International Pilot Study of Schizophrenia: Five-year follow-up findings. *Psychological Medicine* **22**: 131–145.

Lejeune, P. (1982). "The *Autobiographical Contract*" In *French Literary Theory Today*: A Reader, *ed. Tzvetan Todorov, Cambridge: Cambridge University Press*, pp.192–222.

Lewis, A. (1949). Philosophy and Psychiatry, *Philosophy* **24** (89): 99–117.

Lilienfeld, S. O., & Marino, L. (1995). Mental disorder as a Roschian concept: a critique of Wakefield's "harmful dysfunction" analysis. *Journal of abnormal psychology* **104**(3):411–420.

Linge, D. E. (1976). "Editor's Introduction." Hans-Georg Gadamer, Philosophical Hermeneutics. David E. Linge, trans. Berkeley and Los Angeles: University of California Press. pp. xi–lviii.

Locke, J. (1689/1975). *An Essay Concerning Human Understanding*, ed. P. H. Nidditch, Oxford: Oxford University Press.

Lowe, E. J. (1998). *The Possibility of Metaphysics: Substance, Identity, and Time.* New York: Oxford University Press.

Lyubomirsky, S., & Nolen-Hoeksema, S. (1993). Self-perpetuating properties of dysphoric rumination. *Journal of Personality and Social Psychology* **65**: 339–349.

Lyubomirsky, S., Tucker, K. L., Caldwell, N. D., & Berg, K. (1999). Why ruminators are poor problem solvers: Clues from the phenomenology of dysphoric rumination. *Journal of Personality and Social Psychology* **77**: 1041–1060.

McDowell, J. (1981). 'Non-Cognitivism and Rule-Following', in Steven Holtzman and Christopher Leich (eds), *Wittgenstein: to Follow a Rule* (London: Routledge and Kegan Paul, 1981), pp.141–62.

McDowell, J. (1985). Values and Secondary Qualities, in Ted Honderich, ed., *Morality and Objectivity* (Boston: Routledge and Kegan Paul, 1985), pp. 110–129.

McDowell, J. (1996). *Mind and World.* Cambridge: Harvard University Press.

McDowell, J. (1998). "Aesthetic Value, Objectivity, and the Fabric of the World," in *Mind, Value, and Reality* (Cambridge: Harvard University Press).

McEachrane, M. (2003). Capturing emotional thoughts. The philosophy of cognitive-behavioral therapy. In Y. Gustafsson, C. Kronqvist, & M. McEachrane (Eds.), *Emotions and understanding: Wittgensteinian perspectives.* Palgrave Macmillan, pp. 80–101.

McGuire, M. T., & Troisi, A. (1987). Physiological regulation deregulation and psychiatric disorders. *Ethology & Sociobiology* **8**: 9–12.

McGuire, M., & Troisi, A. (1998). *Darwinian psychiatry*, New York: Oxford University Press.

McHugh, P. R., & Slavney, P. R. (1998). *The perspectives of psychiatry*, 2nd edn. Baltimore, MD: Johns Hopkins University Press.

Mackie, J. L. (1977). *Ethics: Inventing Right and Wrong*, New York: Penguin Books.

Mackie, J. L. (1985). "Multiple personality," in *Persons and Values: Selected Papers 2*, Oxford: OUP.

Mackinejad, K., & Sharifi, V. (2006). Wittgenstein's Philosophy and a Dimensional Approach to the Classification of Mental Disorders—A Preliminary Scheme. *Psychopathology* **39**:126–129.

Mackinger, H. F., Kunz-Dorfer, A., Schneider, B., & Leibetseder, M. M. (2000). Episodisches Gedächtnis als Vulnerabilitätsmarker: Eine empirische Untersuchung zur Prognose prämenstrueller Dysphorie. *Zeitschrift für Klinische Psychologie, Psychiatrie und Psychotherapie*, **48**, 45–56.

MacLean, P. D. (1985). Evolutionary psychiatry and the triune brain. Psychological Medicine **15**: 219–221.

Magner, L. N. (2005). *A history of medicine*, 2nd ed. Boca Raton: Taylor & Francis.

Malcolm, N. (1972). Thoughtless brutes. In: *Proceedings and Addresses of the American Philosophical Association* **46**, 5–20.

Marcum, J. A. (2008). *Humanizing Modern Medicine An Introductory Philosophy of Medicine*, Philosophy and Medicine Series, **volume 99**, New York: Springer.

Margolis, E., & Laurence, S. (2011). "Concepts", *The Stanford Encyclopedia of Philosophy* (Fall 2012 Edition), Edward N. Zalta (ed.), URL = <http://plato.stanford.edu/archives/fall2012/entries/concepts/>.

Markova., & Berrios. (2012). Epistemology of Psychiatry, *Psychopathology* **226** (45): 220–227.

Marmar, C. R., Gaston, L., Gallagher. D., & Thompson, L. W. (1989). Therapeutic alliance and outcome in behavioral, cognitive, and brief dynamic psychotherapy in late-life depression. *Journal of Nervous and Mental Disease*, **177**: 464–472.

Mayes, R., & Horwitz, A.V. (2005). DSM-III*and the revolution in the classification of mental illness. Journal of the History* of the *Behavioral* Sciences, **41**(3), 249–267.

Mead, Richard (1762) *The Medical Works of Richard Mead*, London.

Meltzer, H., Gill, B., Petticrew, M., et al. (1995). *The prevalence of psychiatric morbidity among adults living in private households. OPCS surveys of psychiatric morbidity in Great Britain*. ReportI. London: HMSO.

Mercier, C. (1892). "Melancholia" in **Tuke, D. H.** *Dictionary of Psychological Medicine*, **Vol. 1** (London: Churchill), 787–796.

Meyer, J. H., McMain, S., Kennedy, S. H., et al. (2003). Dysfunctional attitudes and 5-HT(2) receptors during depression and self-harm. *Am J Psychiatry.* **167**(1):72–78.

Milgram, E. (1999). "Moral Values and Secondary Qualities," *American Philosophical Quarterly* **36**:3, 253–255.

Mill, J. S. (1843). *A System of Logic, Ratiocinative and Inductive.* **Robson, J. M.** ed.; Toronto: University of Toronto Press.

Miller, G. (2008). Psychiatry as Hermeneutics: Laing's Argument With Natural Science, *Journal of Humanistic Psychology* **48** (1): 42–60.

Miller, G. (2010). Mistreating Psychology in the Decades of the Brain *Perspectives on Psychological Science* **5** no. 6: 716–743

Miller, H. W. (1949). Philosophy and Medicine In Ancient Greece, *The Classical Journal* **44** (5): 309–318

Mills, C. W. (1997). *The Racial Contract*, Ithaca, NY: Cornell University Press.

Mishara, A. L. (1996). Commentary on "Wilhelm Griesinger" *Philosophy, Psychiatry, and Psychology* **3** (3): 165–167.

Moffitt, T.E., et al. (2008). Research Review: DSM-5 conduct disorder: research needs for an evidence base Journal of Child Psychology and Psychiatry **49**:13–33

Moltmann, J. (2002). *Theology of Hope: On the Ground and the Implications of a Christian Eschatology*, London: SCM Press.

Moncrieff, J., & Kirsch, I. (2005). Efficacy of antidepressants in adults. British Medical Journal, **331**, 155–157.

Moran, R. (2001). *Authority and Estrangement: An Essay on Self Knowledge*, Princeton, NJ: Princeton University Press.

Morris, C. (1959). Philosophy, Psychiatry, Mental Illness and Health. Philosophy and Phenomenological Research, **Vol. 20**, No. 1 (Sep., 1959), pp. 47–55

Murphy, D. (2005). Can evolution explain insanity? *Biology and Philosophy* **20**: 745–766.

Murphy, D. (2006). *Psychiatry in the Scientific Image*, Cambridge: MIT Press.

Murphy, D. (2008). "Concepts of Disease and Health," *The Stanford Encyclopedia of Philosophy* Edward N. Zalta (ed.), URL = <http://plato.stanford.edu/archives/sum2009/entries/health-disease/>.

Murphy, D., & Stich, S. (2000). Darwin in the madhouse: Evolutionary psychology and the classification of mental disorders. In *Evolution and the human mind*, ed. P. Carruthers and A. Chamberlain, 62–92. Cambridge: Cambridge University Press.

Murray, T. L., Jr. (2006). The Other Side of Psychopharmacology: A Review of the Literature *Journal of Mental Health Counseling*. **28** (4) 309–337

Nagel, E. (1979). *The Structure of Science*. Indianapolis: Hackett Publishing Company.

Nandrino, J.-L., Pezard, L., et al. (2002). Autobiographical memory in major depression: A comparison between first-episode and recurrent patients. Psychopathology **35**: 335–340.

Nelson, H. L. (2001). *Damaged Identities, Narrative Repair*. Ithaca, NY: Cornell University Press.

Nesse, R. M. (1984). An evolutionary perspective on psychiatry. *Comparative Psychiatry* **25**: 575–580.

Nesse, R. M. (1999). Testing evolutionary hypotheses about mental disorders. In *Evolution in health and disease*, ed. S.C. Stearns, 261–266. New York: Oxford University Press.

Nesse, R. M. (2000). Is depression an adaptation? *Archives of General Psychiatry* **57**: 14–20.

Nesse, R. M., & Williams, G. C. (1995). *Why We Get Sick: The New Science of Darwinian Medicine* New York: Times Books.

Nettle, D. (2004). Evolutionary origins of depression: A review and reformulation. *Journal of Affective Disorders* **81**: 91–102.

Nisbett, R.E., & Cohen, D. (1996). Cultures of Honour: The Psychology of Violence in the South, Boulder: Westview Press.

Nolan, S.A., Roberts, J. E., & Gotlib, I. H. (1998). Neuroticism and ruminative response style as predictors of change in depressive symptomatology. *Cognitive Therapy and Research* **22**: 445–455.

Nolen-Hoeksema, S. (1991). Responses to depression and their effects on the duration of depressive episodes. Journal of Abnormal Psychology **100**: 569–582.

Nolen-Hoeksema, S. (2000). The role of rumination in depressive disorders and mixed anxiety/depressive symptoms. *Journal of Abnormal Psychology* **109**: 504–511.

Nolen-Hoeksema S., Wisco, B.E., & Lyubomirsky, S. (2005). Rethinking rumination. *Perspectives on Psychological Science* **3**: 400–424.

Noonan, J. (2003). Can There be Applied Philosophy Without Philosophy? Interchange, **Vol. 34/1**, 35–49.

Nordenfelt, L. (2001). *Health, Science, and Ordinary Language*. NY: Rodopi.

Norris, C. (2011). "Hawking Contra Philosophy." PHILOSOPHY NOW May/June 2011.<https://owa.liv.ac.uk/owa/?ae=Itemandt=IPM.

Olfson, M., Marcus, S. C., Druss, et al. (2002). National trends in the outpatient treatment of depression. *Journal of the American Medical Association*, **287**: 203–209.

Padesky, C. A., & Beck, A. T. (2003). Science and philosophy: Comparison of cognitive therapy (CT) and rational emotive behavior therapy (REBT). *Journal of Cognitive Psychotherapy: An International Quarterly* **17**, 211–224.

Paik, J. H., Yoon, J. B., Sim, W. Y., et al. (2001). The prevalence and types of androgenetic alopecia in Korean men and women. Br J Dermatol. 2001 Jul;**145**(1):95–99.

Papineau, D. (1993). *Philosophical Naturalism* Oxford: Blackwell.

Parfit, D. (1984). *Reasons and Persons*, Oxford: Clarendon Press.

Pastötter, B., Gleixner, S., Neuhauser, T., et al. (2013). To push or not to push? Affective influences on moral judgment depend on decision frame. *Cognition* **126** (3): 373–377.

Patel, V. (2001). Cultural factors and international epidemiology. *British Medical Bulletin* **57**: 33–45.

Patil, C., & Hadley, C. (2008). Symptoms of anxiety and depression and mother's marital status: An exploratory analysis of polygyny and psychosocial stress. *American Journal of Human Biology* **20**: 475–477.

Pellegrino, E. (1979). *Humanism and the Physician*, University of Tennessee Press, Knoxville.

Perring, C. D. (2007). Mental illness. *The Stanford encyclopedia of philosophy*, ed. E. N. Zalta. Available from: http://plato.stanford.edu

Phillips, J. (1996). Key concepts: Hermeneutics. *Philosophy, Psychiatry, and Psychology* **3**: 61–69.

Phillips, J. (2004). Understanding/explanation. In *The philosophy of psychiatry: A companion*, ed. J. Radden, 180–190. New York: Oxford University Press.

Pierson, R. (1994). The epistemic authority of expertise. In: *Proceedings of the Biennial Meetings of the Philosophy of Science Association*, 1, 398–405.

Pinel, P. (1806). *A treatise on insanity* (Translated by D. D. Davis). Hafner Publishing Co., New York, 1962.

Platter, P. (orig. 1602). *Observationes: Krankheitsbeobachtungen*, edited and translated by Günther Goldschmidt, Berne: Huber, 1963.

Polanyi, M. M. (1962). *Personal knowledge: Towards a post-critical philosophy*. Chicago: IL: University of Chicago Press.

Popper, K. (1962). *Conjectures and refutations. The growth of scientific knowledge*, New York: Basic Books.

Price, J. S. (1972). Genetic and phylogenetic aspects of mood variations. *International Journal of Mental Health* **1**: 124–144.

Price, J. S., & Sloman, L. (1987). Depression as yielding behaviour: An animal model based on Schjelderup-Ebb's pecking order. *Ethology and Sociobiology* **8**: 85–98.

Price, J., Sloman, S., Gardner, L., Gilbert, R., & Rohde, P. (1994). The social competition hypothesis of depression. *British Journal of Psychiatry* **164**:309–315.

Prichard, J. C. (1835). *A Treatise on Insanity and Other Disorders Affecting the Mind.* London: Sherwood, Gilbert and Piper.

Priebe, S., Burns, T., & Craig, T. (2013). The future of academic psychiatry may be social. *British Journal of Psychiatry,* **202**, 319–320.

Puffet, A., Jehin-Marchot, D., Timsit-Berthier, M., & Timsit, M. (1991). Autobiographical memory and major depressive states. *European Psychiatry,* **6**, pp.141–145.

Putnam, H. (1975). The meaning of 'meaning'. In *Mind, Language and Reality: Philosophical Papers,* **Volume 2**, pp. 215–271. Cambridge: Cambridge University Press.

Putnam, H. (1981). *Reason, Truth, and History.* Cambridge: Cambridge University Press.

Putnam, H. (1982). Beyond the Fact-Value Dichotomy, *Crítica: Revista Hispanoamericana de Filosofía* Vol. 14, No. 41 pp. 3–12.

Quine, W. (1969). Natural kinds. In W. Quine *Ontological Relativity and Other Essays.* New York: Columbia University Press, pp.114–38.

Radden, J. (ed.) (2000). *The Nature of Melancholy: From Aristotle to Kristeva*, New York: Oxford University Press.

Radden, J. (ed.) (2004). The Philosophy of Psychiatry: A Companion, Oxford University Press.

Radden, J. (2009). *Moody Minds Distempered: Essays on Melancholy and Depression*, New York: Oxford University Press.

Radden, J., & Varga, S. (2013). "Depression Memoirs: some meta-analysis," in Fulford, KWM. et al. (eds.) *Oxford Handbook of Philosophy and Psychiatry.* Oxford: Oxford University Press.

Randall, V. A. (2010). Molecural basis of Androgenetic Alopecia, in Trueb and Tobin eds. (2010) *Aging Hair,* Springer: Heidelberg, 9–22.

Rawls, J. (1971). *A Theory of Justice.* Cambridge, Mass.: Harvard University Press.

Rawls, J. (1985). Justice as Fairness: Political not Metaphysical, *Philosophy and Public Affairs* **14**: 223–251.

Reynolds, C. F. III, & Lewis, D. A., et al. (2009). The Future of Psychiatry as Clinical Neuroscience *Academic Medicine* **84** (4) 446–450.

Rorty, R. (1989). *Contingency, Irony and Solidarity.* Cambridge: Cambridge University Press.

Rose, N. (1998). *Inventing Our Selves: Psychology, Power, and Personhood.* Cambridge: Cambridge University Press.

Rosenberg, A. (2005). Philosophy of Science: *A Contemporary Introduction.* Routledge, London.

Ross, M. (1989). "The Relation of Implicit Theories to the Construction of Personal Histories," *Psychological Review,* **96**: 341–357.

Roth, A., & Fonagy, P. (2005). *What works for whom? A critical review of psychotherapy research.* New York: The Guilford Press).

Rubin, J. H. (1993). *Religious Melancholy and Protestant Experience in America*, Oxford: OUP.

Ruscio, A. M., & Ruscio, J. (2002). The latent structure of analogue depression: should the BDI be used to classify groups? *Psychological Assessment* **14**: 135–145.

Ruscio, J., & Ruscio, A. M. (2000). Informing the continuity controversy. A taxometric analysis of depression, *Journal of Abnormal Psychology* **109**: 473–487.

Rush, B. (1827). *Medical Inquiries and Observations upon the Diseases of the Mind*, 3rd ed. Philadelphia: J. Grigg.

Sabshin, M. (1990). Turning points in twentieth-century American psychiatry. *Am J Psychiatry* **147**:1267–1274.

Safran, J. D., Muran, J. C., & Proskurov, B. (2009). Alliance, negotiation, and rupture resolution, in *Handbook of Evidence Based Psychodynamic Psychotherapy* (eds R. Levy and S.J. Ablon), Humana Press, New York, pp. 201–205.

Salvio, M., Beutler, L. E., Wood, J. M., & Engle, D. (1992). The strength of the therapeutic alliance in three treatments for depression. *Psychotherapy Research*, **2**(1), 31–36

Sandel, M. (1982). Liberalism and the Limits of Justice. Cambridge, MA: Cambridge University Press.

Sapp, J. P., Eversole, L. R., & Wysocki, G. P. (2004). *Contemporary oral and maxillofacial pathology. 2nd edition.* Mosby; University Park, PA: Pennsylvania State University Press.

Sass, L. A. (1998). "Ambiguity is of the essence: The relevance of hermeneutics for psychoanalysis" Marcus, Paul (Ed); Rosenberg, Alan (Ed), *Psychoanalytic versions of the human condition: Philosophies of life and their impact on practice,* (pp. 257–305). New York, NY, US: New York University Press.

Scadding, J. G. (1967). Diagnosis: the clinician and the computer. *Lancet.* **21**;2(7521):877–882.

Scadding, J. G. (1990). The semantic problems of psychiatry. *Psychological Medicine* **20**: 243–248.

Schacter, D. (2001). *The Seven Sins of Memory*, Houghton Mifflin.

Schleiner, W. (1991). *Melancholy, Genius, and Utopia in the Renaissance.* Wiesbaden: Harrassowitz.

Schmale, A. (1973). The adaptive role of depression in health and disease. In *Separation and depression*, ed. J.P. Scott and F.C. Senay, 187. Baltimore, MD: King.

Schwartz, P. H. (2007). Defining dysfunction: natural selection, design, and drawing a line. *Philosophy of Science* **74**(3):364–385.

Schwitzgebel, E. (2010). "Introspection," *The Stanford Encyclopedia of Philosophy* Edward N. Zalta (ed.), URL = <http://plato.stanford.edu/archives/win2012/entries/introspection/>.

Scott, J., Williams, J. M., & Beck, A. T. (1991). Cognitive therapy in clinical practice: An illustrative casebook. New York: Routledge.

Searle, J. R. (1999). The future of philosophy. *Philosophical Transactions of the Royal Society B: Biological Sciences* **354**, 2069–80.

Segrin, C., & Dillard, J. P. (1992). The interactional theory of depression: A meta-analysis of the research literature. *Journal of Social and Clinical Psychology* **11**: 43–70.

Sena, J. F. (1971). "Melancholy in Anne Finch and Elizabeth Carter: The Ambivalence of an Idea," in *The Yearbook of English Studies* **1**: 108–119.

Shakespeare, W. (1890). *As You Like It.* Ed. H.H. Furness, London: Lippincott.

Shapiro, S. (1983). "Mathematics and Reality," *Philosophy of Science,* **50**(4): 523–548.

Shively, C. A. (1999). Social subordination stress, behavior, and centralmonoaminergic function in cynomolgus monkeys. Biological Psychiatry **44**: 882–891.

Shoemaker, S. (1968). "Self-reference and Self-awareness," *The Journal of Philosophy* **65**:555–567.

Shoemaker, S. (1994). "Self-knowledge and 'Inner-sense'," *Philosophy and Phenomenological Research* **54**:249–314.

Shorter, E. (2005). *A Historical Dictionary of Psychiatry*, New York: Oxford University Press.

Siegel, R. B. (1973). *Galen on Psychology, Psychopathology and Function and Diseases of the Nervous System*. Basel:Karger.

Sikka, S. (2011). *Herder on Humanity and Cultural Difference: Enlightened Relativism*, Cambridge: CUP.

Sloman, L., Gilbert, P., & Hasey, G. (2003). Evolved mechanisms in depression: The role and interaction of attachment and social rank in depression. *Journal of Affective Disorders* **74**(2):107–121.

Smith, B. C. (1998). On knowing one's own language. In C. Wright, B. C. Smith, & C. Macdonald (Eds.), *Knowing our own minds* (pp. 391–428). Oxford: Clarendon Press.

Smith, N. H. (2004). Taylor and the Hermeneutic Tradition, in Abbey, Ruth (2004) *Charles Taylor*, Cambridge: CUP.

Smorti, A., Pananti, B., & Rizzo, A. (2010). Autobiography as tool to improve lifestyle, well being, and self-narrative in patients with mental disorders. *Journal of Nervous & Mental Disease* **198** (8), 564–571.

Snow, C. P. (1990). The Two Cultures, *Leonardo* **23** (2/3), 169–173.

Sommer, R., Clifford, J. S., & Norcross, J. C. (1998). A bibliography of mental patients' autobiographies: An update and classifi cation system. *American Journal of Psychiatry*, **155**: 1261–1264.

Sontag, S. (1989). *Illness as Metaphor and AIDS and Its Metaphors*. New York, NY: Anchor.

Spitzer, M., Uehlein, F. A., & Oepen, G. (Eds.) (1988). Psychopathology and philosophy (pp. 167–183). Berlin/Heidelberg: Springer.

Spitzer, R., Sheehy., & Endicott. (1977). D.S.M.-III guiding principles. In the 1977 Draft of the D.S.M.-III. *Archives of the American Psychiatric Association*. Professional Affairs. Box 16. Folder 177.

Spitzer, R. L. (2011). Psychological Warfare: The DSM-5 Debate, http://www.hcplive.com/publications/mdng-Neurology/2011/february_2011/psychological_warfare_the_dsm5_debate (Retrieved February 2014)

Spitzer, R. L., First, M. B., Williams, J. B., Kendler, K., Pincus, H. A., & Tucker, G. (1992). Now is the time to retire the term "organic mental disorders" *Am J Psychiatry* **149**:240–244.

Stahl, T. (2013). *Immanente Kritik. Elemente einer Theorie sozialer Praktiken*. Frankfurt a. M.: Campus.

Stansfeld, S. A., & Marmot, M.G. (1992). Social class and minor psychiatric disorder in British civil servants: A validated screening survey using the General Health Questionnaire. *Psychological Medicine* **22**: 739–749.

Stansfeld, S. A., Head, J., & Marmot, M. G. (1998). Explaining social class differences in depression and well being. *Social Psychiatry and Psychiatric Epidemiology* **33**: 1–9.

Starobinski, J. (1962). *A History of the Treatment of Melancholy from Earliest Times to 1900*, Basle: Geigy.

Stein, D. J., Phillips, K. A., Bolton, D., Fulford, K. W. M., Sadler, J. Z., & Kendler, K. S. (2010). What is a mental/psychiatric disorder? From DSM-IV to DSM-5. *Psychological Medicine* **40**:1759–1765.

Stempsey, W. E. (2000). A pathological view of disease. Theoretical Medicine, **21**, 321–330.

Stevens, J., & Price, J. (2000). *Evolutionary Psychiatry* (2. Edition) London: Routledge.

Svenaeus, F. (2000). Hermeneutics of clinical practice: the question of textuality, *Theoretical Medicine and Bioethics* **21**: 171–189.

Swain, S., Alexander, J., & Weinberg, J. (2008). "The instability of philosophical intuitions: Running hot and cold on Truetemp." *Philosophy and Phenomenological Research* **76**, 138–155.

Szasz, T. (1960). The Myth of Mental Illness. *American Psychologist*, **15** (February), 113–118.

Szasz, T. (1961). *The Myth of Mental Illness: Foundations of a Theory of Personal Conduct.* New York: HarperCollins.

Szasz, T. (1965). Psychiatry as Ideology, In, Hector Hawton, ed., *The Rationalist Annual.* London: Pemberton Publishing Company, 43–52.

Szasz, T. (2000). Mental disorders are not diseases. *USA Today* January issue, 30–31.

Szasz, T. (2004). *Faith in Freedom: Libertarian Principles and Psychiatric Practices.* New Brunswick, N.J: Transaction Publishers.

Szasz, T. (2012). Varieties of psychiatric criticism, *History of Psychiatry* **23**(3) 349–355.

Szentagotai, A., David, D., Lupu, V., & Cosman, D. (2008). Rational emotive behavior therapy versus cognitive therapy versus pharmacotherapy in the treatment of major depressive disorder: Mechanisms of change analysis. *Psychotherapy* **45**(4), 523–538.

Taylor, C. (1979). *Hegel and* Modern Society, Cambridge: CUP.

Taylor, C. (1982). "The Diversity of Goods." In *Utilitarianism and Beyond*, edited by Amartya Sen and Bernard Williams. Cambridge: Cambridge University Press, 1982. 129–144.

Taylor, C. (1985a). What is human agency? In *Philosophical papers: Vol 1. Human agency and language* (pp. 15–44). Cambridge, England: Cambridge University Press. [jo see first chapter]

Taylor, C. (1985b). Self-interpreting animals. In *Philosophical papers: Vol 1. Human agency and language* (pp. 45–76). Cambridge, England: Cambridge University Press. [jo see first chapter].

Taylor, C. (1989). *Sources of the self.* Cambridge, MA: Harvard University Press.

Taylor, C. (1991a). *The Ethics of Authenticity.* Cambridge: Harvard University Press. [jo see first chapter]

Taylor, C. (1991b). "Comments and Replies," *Inquiry* **34**: 237–254.

Taylor, C. (1994). "The Politics of Recognition," in *Multiculturalism: Examining the Politics of Recognition*, edited by Amy Gutmann, pp. 25–73. Princeton: Princeton University Press.

Taylor, C. (2002). "Gadamer and the Human Sciences." In *The Cambridge Companion to Gadamer.* Cambridge: Cambridge University Press, 2002. 126–142.

Taylor, C. (2007). *A Secular Age.* Cambridge, MA: Belknap Press of Harvard University Press.

ten Have, H. (2000). Bodies of Knowledge, 19–35.

Thornicroft, G., Margolius, O., & Jones, D. (1992). *The TAPS Project. 6: New long-stay psychiatric patients and social deprivation. British Journal of Psychiatry,* **161**, 621–624.

Thornton, T. (2002). Reliability and Validity in Psychiatric Classification: Values and Neo-Humeanism. *Philosophy, Psychiatry, and Psychology* **9**: 229–235.

Thornton, T. (2007). *Essential Philosophy of Psychiatry,* Oxford: Oxford University.

Thornton, T. (2011). *Radical liberal values-based practice. Journal Of Evaluation In Clinical Practice,* **17** (5). pp. 988–991.

Timmons, M. (1999). *Morality Without Foundations: A Defense of Ethical Contextualism* New York: Oxford University Press.

Tollefsen, C. (2000). McDowell's Moral Realism and the Secondary Quality Analogy. Disputatio: International Journal of Philosophy 1 (8):30–42.

Tooby, J., & Cosmides, L. (1992). The psychological foundations of culture. In *The adapted mind: Evolutionary psychology and the generation of culture.* Edited by Barkow JH, Cosmides L, and Tooby J Oxford. England: Oxford University Press, 19–136.

Tooby, J., & Cosmides, L. (1995). Foreword. In: Baron-Cohen S (1995) *Mindblindness: an essay on autism and theory of mind.* Cambridge, MA: MIT Press. pp. xi–xviii.

Treynor, W., Gonzalez, R., & Nolen-Hoeksema, S. (2003). Rumination reconsidered: A psychometric analysis. *Cognitive Therapy and Research* **27**: 247–259.

Tucker, B. P. (1994). "Deafness—Disability or Subculture: The Emerging Conflict." *Cornell Journal of Law and Public Policy* **3**, 265–75.

Tucker, B. P. (1998). "Deaf Culture, Cochlear Implants, and Elective Disability," The Hastings Center Report **vol. 28**, no. 4.

Tuke, S. (1813). *Description of the Retreat.* New York: Alexander.

Tyrer, P., & Steinberg, D. (2003). *Models for mental disorders: Conceptual models in psychiatry.* Chichester: John Wiley and Sons.

Ussher, J. M. (2011). The Madness of Women: Myth and Experience. London: Routledge.

Varga, S. (2011a). "Defining Mental Disorder. Exploring the 'Natural Functions' Approach" *Philosophy, Ethics and Humanities in Medicine,* **6**:1.

Varga, S. (2011b). "Evolutionary Psychiatry and Depression. Testing Two Hypotheses" *Medicine, Healthcare and Philosophy* **15**(1): 41–52.

Varga, S. (2012). Depersonalization and the sense of realness. Philosophy, Psychology and Psychiatry, **19**(2), 103–113.

Varga, S. (2013a). "The Frames of Cognition," *Cognitive Systems Research* **25/26**, 54–60.

Varga, S. (2013b). "The Elephant in the Room. Reply to Radden, Sass and Pienko" *Philosophy, Psychology and Psychiatry.* **20** (2), 165–167.

Varga, S. (2013c). "From Melancholia to Depression. Ideas on a possible continuity" *Philosophy, Psychology and Psychiatry* **20** (2): 141–155.

Varga, S. (2014). "Cognition, Representations and Embodied Emotions: Investigating Cognitive Theory" *Erkenntnis* **79** (1): 165–190.

Wachterhauser, B. R. (1986). Hermeneutics and Modern Philosophy. SUNY Press: NY.

Wakefield, J. C (1992). The concept of mental disorder: On the boundary between biological facts and social values. *American Psychologist*, **47**:373–388.

Wakefield, J. C. (1999a). Evolutionary versus prototype analyses of the concept of disorder. *Journal of Abnormal Psychology* **108**:374–399. [jo see first chapter]

Wakefield, J. C. (1999b). Disorder as a black box essentialist concept. *J Abnorm Psychol* **108**:465–472. [jo see first chapter]

Wakefield, J. C. (2007). The concept of mental disorder: diagnostic implications of the harmful dysfunction analysis, *World Psychiatry* **6**:149–156.

Wakefield, J. C. (2010). Misdiagnosing normality: Psychiatry's failure to address the problem of false positive diagnoses of mental disorder in a changing professional environment. *Journal of Mental Health*, **19** (4), 337–351.

Wallace, E. R. (1994). Psychiatry and its nosology: A historico-philosophical view. In *Philosophical perspectives on psychiatric diagnostic classification*, ed. J. Z. Sadler, O. P. Wiggins, and M. A. Schwartz, 16–86. Baltimore: Johns Hopkins University Press.

Wampold, B. E. (2001). *The Great Psychotherapy Debate: Models, Methods, and Findings.* Mahwah, NJ: Lawrence Erlbaum Associates, Inc.

Wang, P. S., Lane, M., et al. (2005). Twelve-month use of mental health services in the United States: Results from the National Comorbidity Survey Replication. *Archives of General Psychiatry*, **62**: 629–640.

Watson, P. J, & Andrews, P. W. (2002). Toward a revised evolutionary adaptationist analysis of depression: the social navigation hypothesis. *Journal of Affective Disorders*, **72**: 1–14.

Weinberg, J. M., Nichols, S., & Stich S. (2001). "Normativity and Epistemic Intuitions," *Philosophical Topics* **29**: 429–460.

Weissman, M. M. (1987). Epidemiology of depression: Frequency, risk groups, and risk factors. In *Perspectives on depressive disorders: A review of recent research*, 1–22, Rockville, MD: National Institute of Mental Health

Wells, A. (2000). *Emotional disorders and metacognition: Innovative cognitive therapy.* Chichester, UK: Wiley.

Wells, A. (2008). *Metacognitive therapy: A practical guide.* New York: Guilford.

Wenzlaff, R. M., & Luxton, D. D. (2003). The role of thought suppression in depressive rumination. Cognitive Therapy and Research **27**: 293–308.

Werner-Seidler, A., & Moulds, M. L. (2011). Autobiographical memory characteristics in depression vulnerability: Formerly depressed individuals recall less vivid positive memories. Cognition & Emotion, **25**, 1087–1103.

Whitaker, R. (2004). The case against antipsychotic medications: A 50 year record of doing more harm than good. Medical Hypotheses, **62**, 5–13.

Whiting, D. (2006). Why treating problems in emotion may not require altering eliciting cognitions. Philosophy, Psychiatry, and Psychology, **13**(3), 237–246.

Whytt, R. (1768). *The Works of Robert Whytt, M.D.* Edinburgh: Becket, Dehondt, Balfour.

Wilkes, K. V. (1988). *Real People: Personal Identity without Thought Experiments*, Oxford: Oxford University Press.

Wilkins, J. S. (2003). How to be a chaste species pluralist-realist: the origins of species modes and the synapomorphic species concept, Biology and Philosophy **18**: 621–638.

Williams, A. R., & Caplan, A. L. (2012). Thomas Szasz: rebel with a questionable cause, The Lancet **Vol. 380**, Issue 9851, Pages 1378–1379.

Williams, B. (1981). "Persons, Character, and Morality." In: J Rachels (ed.) *Moral Luck: Philosophical Papers*. Cambridge, UK: Cambridge University Press. pp. 1–19.

Williams, J. M., Watts, F. N., MacLeod, C., & Mathews, A. (1997). *Cognitive psychology and emotional disorders* (2nd ed.). Chichester: John Wiley & Sons.

Wilson, A. E., & Ross, M. (2000). The frequency of temporal-self and social comparisons in people's personal appraisals. *Journal of Personality and Social Psychology, 78*, 928–942.

Wilson, A. E., & Ross, M. (2001). From chump to champ: People's appraisals of their earlier and current selves. *Journal of Personality and Social Psychology, 80*, 572–584.

Wilson, A. E., & Ross, M. (2003). "The Identity Function of autobiographical memory: Time is on our side" *Memory* **11**: 137–149.

Wilson, E. O. (1975). *Sociobiology*. Boston: Belknap Press.

Wilson, R. A. (2005). *Genes and the Agents of Life: The Individual in the Fragile Sciences: Biology*, Cambridge University Press.

Wiltshire, J. (2000). Biography, pathography, and the recovery of meaning. *Cambridge Quarterly* **29**: 409–422.

Wolfe, B. E., & Goldfried, M. R. (1988). Research on psychotherapy integration: Recommendations and conclusions from an NIMH workshop. *Journal of Consulting and Clinical Psychology* **56**, 448–451.

Woolfolk. (1999). "Malfunction and Mental Illness," *Monist*, **82**, 658–670.

Wright, C. (1992). *Truth and Objectivity*. Cambridge, Mass: Harvard University Press.

Wright, J. L. (2006). *The Philosopher's I: Autobiography and the Search for the Self* Albany, NY: State University of New York Press.

Wynn, M. (2004). McDowell, Value Recognition, and Affectively Toned Theistic Experience. *Ars Disputandi* **4**, 20–39.

Young, A. (1995). *The Harmony of Illusions: Inventing Post-Traumatic Stress Disorder*. Princeton: Princeton University Press.

Zachar, P. (2000). Psychiatric disorders are not natural kinds. *Philosophy, Psychiatry, and Psychology*. 7: 167–182.

Zachar, P. (2008). Real Kinds but No True Taxonomy, In *Philosophical Issues in Psychiatry*. Edited by Kendler R, Parnas J. Baltimore: John Hopkins University Press, 327–354.

Zachar, P., & Kendler, K. (2007). "Psychiatric Disorders: A Conceptual Taxonomy" *American Journal of Psychiatry* **164**: 557–565.

Index

f indicates footnotes

The manufacturer's authorised representative in the EU for product safety is Oxford University Press España S.A. of el Parque Empresarial San Fernando de Henares, Avenida de Castilla, 2 – 28830 Madrid (www.oup.es/en or product.safety@oup.com). OUP España S.A. also acts as importer into Spain of products made by the manufacturer.

www.ingramcontent.com/pod-product-compliance
Lightning Source LLC
Chambersburg PA
CBHW071322180926
51611CB00002B/30
* 9 7 8 0 1 9 8 7 4 7 2 5 3 *